New England Family Histories

State of Connecticut

Lu Verne V. Hall

and

Donald O. Virdin

HERITAGE BOOKS
2015

HERITAGE BOOKS

AN IMPRINT OF HERITAGE BOOKS, INC.

Books, CDs, and more—Worldwide

For our listing of thousands of titles see our website
at
www.HeritageBooks.com

Published 2015 by
HERITAGE BOOKS, INC.
Publishing Division
5810 Ruatan Street
Berwyn Heights, Md. 20740

International Standard Book Numbers
Paperbound: 978-0-7884-1394-0
Clothbound: 978-0-7884-6177-4

CONTENTS

A

AASEN – Aasen, Lawrence O.
A look back... to Ole and Mary Aasen, their children and the early days.
By Lawrence O. Aasen. Westport, Conn., 1971. (LoC)

ABBE – Abbe, Cleveland
Abbe-Abbey genealogy. New Haven, Conn.: Tuttle, Morehouse & Taylor,
1916. (DAR)

ABBEY –
Abbe-Abbey genealogy, in memory of John Abbe and his descendants. By
Cleveland Abbe and Josephine Genung Nichols. New Haven, Conn., The
Tuttle, Morehouse & Taylor Company, 1916. (LoC)

ABBEY – Freeman, Alden
Memorial of Captain Thomas Abbey, his ancestors and descendants of the
Abbey family, pathfinders, soldiers and pioneers, settlers of Connecticut,
its Western Reserve in Ohio and the great West... By Alden Freeman.
(East Orange, N. J., The Abbey print shop, 1916?). (LoC)

ABBEY – Freeman, Alden
Memorial of Captain Thomas Abbey, his ancestors and descendants of the
Abbey family, pathfinders, soldiers and pioneers, settlers of Connecticut,
its Western Reserve in Ohio and the great West... 2nd Ed. By Alden
Freeman. (East Orange, N. J., The Abbey print shop, 1917). (LoC)

ABBEY – Freeman, Alden
Memorial of Captain Thomas Abbey, his ancestors and descendants of the
Abbey family, pathfinders, soldiers and pioneer settlers of Connecticut,
also Freeman family. East Orange, N. J. ?1916. (NGS)

ABBOTT –
A genealogical record of the descendants of George Abbot, of Andover;
George Abbot, of Rowley; Thomas Abbot, of Andover; Arthur Abbot, of
Ipswich; Robert Abbot, of Branford, Ct.; and George Abbot, of Norwalk,
Ct. Comp. by Rev. Abiel Abbot, D. D. and Rev. Ephraim Abbot. Boston,
J. Munroe and Company, 1874. (LoC)

ABBOT – Abbot, Abiel
A genealogical register of the descendants of George Abbot of Andover,
George Abbot of Rowley, Thomas Abbot of Andover, Arthur Abbot of
Ipswich, Robert Abbot of Branford, Ct., and George Abbot of Norwalk, Ct.
Boston: James Munroe and Co., 1847. (DAR)

1

ABBOTT – Abbott, John Thos.
...Pedigree of Abbott of Suffolk, and elsewhere. Comp. by John Thos. Abbott of Darlington, from documents in British museum and at Herald's College, wills at Bury St. Edmunds, Doctor's Commons, Norwich, and Ipswich, and the various parish registries mentioned. Abridged. (n.p., 1862). (LoC)

ABBOTT – Abbott, Maj. Lemuel Abijah
Descendants of George Abbott, of Rowley, Mass., of his joint descendants with George Abbott, Sr., of Andover, Mass., of the descendants of Daniel Abbott, of Providence, R. I.; of some of the descendants of Capt. Thomas Abbott, of Andover, Mass.; of George Abbott, of Norwalk, Ct.; of Robert Abbott, of Branford, Ct.; with brief notes of many others of the name, original settlers in the United States. By Maj. Lemuel Abijah Abbott... Published by the compiler. (Boston, T. R. Mavin & Son, printers), 1906. (LoC)

ABELL – Abell, Horace A.
Ancestors and descendants of Jonathan Abell who came from Connecticut and settled in Schenectady County, New York, about 1812. (by) Horace A. Abell. Rochester, N. Y., 1933. (LoC)

ABELL – Bliss, J. Homer
Genealogy: family of Abell, descendants of Rebecca Shuman and John Abell of Lebanon, Conn. By J. Homer Bliss. (Plainfield, Conn., 1904). (FW)

ABORN –
Aborn genealogy. (Everett Anderson Aborn). (Rockville, Conn., T. F. Rady & Co., 1921). (LoC)

ADAMS –
Adams Family of Hartford (1905), 8 pgs. [1]

ADAMS –
Memoir of the Rev. William Adams of Dedham, Mass., and of the Rev. Eliphalet Adams, of New London, Conn. (and their descendants, with the journal of William Adams, 1666-1682). Cambridge, 1849. (FW)

ADAMS –
Jeremy Adams of Cambridge, Mass., and Hartford, Conn., and his descendants. Boston, 1955. (LoC)

2

ADAMS –
Adams in Massachusetts, Rhode Island and Connecticut: Adams addenda descriptive index (Volumes I-XII. 1971-1982. Adams addenda). St. Louis, Mo. Adams addenda. Genealogical R. & P. (1983). (LoC)

ADAMS – Adams (Arthur)
Jeremy Adams of Hartford, Conn., and some of his descendants. By (Arthur) Adams. Boston, D. Clapp & Son, 1905. (NY)

ADAMS – Adams, Arthur
Jeremy Adams of Cambridge, Mass., and Hartford, Conn.., and his descendants. Boston, Mass., 1955. (NGS)

ADAMS – Adams, Elmo W.
Genealogy of the family of Charles Adams... of Farmington, Conn. .... Comp. and ed. by Elmo W. Adams. Burlingame, Calif., 1969. (SU)

ADAMS – Adams, Enid Eleanor Smith
Ancestors and descendants of Jeremiah Adams, 1794-1883, of Salisbury, Ct., Sullivan County, N. Y., Harbor Creek, Pa., and Vermillion, Oh., and descendants of his brothers and sisters: 7th in descent from Henry Adams of Braintree, Ma. Victor, ID, 1974. (NGS)

ADAMS – Adams, Frank M.
The Adams family of Wethersfield, Conn. By Frank M. Adams. Glendora, Cal., 1927. (LA)

ADAMS – Leighton, Perley M.
Ancestry of Laura Adams, wife of Owen Cotton, 1807-1873: nineteen families, mainly of Simsbury, Conn. Compiled by Perley M. Leighton. Westbrook, Me. P. M. Leighton, 1984.

ADAMS – Swantak, Isabella Adams
Abraham's flock, 1719-1954; a history of one branch of the Adams family. By Isabella Adams Swantak. Middletown, Conn. Indexed and printed by Mr. and Mr.? W. T. Many, 1966. (LoC)

ADAMS – Todd, Charles Burr
The history of Redding, Conn., from its first settlement to the present time. With notes on the Adams, Banks... Stow families. By Charles Burr Todd... New York, The J. A. Gray press, 1880. (LoC)

ADGATE – Perkins, Mary E.

Old famlies of Norwich, Connecticut, 1660-1800. Comp. by Mary E. Perkins. Genealogies. Vol.. 1, pt. 1... Norwich, Conn., 1900. (LoC)

ADSIT –
Descendants of John Adsit of Lyme, Connecticut. (n.p., 195-). (LoC)

ADSIT –
Descendants of John Adsit of Lyme, Conn. (NY)

ADSIT – Adsit, Newman Ward
Descendants of John Adsit of Lyme, Connecticut. S.1.:Adsit? 195-? (DAR)

AIKEN – Boas, Norman F.
Jane M. Pierce (1806-1863): the Pierce-Aiken papers: letters of Jane M. Pierce, her sister Mary M. Aiken, their family and President Franklin Pierce, with biographies of Jane Pierce, other members of her family, and genealogical tables. By Norman F. Boas. Stonington, Conn.: Seaport Autographs, c1983. (LoC)

AIKEN – Boas, Norman F.
Jane M. Pierce (1806-1863): the Pierce-Aiken papers supplement. By Norman F. Boas. Mystic, Conn.: Seaport Autographs, c1989. (LoC)

ALBRO – States Historical Society, Inc.
William C. Albro, Theodore Rogers Albro. Hartford, Conn.: The Society, 1937. (DAR)

ALDEN – Wallace, Robert N.
Twelve generations of descendants of John Alden and of John Clarke of Hartford, Connecticut. Joliet, Ill.: Wallace, 1940. (DAR)

ALEXANDER – Alexander, Winthrop
Genealogy of the Alexander family of the Connecticut Valley. 1931. (DAR)

ALLEN –
Allen Family of Watertown (1900), 35 pgs. [1]

ALLEN –
Allen Family of Windsor, Ct. (1876), 76 pgs. [1]
Allen Family of New Haven, Ct. (1899), 317 pgs. [1]

4

ALLEN –
Family of Roger Allen or Alling, English ancestry of New Haven, 1639.
(Norwich, Conn., n.d.). (PW)

ALLEN –
A genealogy of Samuel Allen of Windsor, Connecticut, and some of his
descendants. Boston, Priv. print. (D. Clapp & Son), 1876. (LoC)

ALLEN –
A brief history of Lewis Allen, of Fisher's Island and New London, Conn.,
and his descendants from 1699 to 1954. Rutland, Vt., Tuttle Pub. Co.
(1954). (LoC)

ALLEN –
Genealogical sketches of Roger Alling, of New Haven, Conn., 1639,
Gilbert Allen, of Morristown, N. J., 1736, and Thomas Bancroft, of
Dedham, Mass., 1640, and some of their descendants. Prepared by Jno. K.
Allen and Edwin Salter. Lansing, Mich. Journal steam printing house,
1883. (LoC)

ALLEN – Allen, Augustus L.
Brief history of the family of Nathan Allen and Mary Putnam, his wife,
late of Fort Plain, Montgomery County, N. Y., and of the families of Rev.
Aaron Putnam of Pomfret, Conn., the Bulkeley, Prescott, Hall, Grosvenor,
and other families… By Augustus L. Allen. Poughkeepsie, N. Y., 1895.
(FW)

ALLEN – Allen, George P.
A history and genealogical record of the Alling-Allens of New Haven,
Conn.: the descendants of Roger Alling, first, and John Alling, Sen., from
1639 to the present time. Compiled by George P. Allen. Mt. Airy, Md.
Libra Publications, 1977. (LoC)

ALLEN – Allen, George P.
A history and genealogical record of the Alling-Allens of New Haven,
Conn., the descendants of Roger Alling, first, and John Alling, sen., from
1639 to the present time… Comp. by George P. Allen… New Haven,
Conn., The Price, Lee & Adkins Co., 1899. (LoC)

ALLEN – Allen, Orrin Peer
The Allen memorial. Second series. Descendants of Samuel Allen of
Windsor, Conn., 1640-1907. By Orrin Peer Allen… Palmer, Mass., The
author, 1907. (LoC)

ALLEN – Allen, Willard S.
A genealogy of Samuel Allen of Windsor, Connecticut. Boston: David
Clapp & Son,, Printers, 1876. (DAR)

ALLEN – Bolton, Charles Knowles
The ancestry of Margaret Wyatt, wife of Matthew Allyn of Braunton in
Devon, and later of Windsor in Connecticut... (By) Charles Knowles
Bolton. (Boston, 1898). (LoC)

ALLEN – Lainson, Dorothy A. S.
Roger Alling (Allen) and John Alling (Allen) Sr. Cousins and pioneer
settlers of New Haven, Conn., and some of their descendants. By Dorothy
A. S. Lainson. Huntsville, Ark., Cent. Enterprises Geneal. Ser., 1971.
(FW)

ALLEN – Phinney, Mary A.
Allen genealogy. A brief history of Lewis Allen... (Conn.)... 1699-1954.
By Mary A. Phinney. Rutland, Vt., Tuttle Pub. Co. (1954). (SP)

ALLEN – Sastrom, Theodore M.
The Pequonneck Allen family. (Bridgeport, Conn.). By Theodore M.
Sastrom. Fairfield, Conn. (1962?). (FW)

ALLING – Allen, George P.
A history and genealogical record of the Alling-Allens of New Haven,
Conn. New Haven, Conn.: Price, Lee & Adkins Co., 1899. (DAR)

ALLIS – Allis, Horatio D.
Genealogy of William Allis. Hartford, Conn.: Allis, 192-? (DAR)

ALLYN – Sastrom, Theodore M.
Matthew Allyn of Windsor, Connecticut. Brooklyn, N. Y.?: Sastrom,
197-? (DAR)

ALSOP – Leffingwell, Douglas
Alsop genealogy, being a brief account of the descendants of Richard
Alsop, who first appeared in Middletown, Connecticut, in 1750, grandson
of Richard Alsop and Hannah Underhilll. Done in typewriting for Mary
Alsop Cryder by Douglas Leffingwell. (n.p.) 1928. (LoC)

ALVORD – Alvord, Samuel Morgan
A genealogy of the descendants of Alexander Alvord. Hartford, Conn.:
Alvord, 1908. (Webster, N. Y.: A. D. Andrews). (DAR)

ALVORD – Alvord, Samuel Morgan
A genealogy of the descendants of Alexander Alvord, an early settler of Windsor, Conn. and Northampton, Mass. Comp. by Samuel Morgan Alvord. Webster, N. Y.: A. D. Andrews, Printer, 1908. (LoC)

AMELUNG – Amelung, Charlotte Hill
Amelungs in America: a family records. Compiled by Charlotte Hill Amelung. (Fairfield, Conn.): C. H. Amelung, 1980. (LoC)

AMES – DeLong, Kathy L. (Kathy Louise)
Descendants of Benjamin and Dorcas Ames of Connecticut, 1786-1979: a genealogy. By Kathy L. DeLong. Reseda,Calif., Mojave Books, c1980. (LoC)

ANABLE – Anable, Anthony
The Anable family in America, 1623-1967. Stamford, Conn.: Priv. print. by Demarest Associated Services, 1967. (DAR)

ANDREW – Elmer, Adelia (B.)
History of the Andrew family, from various sources. Written and comp. by Adelia (B.) Elmer. Ansonia,Conn., Press of the Evening Sentinel, 1889. (NY)

ANDREWS –
Andres Family of Farmington, Ct. (1872), 652 pgs. [1]

ANDREWS – Andrews, Alfred
Genealogical history of John and Mary Andrews who settled in Farmington, Conn., 1640, embracing their descendants to 1872... Chicago, Ill.: A. H. Andrews & Co., 1872. (DAR)

ANDREWS – Andrews, Alfred
Genealogical history of John and Mary Andrews, who settled in Farmington, Conn., 1640: embracing their descendants to 1872; with an introduction of miscellaneous names of Andrews, with their progenitors as far as known; to which is added a list of some of the authors, clergymen, physicians and soldiers of the name. By Alfred Andrews... Chicago, Ill.: A. H. Andrews & Co., 1872. (LoC)

ANDREWS – Andrews, Frank H. (Frank Herbert)
William Andrews of Hartford, Conn., and his descendants in the direct line to Asa Andrews of Hartland, Conn., and Hartford, Ohio: Chester Andrews and descendants, Rev. Wells Andrews and descendants, Nelson Andrews and descendants, Sherman and Schuyler Andrews. Prepared by Frank H.

7

Andrews. [Illinois: s.n., 1938]. (Washington, Ill.: Tazewell County Reporter). (LoC)

ANDREWS – Andrews, Frank H.
William Andrews of Hartford, Conn. Washington, Ill.: Tazewell County Reporter, 1938. (DAR)

ANDREWS – Andrews, Frank A.
WilliamAndrews of Hartford, Conn. and his descendants in the direct line to Asa Andrews of Hartland, Conn., and Hartford, Ohio. By Frank A. Andrews. Washington, Ill., Tazewell County Reporter. 1938. (FW)

ANDREWS – Goodwell, Harriet A.
John Andrews of Ipswich, Mass. and Norwick, Conn. and some of his descendants... By Harriet A. Goodwell. Boston (F. H. Gilson). 1916. (FW)

ANDREWS – Moore, Cora (A.)
Genealogical history of Wm. Andrews and wife who settled in New Haven, Conn., 1638... (FW)

ANDREWS – Porter, George S.
Genealogy: family of Andrews-Giddings. By George S. Porter. Norwich, Conn., n.d. (FW)

ANDRUS – Lee, Elizabeth Duncan
Some descendants of John and Grace (Rood) Andrus of Preston, Connecticut, Lebanon, New Hampshire, Clesea, Vermont. Compiled by Elizabeth Duncan Lee. Rev. St. Louis, Mo.: Genealogical R. & P., 1982. (LoC)

ANTISELL – Wyman, Mary Elizabeth Tisdel
The genealogy of the descendants of Lawrence and Mary Antisell of Norwich and Willington, Conn. Painesville, Ohio: Wyman (Columbus, Ohio: Champlin Printing Co.), 1908. (DAR)

ANTISELL – Wyman, Mary Elizabeth Tisdel
The genealogy of the descendants of Lawrence and Mary Antisell of Norwich and Willington, Conn., including some records of Christopher Antisell of Sraduff, Birr (Kings Co.) Ireland. By Mary Elizabeth Tisdel Wyman. (Columbus, O., The Chaplin Printing Co.) 1908. (LoC)

ARNOLD – Hook, James W.

The John Arnold family of Haddon and E. Haddon, Conn. By James W. Hook. New Haven, Conn., 1952. (SP)

ASHLEY – Trowbridge, Francis Bacon
The Ashley genealogy. New Haven, Conn.: Trowbridge (Tuttle, Morehouse & Taylor) 1896. (DAR)

ATKINS – Cuccio, Jane
The Atkins chronicles: seven generations of the family in New England, from William Adkins of Connecticut to John Atkins, III, of Vermont and Illinois, together with a survey of seven generations of the latter's descendants throughout the United States. Compiled by Jane Cuccio; with illus. and assistance by Earl Hill. (Greenfield Center, N. Y.), Cuccio, 1977. (LoC)

ATKINSON – Atkinson, Mrs. Adelaid C.
Account of Stephen Atkinson and his descendants. By Mrs. Adelaid C. Atkinson. Meriden, Conn., 1896. (PH)

ATWATER –
Memoirs of Francis Atwater, half century of recollections of an unusually active life. Considerable space devoted to the progess of the City of Meriden and its people. Enterprises organized in many places, covering varied lines of business... (Meriden, Conn., Horton Printing Co., 1922). (LoC)

ATWATER –
Atwater history and genealogy. Meriden, Conn. Printed by the Journal Publishing Co., 1901. (LoC)

ATWATER –
A genealogical register of the descendants in the male line of David Atwater, one of the original planters of New Haven, Conn., to the sixth generation. New Haven, Tuttle, Morehouse & Taylor, 1873. (LoC)

ATWATER – Atwater, Edward Elias
A genealogical record of the descendants in the male line of David Awater, one of the original planters of New Haven, Conn., to the sixth generation. New Haven, Ct., 1873. (NGS)

ATWATER – Atwater, Edward Alias
A genealogical register of the descendants in the male line of David Atwater, one of the original planters of New Haven, Conn., to the fifth

generation. By Edward Alias Atwater. New Haven, Conn., J. H. Benham, 1851. (LoC)

ATWATER –Atwater, Edward E.
A genealogical register of the descendants in the male line of David Atwater. New Haven, Conn.: Tuttle, Morehouse & Taylor, 1873. (DAR)

ATWATER – Atwater, Francis
Atwater history and genealogy. S.1.:Atwater, 1901-1927 (Meriden, Conn.: Journal Publishing Co.). (DAR)

ATWELL – Atwell, Charles Beach
The genealogy of the Atwell family, formerly of New London, Conn. Prepared by Charles Beach Atwell. Evanston, Ill., 1896. (LoC)

AUGUR – Augur, Edwin P.
Family history and genealogy of the descendants of Robert Augur of New Haven Colony. Middletown, Conn.: Augur, 1904. (DAR)

AUGUR – Augur, Edwin P.
Family history and genealogy of the descendants of Robert Augur of New Haven colony. Comp. by Edwin P. Augur. Middletown, Conn. (Press of Pelton & King), 1904. (LoC)

AUSTIN – Moore, Edith Austin
John Austin of Greenwich, Connecticut, 1963. (DAR)

AUSTIN – Moore, Edith Austin
John Auston (i. e. Austin) of East Haven, Conn. 1963. (DAR)

AUSTIN – Moore, Edith Austin
Descendants of John Austin of Greenwich, Connecticut: Vermont migration to New York and west. By Edith Austin Moore; with additions by Marion Wright Jones. (Silver Creek, N. Y.): M. W. Jones (1981?). (LoC)

AUSTIN – Moore, Edith A.
John Austin of Stamford, Connecticut. By Edith A. Moore. (St. Petersburgh, Fla., 1973?). (NY)

AVERY –
Genealogy of the descendants of Avery, Chesebrough, Palmer and Miner families who settled Stonington, Conn., early 1600s, also Kniffen, Weeks, Whitbeck, Wrigley families. Arden, N. C., 1983. (NGS)

AVERY – Avery, Amos G.
Clockmaker and craftsmen of the Avery family in Connecticut. By Amos
G. Avery. Hartford: Connecticut Historical Society, 1987. (LoC)

AVERY – Avery, Samuel Putnam
The Avery, Fairchild & Park families of Massachusetts, Connecticut &
Rhode Island, with a short narration of facts concerning Mr. Richard
Warren, Mayflower passenger, and his family connections with Thomas
Little. Hartford, Ct., 1919. (NGS)

AVERY – Avery, Samuel Putnam
The Avery, Fairchild & Park families. Hartford, Conn.: Avery, 1919.
(DAR)

AVERY – Avery, Samuel Putnam
The Avery, Fairchild & Park families of Massachusetts, Connecticut &
Rhode Island, with a short narration of facts concerning Mr. Richard
Warren, Mayflower passenger, and his family connections with Thomas
Little... By Samuel Putnam Avery. Hartford, Conn., 1919. (LoC)

AVERY – Wrigley, Harold Chandler
Genealogy of the descendants of Avery, Chesebrough, Palmer & Miner
families who settled in Stonington, Conn., early 1600s: also relating
families of Kniffen, Weeks, Whitbeck & Wrigley. Compiled by Harold
Chandler Wrigley, May 14, 1983. Arden, N. C., H. C. Wrigley (1983).
(LoC)

AXTELL – Axtell, Carson A.
Axtell genealogy. New Bedford, Conn. Darwin Press, 1945, 1962.
(DAR)

AXTELL – Corbett, Helene (Ann)
More about the Axtells: Augustus Ellridge and his descendants. Compiled
by Helene A. Corbett and Gretchen L. Defabaugh. [East Hartford, Conn.:
G. L. Defabaugh], c1989. (LoC)

AYER – Connecticut DAR, G. R. C.
Ayer family Haverhill, Massachusetts to Ayer's Gap, Franklin,
Connecticut. 1957. (DAR)

AYER – States, James Noyes
Genealogy of the Ayres family of Fairfield County, Conn. Comp. by
James Noyes States. New Haven, Conn., 1916. (LoC)

AYERS – States, James Noyes
Genealogy of the Ayers family of Fairfield County, Conn. New Haven,
Conn.: States, 1916. (DAR)

AYRES – States, James N.
Genealogy of the Ayres family of Fairfield County, Conn. Comp. by
James N. States... New Haven, Conn., 1916. (LI)

B

BABCOCK – deForest, Louis Effingham
Babcock and allied families. S.1.: deForest, 1928. (New Haven,Conn.:
Tuttle. Morehouse & Taylor). (DAR)

BACKHOUSE – Backus, William W.
A genealogical memoir of the Backus family, with the private journal of
James Backus, together with his correspondence bearing on the first
settlement of Ohio, at Marietta, in 1788. Also, papers and correspondence
of Elijah Backus, showing the character and spirit of the times during the
revolutionary period. In two parts. Part I. Genealogical, including journal
of James Backus, and poems by Miss Sarah Backus. Part II. Historical,
containing sketches of the first settlements of Connecticut and Ohio, with
miscellaneous papers of historic interest. By William W. Backus.
(Norwich, Conn., Press of The Bulletin Co.), 1889. (LoC)

BACKUS – Backus, William W.
A genealogical memoir of the Backus family. Norwich, Conn.: Backus
(The Bulletin Co.), 1890. (DAR)

BACKUS – Backus, William W.
A genealogical memoir of the Backus family. By William W. Backus.
(Norwich, Conn.), 1889. (LI)

BACKUS – Thomas, Edwin Backus
Backus manuscript, tracing descendants of William Backus, Senior, from
Saybrook, Ct., 1637 to Toledo, Ohio, 1928. Naples, Fl., 1976. (NGS)

BACON – Porter, George S.
Genealogy: family of Bacon, John, and wife Hannah family records. By
George S. Porter. Norwich, Conn., ca.1713. (Norwich, Conn., 1907).
(FW)

12

BAILEY –
Thomas Bailey family (of Groton, d. 1709). N.p.:n.d. (FW)

BAIRD – Beard, Ruth
Agenealogy of the descendants of Widow Martha Beard of Milford, Conn.
By Ruth Beard. Ansonia, Conn., The Emerson Publishing Co., 1915.
(LoC)

BALDWIN – Baldwin, George E.
The descendants of Deacon Aaron Baldwin of North Branford, Conn.,
1724-1800. Forestville, N. Y.: Baldwin, 1907. (DAR)

BALDWIN – Baldwin, Geo. E.
The descendants of Deacon Aaron Baldwin of North Branford, Conn.,
1724-1800; with a brief account of his ancestors. Compiled and arranged
by Geo. E. Baldwin... Forestville, N. Y. 1907? (LoC)

BALDWIN – Baldwin, Henry
The Baldwin family from Joseph of Milford, Conn., with the line of Isaac
(6) complete. By Henry Baldwin. Bath, N. Y., 1915. (LI)

BALDWIN – Baldwin, John D.
A record of the descendants of John Baldwin, of Stonington, Conn., with
notices of other Baldwins who settled in America in early colony times.
Worcester, Mass.: Tyler & Seagrave, 1880. (DAR)

BALDWIN – Baldwin, John D.
A record of the descendants of John Baldwin, of Stonington, Conn.; with
notices of other Baldwins, who settled in America in early colony times.
Prepared by John D. Baldwin... Worcester, Printed by Tyler & Seagrave,
1880. (LoC)

BALDWIN – Horne, Mary Virginia
Descendants of Jesse Baldwin of Richmond County, North Carolina, and
Baldwin family history in New Jersey and Connecticut. 1975. (DAR)

BALDWIN – Perkins, Mary E.
Old families of Norwich, Connecticut, 1670-1800. Comp. by Mary E.
Perkins. Genealogies. Vol. 1, pt. 1... Norwich, Conn., 1900. (LoC)

BALDWIN – Snow, Helen F.
The ancestry of Francis Baldwin. Madison, Conn.: Snow, 1971? (DAR)

BALDWIN – Snow, Helen

13

The ancestry of Francis Baldwin. By Helen F. Snow. Madison, Conn., n.d. (FW)

BALL – Ball, D. A. S.
Alling Ball of London, England and some of his descendants in Conn., U. S. A. By D. A. S. Ball. Huntsville, Ark. Cent. Enterprises, 1971. (FW)

BALLARD –
The Ballard history from 1420 to 1903. (Thompson? Conn., Priv. print., 1903). (LoC)

BANKS – Jockum, Helen Parker
Recollections. By Helen Parker Jockum, illustrations by Janet Konther Monteith. [Bloomfield, Conn.]: H. P. Jockum, c1988. (LoC)

BANKS – Todd, Charles Burr
The history of Redding, Conn., from its first settlement to the present time. With notes on the Adams, Banks... Snow families. By Charles Burr Todd... New York, The J. A. Gray Press, 1880. (LoC)

BANNING –
Banning-Bradley and allied families: genealogical, biographical. Hartford, Conn., States Historical Society, Inc., 1930. (LoC)

BANNING –
Banning-Bradley and allied families, genealogical, biographical. Hartford, Conn., States Historical Co., Inc., 1930. (FW)

BARBER – Barbour, Sylvester
Newspaper clippings on the Barbour family, from Hartford,Conn., 1911-1912 newspapers. By Sylvester Barbour. (n.d.). (FW)

BARBER – Barbour, Sylvester
Reminiscences, by Sylvester Barbour, a native of Canton, Conn. Fifty years a lawyer and appendix, containing a list of the officers and members, and a copy of the by-laws of Phoebe Humphrey Chapter, Daughters of the American Revolution of Collinsville, Connecticut. Hartford, The Case, Lockwood & Braindard Company, 1908. (LoC)

BARBOUR – Barbour, Hemen H.
My wife and my mother. By Hemen H. Barbour. Hartford, Press of William, Wiley and Waterman, 1864. (CH)

14

BARKER –
Barker Family of Pomfret, Ct. (1897), 36 pgs. [1]

BARKER – Barker, Elizabeth Frye
Barker genealogy; Robert of Plymouth Colony, 1628; John of Duxbury,
Mass., 1628; James of Rhode Island, 1634; James of Rowley, Mass., 1638;
Edward of Bradford, Conn., 1640; Richard of Andover, Mass., 1643;
Samuel of Delaware, 1682; Virginia Barkers, 1700. (By) Elizabeth Frye
Barker. New York, Frye Pub. Co., 1927. (LoC)

BARLOW – Williams, George Ebenezer
A genealogy of the descendants of William Howard Barlow of Naugatuck,
Connecticut. By Geo. E. Williams. West Hartford, Ct., G. E. Williams
(198?). (LoC)

BARNES – Barnes, Clair Elmer
Barnes: the westward migration of one line of the descendants of the
Thomas Barnes of Hartford and Farmington, Connecticut: including the
vital records of the descendants of Julius Elizer Barnes and Sylvina Harriet
Vought. By Clair Elmer Barnes. Long Beach, Calilf., 1966. (LoC)

BARNES – Barnes, Frederick R.
Thomas Barnes (ca. 1615-1689/90) of Hartford and Farmington,
Connecticut in relation to inheritable tendencies. Minneapolis, Minn.:
Barnes, 1943. (DAR)

BARNES – Barnes, Frederick R.
Thomas Barnes, ca1615-1689/90 of Hartford and Farmington, Conn., in
relation to inheritable tendencies. (Minneapolis, Minn., 1943). (FW)

BARNES – Barnes, Fuller F.
Ten generations of the Barnes family in Bristol, Conn. Privately printed
and distributed by Fuller F. Barnes... (Worcester, The Davis Press), 1946.
(FW)

BARNHART –
Genealogical sketch of the family of Jeremiah Barnhart (1758-1834).
Middletown, Conn., Felton and King, 1891. (LI)

BARRETT – Marks, Jeannette Augustus
The family of the Barrett, a colonial romance. Westport, Conn.:
Greenwood Press [1973, c1938]. (LoC)

BARRETT – Porter, George Shepard

English ancestry of Margaret Baret, wife first, of Simon Huntington, who died on the passage to New England in 1633, and secondlly, of Lieut. Thomas Stoughton of Dorchester, Mass., in 1630, and of Windsor, Conn., in 1635. By George Shepard Porter. Norwich, Conn., 1906. (LoC)

BARTHOLOMEW -
A collection of family records from Bartholomew, Botsford, and Winston lines of genealogy...Hartford, Hartford Press, 1899. (LoC)

BARTHOLOMEW –
Address of the Hon. Andrew J. Bartholomew... delivered Aug. 10, 1882, at Stony Creek, Conn., on the occasion of the first reunion of the descendants of Lieut. William Bartholomew. Boston. Press of Coburn Brothers, 1882. (LoC)

BARTHOLOMEW – Pond, Sarah Annis Winston
A collection of family records from Bartholomew, Botsford and Winston. Hartford, Conn.? Hartford Press (The Case, Lockwood & Brainard Co.), 1899. (DAR)

BARTLETT –
The Bartletts. Ancestral, genealogical, biographical, historical. Comprising an account of the American progenitors of the Bartlett family, with special reference to the descendants of John Bartlett, of Weymouth and Cumberland. New Haven, Conn., Press of the Stafford Printing Co., 1892. (LoC)

BARTLETT - Bartlett, Thomas Edward
The Bartletts. Descendants of John Bartlett, of Weymouth and Cumberland. New Haven, Ct., 1892. (NGS)

BARTLETT – Bartlett, Thomas Edward
The Bartletts, ancestral, genealogical, biographical, historical. New Haven, Conn.: Bartlett. (Stafford Printing Co.), 1892. (DAR)

BARTRAM – Bartram, Evelyn R.
The Bartrams of Connecticut; genealogy of a Puritan family, 1658-1953. By Evelyn R. Bartram. Brooklyn, N. Y., 1953. (NY)

BASS – Manchester, Irving E.
The history of Colebrook, by Irving E. Manchester, and other papers. (Winstead, Conn., The Citizen Printing Company), 1935. (LoC)

BASSETT –
Report of the proceedings of the 1st-4th reunions of the Bassett Family Assoc. of America, 1897-1902. New Haven & Seymour, Conn. (1897-1902). (LI)

BASSETT –
...Report of the proceedings of the first reunion of the Bassett family association of America... 1897... New Haven, Conn., Press of the Price, Lee & Adkins Co. (1897-19--). (LoC)

BASSETT – Bassette, Buell Burdett
One Bassett family in America, with all connections in America and many in Great Britain and France. New Britain, Conn.: Bassette, 1926. (DAR)

BASSETT – Preston, Belle
Bassett-Preston ancestors. New Haven, Conn,: Tuttle, Morehouse & Taylor, 1930. (DAR)

BASSETT – Preston, Belle
Bassett-Preston ancestors; a history of the ancestors in America of Marion Bassett Luitweiler, Howard Murray Bassett, Preston Rogers Bassett, Isabel Bassett Wasson, and Helen Bassett Hauser, children of Edward M. and Annie (Preston) Bassett. By Belle Preston... New Haven, Conn., The Tuttle, Morehouse & Taylor Co., 1930-(36). (LoC)

BATEMAN – Ridge, Bradley B.
The Bateman connection: the known descendants of William Bateman "of London, England, Charleston and Concord, Massachusetts, and Fairfield, Connnecticut." By Bradley B. Ridge. San Francisco, Ralling Hall, 1978. (LoC)

BATES – Bates, Albert Carlos
Ancestral line for eight generations of Capt. Lemuel Bates, 1729-1820. Hartford, Conn.: Bates? 1943. (DAR)

BATES – Bates, Albert Carlos, M. A.
Ancestral line for eight generations of Capt. Lemuel Bates, 1729-1820, with some records of his descendants. By Carlos Bates, M. A. Hartford, 1943. (LoC)

BATES – Cunningham, Mildred Bates
Some Bates from Connecticut, New York, Ohio, and beyond. Kalamazoo, Mi., 1983. (NGS)

BATES – Cunningham, Mildred Bates
Some Bates and their wives following: Henry and Elias of Connecticut;
Benjamin of Connecticut and New York; Calvin and Rufus of Ohio,
descendants of Rufus Bates. By Mildred Bates Cunningham... [et al.].
Alice Grandy Robinson, ed. Kalamazoo, Mi., A. G. Robinson [1983].
(LoC)

BATES – Deacon, Edward
Bates, bears and Bunker Hill with a correction or two. By Edward
Deacon. Bridgeport, Conn., Press of the Automatic Printing Co., 1911.
(LoC)

BATTERSON – Sastrom, Berniece G.
The Batterson family of Old Fairfield, Connecticut. Brooklyn, N. Y.:
Sastrom, 1973. (DAR)

BAYLEY – Bayley, Lewis D.
Souvenir 100th anniversary of the birth of Joshua Bayley (Bayley
genealogy). By Lewis D. Bayley. Hartford, Conn., 1907. (LI)

BEACH –
The Reverend John Beach and his descendants; together with historical
and biographical sketches and the ancestry and descendants of John
Sanford, of Redding,Connecticut. By Rebecca Beach and Rebecca
Donaldson Gibbons. New Haven, The Tuttle, Morehouse & Taylor
Press, 1898. (LoC)

BEACH –
The descendants of Thomas Beach of Milford, Connecticut. Hartford,
Conn., The Case, Lockwood & Brainard Company, 1912. (LoC)

BEACH –
Beach in America; containing general information regarding the three
brothers, Richard Beach, John Beach and Thomas Beach, planters in
the original settlements of New Haven Colony, Wallingford Colony
and Milford Colony, Connecticut, 1638 to 1641, and genealogical
record on a portion of the descendants of Richard Beach, together with
notes on pioneer Beaches of Michigan, and an index of all known male
descendants of Planter Richard Beach, signer of the Fundamental
Compact of New Haven Colony, 1639. (Kalamazoo, Mich., Ihling
Bros. Everard Co., 1923). (LoC)

BEACH – Beach, David Nelson

Beach family reminiscences and annals. By David Nelson Beach.
Meriden, Conn., The Journal Press, 1931. (LoC)

BEACH – Beach, Mary E.
The descendants of Thomas Beach of Milford, Connecticut. Hartford,
Conn.: Case, Lockwood and Brainard Co., 1912. (DAR)

BEACH – Beach, Rebecca Donaldson
The Reverend John Beach and his descendants. New Haven, Conn.:
Tuttle, Morehouse & Taylor, 1898. (DAR)

BEACH – McClaughry, Charles C.
Genealogy of the Beach family of Connecticut. S.1.: McClaughry?
191-? (DAR)

BEACH – McClaughry, Charles C.
Genealogy of the Beach family of Connecticut, with portions of the
genealogies of the allied families of Demmond, Walker, Gooding and
Carpenter... Comp. by Charles C. McClaughry. (n.p. 19--?). (LoC)

BEAMAN – Bjorkman, Gwen Boyer
The descendants of Thomas Beeman of Kent, Connecticut. By Gwen
Boyer Bjorkman. Seattle, Wash., 1971. (LoC)

BEARD – Beard, Ruth
A genealogy of the descendants of Widow Martha Beard of Milford,
Conn. Ansonia, Conn.: Emerson Pub. Co., 1915. (DAR)

BEARD – Beard, Ruth
A genealogy of the descendants of widow Martha Beard of Milford,
Conn. By Ruth Beard. Ansonia, Conn., Emerson Pub. Co., 1915.
(NY)

BEARDSLEY – Beardsley, E. Edwards
A sketch of William Beardsley: one of the original settlers of Stratford,
Conn., and a record of his descendants to the third generation; and of
some who bear his name to the present time. By E. Edwards
Beardsley... New Haven, Bassett & Barnett, 1867. (LoC)

BEARSE – Newcomb, John Bearss
A contribution to the genealogy of the Bearse or Bearss family in
America: 1618-1871. Ancestry and descendants of Dea. John Bearss
and his wife, Molly (Beardsley) Bearss, of New Fairfield, Ct., and

Westmoreland, N. Y. By John Bearss Newcomb... Elgin, Ill., 1871. (LoC)

BECHTEL – Hook, James William
Judge Karl Bechtel of Hanau, Germany, his forbears and some of his descendants, including notes on the families of Dufay, Serrurier, Laufer, Waldburger, Leopoldt and Kampe, with which the Bechtels and others in the direct line intermarried, Compiled by James William Hook. (New Haven, The Tuttle, Morehouse & Taylor Company, 1936). (LoC)

BECK – Massey, George Valentine
Clayton-Hambly ancestry of Thomas Beach, Esq. By George Valentine Massey. (Wilton, Conn.), 1948. (LoC)

BECKLEY –
The descendants of Richard Beckley of Wethersfield, Connecticut. Hartford, Connecticut Historical Society, 1948. (LoC)

BECKLEY – Sheppard, Caroleen Beckley
The descendants of Richard Beckley of Wethersfield Connecticut. Hartford, Conn.: Connecticut Historical Society, 1948. (DAR)

BECKWITH –
Matthew Beckwith (of Hartford, Conn.). N.p., n.d. (FW)

BECKWITH – Beckwith, Frederick H.
Additional Beckwith notes. Stratford, Conn.: Beckwith, 1956. (DAR)

BECKWITH – Beckwith, Frederick H.
Additional Beckwith notes including Every, Ely, Holms, Lee, Smith (Nehemiah, Richard and Simon), Southerland, Wightman and Williams families with miscellaneous historical data. By Frederick H. Beckwith. Stratford, Conn., 1956. (FW)

BEEBE – Hunt, Mitchell J.
The mysterious Beebe families of Beebe, Vermont – Quebec: with genealogy of the Beebe brothers of New London, Connecticut, in lines which went to Vermont, and notes on the House families of Vermont and Quebec. By Mitchell J. Hunt. Nov. 1979 revisions. Willow Grove, Pa., M. J. Hunt, 1979. (LoC)

BEECHER –
Portraits of a nineteenth century family: a symposium on the Beecher family. Edited by Earl A. French and Diana Royce. Hartford, Stowe-Day Foundation, 1976. (LoC)

BEECHER – Caskey, Marie
Chariot of fire: religion and the Beecher family. By Marie Caskey. New Haven, Yale University Press, 1978. (LoC)

BEECHER – Hughes, Reuben Beecher
Genealogy of a branch of the Beecher family. Comp. by Reuben Beecher Hughes. New Haven, Conn., November, 1898. New Haven, Hoggson & Robinson Printers, 1898. (LoC)

BEEMAN – Bjorkman, Gwen B.
The descendants of Thomas Beeman of Kent, Connecticut. By Gwen B. Bjorkman. Seattle, Wash., 1971. (FW)

BEEMAN – Bjorkman, Gwen Boyer
The descendants of Thomas Beeman of Kent, Connecticut. Seattle, Wa., 1971. (NGS)

BEERS – Dutton, Samuel W. S.
An address at the funeral of Deacon Nathan Beers, on the 14th of February, 1849. By Samuel W. S. Dutton... New Haven, W. H. Stanley, Printer, 1849. (LoC)

BEERS – Regan, Mary Louise
The descendants of Anthony Beers of Fairfield, Connecticut through his son Barnabas. By Mary Louise Regan. Palatine, Ill., Regan Genealogical Pub. Co., 1982. (LoC)

BEERS – Regan, Mary Louise
The descendants of Anthony Beers, of Fairfield, Connecticut, through his son Ephraim. By Mary Louise Regan; containing a report on her search for the English ancestry of Anthony Beers by Josephine Wakeman Beers. Palatine, Ill. Regan Genealogical Pub. Co., 1978. (LoC)

BEHAIM –
Three Behaim boys: growing up in early modern Germany: a chronicle of their lives. Edited and narrated by Steven Ozment. New Haven: Yale University Press, c1990. (LoC)

BELDING – Whitney, Charles C.
Some Belding genealogy; being some of the descendants of Richard
Belding, of Staffordshire, England, one of the earliest settlers of
Wethersfield, Conn. Comp. by Charles C. Whitney. Printed privately.
New York, 1896. (LoC)

BELOTE – Macdonald, Donald B.
Belote family, Connecticut and New York. Compiled by Donald B.
Macdonald... Kingston, Pa., 1935. (MH)

BENJAMIN – Baker, Ellis Benjamin
Genealogy of the Benjamin family in the United States of America
from 1632 to 1898. New Haven, Conn.: Baker (Tuttle, Morehouse &
Taylor), 1898. (DAR)

BENNET –
Descendants of James Bennet of Norwich, Conn. N.p. (1912?) (NY)

BENNETT – Bennett, Edgar B.
The Bennett family, 1628-1910. East Berlin, Conn.: E. B. Bennett,
1910. (DAR)

BENNETT – Bennett, Edgar B.
The Bennett family, 1628-1910. By Edgar B. Bennett. East Berlin,
Conn.: E. B. Bennett, 1910. (LoC)

BENNETT – Bennett, Edgar B.
Bennett history, 1833-1908. (By Edgar B. Bennett). East Berlin,
Conn., 1908. (FW)

BENNETT – Wright, John Calvin
The genealogy of Calvin Goddard Bennett of Gypsum, Kansas, a lineal
descendant of John Bennett of Stonington, New London County,
Connecticut. 1945. (DAR)

BENTLEY – Bentley, Mrs. Edward M.
William Bentley of Lebanon, Connecticut, 16**-1751 and his
descendants. 1925. (DAR)

BENTON – Fowler, Sarah B.
Ancestral register of... Arthur Hotchkiss Benton... By Sarah B.
Fowler. Guilford, Conn., 1918. (NY)

BERRY – Berry, June

Descendants of Hosea Berry of Sharon, Conn. By June Berry.
[Kearns, Utah]: J. Berry, 1987. (LoC)

BERTRAND –
Bartram branches: genealogy of the families of West Virginia,
Connecticut, and Pennsylvania. By Violet W. Bartram and D. Kent
Bartram, Jr. Baltimore: Gateway Press, 1984. (LoC)

BETTS – Chamberlain, Marjorie Dikeman
The ancestors and descendants of Annie Rebecca Betts, 1850-1916.
Wilton, Connecticut. By Marjorie D. Chamberlain. (East Poland?
Me.) M. D. Chamberlain (1982). (LoC)

BILLARD – Edwards, William Hopple
Ancestors of Mary Elizabeth Billard; Part 1, Billard family. Meriden,
Conn.: Edwards, 1959. (DAR)

BINGHAM – Bingham, Charles E.
Thomas Bingham, Connecticut pioneer; a story of very early colonial
times, 1658-1730, based on records. By Charles E. Bingham. Essex,
Conn., Pequot Pr. (1968). (FW)

BINGHAM – Bingham, Theodore A.
The Bingham family in the United States, especially of the state of
Connecticut. Easton, Pa.: Bingham Assoc., 1927-30. (DAR)

BINGHAM – Bingham, Theodore A.
Genealogy of the Bingham family in the United States especially of the
state of Connecticut. Harrisburg, Pa.: Harrisburg Pub. Co., 1898.
(DAR)

BINGHAM – Bingham, Theodore A.
The Bingham family in the United States, especially of the state of
Connecticut; including notes on the Binghams of Philadelphia and of
Irish descent; medieval records; armorial bearings, etc. Compiled by
Theodore A. Bingham... Easton, Pa., The Bingham Association, 1927.
(LoC)

BINGHAM – Bingham, Theodore A.
Bingham and other genealogies; the Bingham family in the United
States, especially of the state of Connecticut; including notes on the
Binghams of Phialdephia & of Irish descent; mediaeval records;
armorial bearings. &c. also partial genealogies of the following

intemarried families: Rutherfurd, Tison, DeLaBeaume, Grew, Johnson, Deming, Foote, Clark, Whiting. Compiled by Theodore A. Bingham... (n.p.) 1920. (LoC)

BINGHAM – Bingham, Theodore A.
Genealogy of the Bingham family in the United States, especially of the state of Connecticut; including notes on the Binghams of Philadelphia and of Irish descent, with partial genealogies of allied families. Comp. by Theodore A. Bingham. Harrisburg, Pa., Harrisburg Pub. Co., 1898. (LoC)

BINGHAM – Bingham, Theodore A.
A reconstruction of old Windham Street, Conn., 1686-1916, from original sources, by Theodore A. Bingham. (New York? 1916). (NY)

BINGHAM – Bingham, Theodore A.
The Bingham family in the United States, especially of the state of Connecticut; including notes on the Binghams of Philadelphia and of Irish decent... By Theodore A. Bingham... Easton, Pa., The Bingham Assoc., 1927-30. (NY)

BIRCHARD –
The Birchard-Burchard genealogy, with history and records of the kindred in North America, descendants (!) of Thomas Birchard (1636) Norwich, Connecticut. Mrs. Elizabeth Birchard, publisher; Mr. Casius Birchard, secretary. Philadelphia, 1927. (LoC)

BIRD –
Bird Family of Hartford (1855), 24 pgs. [1]

BIRD – Bird, Frederick J.
Genealogical plot of the Bird family origin. By Frederick J. Bird. Hartford, Conn. (1944?). (FW)

BIRD – Bird, Isaac
Genealogical sketch of the Bird family, having its origin in Hartford, Conn. (By Isaac Bird). Hartford, E. Geer, Steam Printer and Stationer, 1855. (LoC)

BISHOP –
Record of the descendants of John Bishop, one of the founders of Guilford, Connecticut in 1639. Compiled by William Whitney Cone and George Allen Root. Nyack, N. Y., J. G. Bishop, 1951. (LoC)

BISHOP. See also: Benton, 1904 Galeener, 1965
Benton, 1906 Venn, 1904
Converse, 1905 Wayne, 1927

BISHOP – Cone, William Whitney
Record of the descendants of John Bishop, one of the founders of
Guilford, Connecticut, in 1639, also by George A. Root. Nyack, N. Y.,
1951. (NGS)

BISHOP – Cone, William Whitney
Record of the descendants of John Bishop, one of the founders of
Guilford, Connecticut in 1639. Nyack, N. Y.: John Guy Bishop, 1951.
(DAR)

BISHOP – Lainson, Dorothy A. S.
James Bishop, immigrant ancestor to New Haven, Conn., ca. 1648, and
some of his descendants. By Dorothy A. S. Lainson. Huntsville, Ark.,
Century Enterprises Geneal. Ser., 1973. (FW)

BISHOP – Wait, John C.
Some descendants of Revd. John Bishop (1643-1694) of Stamford,
Conn. By John C. Wait. New York, J. C. Wait, 1930. (LoC)

BISSELL – Jones, Edward Payson
Genealogy of the descendants of John Bissell of Windsor, Connecticut.
By Edward Payson Jones. (S.1) R. B. Jones (1975?). (LoC)

BLACKMORE – Smith, Rev. Alven Martyn
Three Blackmore genealogies. William Blackmore of Scituate, Mass.,
James Blackmore of Providence, R. I., Rev. Adam Blackman
(Blackmore) of Stratford, Conn., and probably related lines of Samuel
Blackmer of Bennington, Vt., and David Blackmer of Rhode Island;
also unattached lines of Reuben Blackmer of Belchertown, Mass., and
David Blackmer of Nova Scotia. Compiled and edited by Rev. Alven
Martyn Smith. So, Pasadena, Calif., A. M. Smith, 1930. (LoC)

BLACKSTONE –
The Blackstone family. Norwich, Conn.: Courier Office, 1857. (DAR)

BLACKSTONE –
Exercises at the opening of the James Blackstone library, Branford,
Conn. ... 1896. New Haven, Tuttle, 1897. (DP)

BLACKSTONE – Sargent, Lucius Manlius

The Blackstone family: being sketches, biographical and genealogical, of William Blackstone, and his descendants. By Lucius Manlius Sargent). Norwich, Conn., Courier Office, 1857. (LoC)

BLAKE –
Blake Family of Middletown, Ct. (1895), 39 pgs. [1]

BLAKE –
Our folks. (Second preliminary draft). Descendants of John Blake, of Middletown, Conn. Rockford, Ill., W. P. Lamb, Printer, 1895. (LoC).

BLAKE – Blake (Edwin M.)
Genealogical descent of Amos S. Blake of Waterbury, New Haven county, Conn. By (Edwin M.) Blake. (Tucson, Arizona, the author, 1908). (NY)

BLAKE – Hazard, Alida Blake
The Blakes of 77 Elm Street; a family sketch. By Alida Blake Hazard. (New Haven, Conn., Quinnipiack Press, Inc.), 1924. (LoC)

BLAKESLEY – Shepard, James
Samuel Blakesley of New Haven, Conn., and his descendants. By James Shepard... Boston, Press of D. Clapp & Son, 1902. (LoC)

BLANKMAN – Blankman, Donald Warren
The Blankman genealogy: the descendants in Holland and America of Pieter Blankman of North Holland (ca. 1680). Compiled by Donald Warren Blankman. Woodbury, Ct.: D. W. Blankman, 1979. (LoC)

BLIN –
Blinn-Pollard-Winkley and allied families; genealogical biographical. States Historical Co., Inc. Hartford, Conn., author, 1945. (FW)

BLIN – Hill, James W.
Blin, a short genealogy of one line of the Blin family descended from Peter Blin, the settler of Wethersfield, Connecticut. 1914. (DAR)

BLIN – Hill, James W.
Blin, a short genealogy of one line of the Blin family, descended from Peter Blin, the settler of Wethersfield, Connecticut; with a few notes on the Tibbetts family. By James W. Hill... Peoria, Ill., 1914. (LoC)

BLIN – Hill, James W.

Blin; a short genealogy of one line of the Blin family descended from
Peter Blinn, the settler, of Wethersfield, Conn., with a few notes on the
Tibbits family. By James W. Hill... (Buffalo, N. Y., Niagra Frontier
Pub. Co.), 1914. (NY)

BLINN –
Blinn – Pollard – Winkley and allied families. Hartford, Conn.: States
Hiistorical Co., 1945. (DAR)

BLISH – Blish, Matthew Rhodes
Supplement to genealogy of the Blish family in America. Fairfield,
Conn.: Blish, 1957. (DAR)

BLISS –
English ancestry of Thomas Bliss of Braintree, Mass. in 1635 and of
Hartford, Conn. (Norwich, Conn., 1907?). (FW)

BLISS – Dayton, Elinor B.
Bliss and Holmes descendants; genealogical data and biographical
sketches of the descendants of Ephraim Bliss of Savoy, Mass. and
Israel Holmes of Waterbury, Conn., and related families. By Elinor B.
Dayton. New Haven, New Haven Colony Hist. Soc., 1961. (FW)

BLISS –Hoppin, Charles Arthur
The Bliss book. Hartford, Conn.: Hoppin, 1913. (DAR)

BLODGETT –
Ancestry of Hon. William A. Blodgett... Hartford, Conn. State Lib.
(LA)

BOARDMAN – Boardman, William F. J.
The ancestry of William Francis Joseph Boardman, Hartford,
Connecticut; being his lineage in all lines of descent from the emigrant
ancestors in New England. By William F. J. Boardman... Hartford,
Conn., Priv. print. (The Case, Lockwood & Brainard Company), 1906.
(LoC)

BOARDMAN – Boardman, William Francis Joseph
The ancestry of William Francis Joseph Boardman. Hartford,
Connecticut. Hartford, Conn.: Boardman (Case, Lockwood &
Brainard), 1906. (DAR)

BOARDMAN – Goldthwaite, Charlotte

Boardman genealogy, 1525-1895. The English home and ancestry of
Samuel Boreman, Wethersfield, Conn., Thomas Boreman, Ipswich,
Mass. With some account of their descendants (now called Boardman)
in America... Comp. by Charlotte Goldthwaite... Pub. by William F.
J. Boardman. Hartford,Conn., Press of the Case, Lockwood &
Brainard Company, 1895. (LoC)

BOARDMAN – Goldthwaite, Charlotte
Boardman genealogy, 1525-1895. Hartford, Conn.: William F. J.
Boardman (Case, Lockwood & Brainard), 1895. (DAR)

BOGUE – Deming, Flora Bogue
Bogue genealogy, descendants of John Bogue of East Haddam, Conn.,
and wife Rebecca Walkley. Rutland, Vt.: Tuttle, 1944. (DAR)

BOGUE – Deming, Flora Bogue
Bogue genealogy; descendants of John Bogue of East Haddam, Conn.,
and wife, Rebecca Walkley; also the North Carolina Bogues and
miscellaneous Bogue records; ancestors of James Hubbard Bogue and
wife, Polly Adelaide Phillips, their royal lines. By Flora Bogue
Deming. Rutland, Vt.: The Tuttle Publishing Company, Inc. (1944).
(LoC)

BOGUE – Deming, Flora Lucinda (Bogue)
Bogue genealogy; descendants of John Bogue of East Haddam, Conn.,
and wife, Rebecca Walkley. Rutland, Vt., 1944. (NGS)

BOLTON – Bolton, Arthur L.
James Bolton of Bolton, his descendants and an industrial heritage. By
Arthur L. Bolton. (Clinton, Conn.), 1972. (FW)

BOLTON – Bolton, Henry Carrington
The family of Bolton in England and America, 1100-1894. New York.
Bolton: Bolton (New Haven, Conn.: Tuttle, Morehouse & Taylor),
1895. (DAR)

BONAPARTE – Aronson, Theo
Golden bees; the story of the Bonapartes. By Theo Aronson.
Greenwich, Conn., New York Graphic Soc. (1964). (FW)

BOND –
American pedigree of Rev. Alvan Bond, D. D., of Norwich,
Connecticut. (Norwich, 1896). (LoC)

BONTECOU – Morris, John E.
The Bontecou genealogy. Hartford, Conn.: Case. Lockwood & Brainard, 1885. (DAR)

BONTECOU – Morris, John E.
The Bontecou genealogy. A record of the descendants of Pierre Bontecou, a Huguenot refugee from France, in the lines of his sons. Comp. by John E. Morris. Hartford, Conn., Press of the Case, Lockwood & Brainard Company, 1885. (LoC)

BOOTH –
Booth Family of Stratford, Ct. (1862), 64 pgs. [1]
Booth Family of Stratford, Ct. (1892), 27 pgs. [1]
Booth Association (1868), 40 pgs; (1869), 19 pgs. [1]

BOOTH –
The family of Richard Boothe (an original settler in Stratford, Conn.), traced through some branches of his posterity, and introduced by fragmentary notes on ancient Stratford. New York, C. S. Westcott & Co., Printers, 1862. (LoC)

BOOTH – Booth, Walter
Genealogy of the Booth family in England and the United States. Being a compilation of the pedigrees of the English line, and of the descendants of Richard Booth of Connecticut, U. S. A., down to the family of the compiler. By Walter Booth. Minneapolis, Minn. (W. S. Booth & Son, Printers and Publishers), 1892. (LoC)

BOOTH – Fennell, Lela Brooks
Nathaniel Brooks of Ashford, Connecticut: revolutionary war pensioner, some of his ancestors and descendants, plus genealogies of four allied lines, Aldrich, Boothe, Cornwall, Killoran-Gurry. By Lela Brooks Fennell. Baltimore: Gateway Press; Wilmington, De., 1989. (LoC)

BOOTH – Jacobus, Donald Lines
The genealogy of the Booth family; Booth families of Connecticut for six or more generations. Pleasant Hill, Mo., 1952. (NGS)

BOOTH – Jacobus, Donald Lines

The genealogy of the Booth family; Booth families of Connecticut for six or more generations. By Donald Lines Jacobus. Pleasant Hill, Mo., E. C. Booth, 1952. (LoC)

BOSTWICK – Bostwick, Henry Anthon
Genealogy of the Bostwick family in America. The descendants of Arthur Bostwick, of Stratford, Conn. Comp. by Henry Anthon Bostwick, New York. (Hudson, N. Y., Bryan Printing Company), 1901. (LoC)

BOSTWICK – Coddington, John I.
Additions and corrections to the Bostwick genealogy (by Henry Anthon Bostwick, New York, 1901) by John I. Coddington... (New Haven, 1938). (LoC)

BOSTWICK. See also: Smith, 1931
                             Starkweather, 1925

BOTSFORD –
Origins of the Botsford family, a supplement to "An American family" (1933)... (New Haven, Conn., The Tuttle, Morehouse & Taylor Company, 1937). (LoC)

BOTSFORD – Jacobus, Donald Lines
An American family, Botsford-Marble ancestral lines. New Haven, Conn.: Jacobus (Tuttle, Morehouse & Taylor), 1933. (DAR)

BOUGHTON –
Bouton-Boughton family; descendants of John Boution, a native of France, who embarked from Gravesend, Eng., and landed at Boston in December, 1635, and settled at Norwalk, Ct. Albany, J. Munsell's Sons, 1890. (LoC)

-    An informative index; the names of persons and their essential genealogical data. Compiled by Willis A. Boughton. Fort Lauderdale, Fla., 1958. (LoC)

BOURNE – Lee, Helen Bourne Joy
The Bourne genealogy. Chester, Conn., Pequot Press, 1972. (DAR)

BOWEN –
Bowen Family of Woodstock, Ct. (1893), 272 pgs. [1]
Bowen Family of Woodstock, Ct. (1897), 245 pgs. [1]

BOWEN – Bowen, Arthur L.

Bowen's Court, by Elizabeth Bowen (Mrs. Donald Cameron). (A review). With notes on the Bowens of Rhode Island and Connecticut, hatched, matched & dispatched by Arthur L. Bowen. Research by Philip Mack Smith... Washington, 1943. (LoC)

BOWEN – Bowen, Daniel

The family of Griffith Bowen, gentleman, Welsh Puritan immigrant, Boston, Mass., 1638-9, especially the branch of Esquire Silas Bowen, born in Woodstock, Conn., 1722. By Daniel Bowen... Jacksonville, Fla., Da Costa Printing Company, 1893. (LoC)

BOWEN – Bowen, Edward Augustus

Lineage of the Bowens of Woodstock, Connecticut. Woodstock, Conn.: Bowen (Cambridge, Mass.: Riverside Press), 1897. (DAR)

BOWEN – Bowen, Georgene Esther

Bowen; the acestry of Griffith Bowen of "Burryhead," Llangenydd Parish, Glamorgan County, Wales, and one line of American descendants through the Bowens of Woodstock, Connecticut, and the Bowens of Charlestown, New Hampshire. By Georgene Esther Bowen. (Philadelphia?? 1960?). (LoC)

BOWER – Baldwin, C. C.

Rev. John Bower, first minister at Derby, Conn., and his descendants. By C. C. Baldwin... Reprinted from W. C. Sharpe's History of Seymour, Conn. (Seymour, Conn.), 1879. (LoC)

BOWNE – Coddington, John Insley

A Bowne problem. By John Insley Coddington... (New Haven, 1943). (LoC)

BRADFORD – Shepard, James

Governor William Bradford, and his son, Major William Bradford. New Britain, Conn.: Shepard (Herald, Print), 1900. (DAR)

BRADFORD – Shepard, James

Governor William Bradford, and his son, Major William Bradford. By James Shepard. New Britain, Conn., J. Shepard, 1900. (LoC)

BRADLEY –

Bradley Family of Guilford (1879), 46 pgs. [1]
Bradley Family of Fairfield (1894), 69 pgs. [1]

BRADLEY –
Genealogy. Family of Aaron and Sarah Bradley, of Guilford, Conn. ...
Hartford, Conn., Press of Case, Lockwood & Brainard Co., 1879.
(LoC)

BRADLEY –
(Account of) the Bradley Society. Organized at Southport, Conn., Dec.
22, 1914. Southport, Conn., 1914. (NY)

BRADLEY –
Treasure of old Watertown house. Relics of Bradley family well
preserved. (Waterbury, Conn., 1915). (MH)

BRADLEY –
Bradley family, genealogical biographical. Hartford, Conn., States
Hist. Soc., 1931. (FW)

BRADLEY –
Descendants of Isaac Bradley of Branford and East Haven,
Connecticut, 1650-1898. New York: J. M. Andreini, 1917. (DAR)

BRADLEY – Bradley, Leland S.
The ancestors of Leland Bradley, Putnam, Conn. (By Leland S.
Bradley. Putnam, Conn., 1967?). (LoC)

BRADLEY – Bradley, Leonard Abram
Descendants of Isaac Bradley of Branford and East Haven,
Connecticut, 1650-1898; together with a brief history of the various
Bradley families in New England. By Leonard Abram Bradley... New
York, Priv. print., 1917. (LoC)

BRADLEY – Lloyd, A. P.
Genealogy, family of Aaron and Sarah Bradley, of Guilford, Conn.
Hartford, Conn.: Lloyd (Case, Lockwood & Brainard), 1879. (DAR)

BRADLEY – Lloyd, Abigail Parkman
Genealogy. Family of Aaron and Sarah Bradley, of Guilford, Conn. ...
(By Abigail Parkman Lloyd). Hartford, Conn., Press of the Case,
Lockwood & Brainard Co., 1879. (LoC)

BRAINARD – Brainard, Lucy Abigail
The genealogy of the Brainerd – Brainard family in America, 1649-1908. Hartford, Conn.?: Case, Lockwood & Brainard (Hartford Press), 1908. (DAR)

BREED –
Breed Family of Stonington (1900), 15 pgs. [1]

BREED – Coates, Julia Beebe
Principal facts of interest concerning the Breed family in America, with the genealogy of the Stonington, Conn. branch. (By Julia Beebe Coates). Portland, Or., C. H. Crocker Printing Co., 1900. (LoC)

BREWER – Brewer, Duane E.
A genealogical record of the descendants of Erastus Brewer and Nancy Noble. By Duane E. Brewer. Bridgeport, Conn., 1880. (LI)

BREWSTER –
Account of the golden wedding of James and Mary Brewster, 1860. New Haven, 1860. (FW)

BREWSTER – Brewster, James
Brewster genealogy of the tenth to twelfth generation. By Emma C. Brewster Jones. New ed. comp. by James Brerwster. Litchfield (Conn.), 1960. (SL)

BREWSTER – Porter, G. S.
Genealogy: family of Brewster; William Brewster, the pilgrim. By G. S. Porter. Norwich, Conn., n.d. (FW)

BRIGHT – Porter, G. S.
English ancestry of Henry Bright of Charlestown in 1630... By G. S. Porter. Norwich, Conn., n.d. (FW)

BRINLEY – Porter, G. S.
English ancestry of Grissell Brinley, wife of Nathaniel Sylvester, of Shelter Island, 1652. By G. S. Porter. Norwich, Conn., n.d. (FW)

BRISTOL – Bristol, Warren Edwin
Bristol genealogy. Comp. Warren Edwin Bristol. Prepared for publication by Morris W. Abbott and Susan W. Abbott. (Milford, Conn.), Bristol Family Association, 1967. (LoC)

-    Supplement 1 – Prepared by the Bristol Family Association. (Editors: Alan Hefflon and Patricia Hefflon. Milford, Conn.), 1971. (LoC)

BRITTON – L. H. B. (Lewis Hotchkiss Brittin)
The ancestry of Lewis Hotchkiss Brittin, 1942, showing lines of descent from William Brittaine of Mespat, married 1660, William Howell of Wedon, married 1536, Samuel Hotchkiss of New Haven, married 1642, George Hull of Dorchester, married 1614. Compiled by L. H. B. (Lewis Hotchkiss Brittin). (Washington?), 1942.

BRITTON. See also: Bailey, 1962
                              Brittin
                              Wilson, 1929

BROCKETT –
The descendants of John Brockett, one of the original founders of New Haven colony. Illustrated with portraits and armorial bearings; an historical introduction relating to the settlement of New Haven and Wallingford, Connecticut. The English Brockettes. "A pedigree of Brockett," published in England in 1860, comp. by Edward J. Brockett, assisted by John B. Koetteritz and Francis E. Brockett. East Orange, N. J. (The Orange Chronicle Company, Printers), 1905. (LoC)

BROCKETT – Brockett, Edward J.
The descendants of John Brockett, one of the original founders of New Haven Colony. East Orange, N. J.: Orange Chronicle Co., 1905. (DAR)

BROCKWAY – Brockway (Asahel N.)
Genealogy of a branch of the descendants of Wolston Brockway, who settled in Lyme, Conn., about 1660. By (Asahel N.) Brockway. Watertown, N. Y., Brockway & Sons, Printers, 1888. (FW)

BROCKWAY – Brockway, Beman
Genealogy of a branch of the descendants of Wolston Brockway, who settled in Lyme, Conn., about 1660. Comp. by Beman Brockway. Watertown, N. Y., Brockway & Sons' Daily Times Print, 1887. (LoC)

BROMLEY – Bromley, J. Robert
The Bromley line: freedom in America as seen through the lives of 10 generations, from 1648 to 1982. By J. Robert Bromley. Stamford, Conn., (Meade, Bromley, and Bishop): J. R. Bromley, c1983. (LoC)

BROMLEY – Bromley, Viola A.

The Bromley genealogy; being a record of the descendants of Luke Bromley of Warwick, R. I., and Stonington, Conn. By Viola A. Bromley... New York, F. H. Hitchcock (c1911). (LoC)

BRONSON – Tracy, Eliza H.
Bronson-Brownson-Brunson: some descendants of John Bronson of Hartford (1636) who migrated to Vermont, New Hampshire, New Jersey (and) Pennsylvania... with some brief accounts of their relationship to Canfield, Chittenden, French, Howlett, Morris, and Tracy families. By Eliza H. Tracy. La Jolla, Calif., 1973. (NY)

BROWN – Brown, Avery
Thomas Brown of Stonington, Conn., and his descendants. 1928. (DAR)

BROWN – Grobel, Kendrick
David Arms Brown and Cleora August Towne, their ancestry and descendants. Compiled by Kendrick Grobel. Stafford Springs, Conn., 1940. (LoC)

BROWN – Wright, Helen M.
John Browne of Milford, Conn., and Newark, New Jersey, 1648, through Max L. Brown, Franklin, Indiana, 1962. By Helen M. Wright. (Montclair? N. J.), 1962. (NY)

BROWNE – Browne, Florence A.
Brown, Foster and related families. Compiled by Florence A. Browne. West Hartford, Conn., 1967. (LoC)

BROWNELL –
Brownell Family, Danbury, Ct. (1903), 53 pgs. [1]

BROWNSON –
The Brownsons of Derbyshire, England: the family of John and Richard of Hartford, Connecticut, 1836. Dallas, Ore., author, 1929. (OS)

BRYAN – Baldwin, C. C.
Alexander Bryan of Milford, Connecticut, his ancestors and his descendants. By C. C. Baldwin... Cleveland, O. (Leader Printing Co.), 1889. (LoC)

BUCK –
Buck Family of Conn. (1889), 273 pgs. [1]

Buck Family of Conn. (1894), 54 pgs. [1]

BUCK – Buck, Horace B.
Genealogy of the Samuel Buck family, of Portland, Conn., to the year
1894. By Horace B. Buck. Worcester, Mass., O. B. Wood, 1894.
(LoC)

BUCK – Cody, Edward Perrine
Genealogy of Emanuel Buck family of Wethersfield, Conn. By
Edward Perrine Cody. (Wethersfield? 1949). (LoC)

- Addictions to Buck family genealogy. Addictions through Thomas,
the son of Emanuel Buck and his wife, Mary Kirby, of Wethersfield,
Conn. (Wethersfield? 1950?). (LoC)

BUCKINGHAM – Chapman, F. W.
The Buckingham family. Hartford, Conn.; Case, Lockwood &
Brainard, 1872. (DAR)

BUCKINGHAM – Chapman, Rev. F. W.
The Buckingham family; or, The descendants of Thomas Buckingham,
one of the first settlers of Milford, Conn. Comp. at the request of
William A. Buckingham, of Norwich, Conn., by Rev. F. W.
Chapman... Hartford, Conn., Case, Lockwood & Brainard, 1872.
(LoC)

BUDINGTON – Nielson, Richard Walter
The Budington Buddington family: family pedigree. By Richard
Walter Nielson, assisted by Ruth Buddington Leighton. Westport, Ct.:
Nielson Pub. Co., 1989. (LoC)

BULKELEY – Chapman, Frederick W.
The Bulkeley family. Rocky Hill, Conn.: Chapman (Hartford, Conn.:
Case, Lockwood & Brainard), 1875. (DAR)

BULKELEY – Deacon, Edward
Bates, bears and Bunker Hill with a correction or two. By Edward
Deacon. Bridgeport, Conn.: Press of the Automatic Printing Co., 1911.
(LoC)

BULKELEY – Jacobus, Donald Lines
The Bulkeley genealogy, Rev. Peter Bulkeley. New Haven, Conn.:
Jacobus (Tuttle, Morehouse & Taylor), 1933. (DAR)

BULL –
Descendants of Captain Thomas Bull (1610-1684) original proprietor of Hartford, Connecticut. By Virginia B. Pope and Mary Louise B. Todd. (n.p.), 1939. (LoC)

BULL – Pope, Virginia B.
An outline of the descendants of Captain Thomas Bull (1610-1684) of Hartford, Conn. By Virginia B. Pope. Lake Forest, Ill., Mrs. Wm. G. Todd, 1962. (NY)

BULL – Todd, Mary Louise Buell
Thomas and Susannah Bull of Hartford, Connecticut, and some of their descendants in the first five generations. Compiled by Mary Louise B. Todd. Lake Forest, Ill. Heitman Printers, 1981 (1985). (LoC)

BUNCE – Howard, Alice K.
Genealogy of the Bunce family of Connecticut. By Alice K. Howard. (Marion? Mass., A. K. Howard, 197-). (NY)

BURBANK – Dewey, Louis M.
John Burbank of Suffield, Connecticut, and some of his descendants. By Louis M. Dewey. Westfield, Mass., n.d. (FW)

BURNHAM –
Burnham Family of Hartford (1884), 292 pgs. [1]

BURNHAM – Burnham, Roderick H.
The Burnham family. Hartford, Conn.: Press of Case, Lockwood & Brainard, c1869. (DAR)

BURNHAM – Burnham, Roderick H.
Genealogical records of Thomas Burnham, the emigrant. Hartford, Conn.: Case, Lockwood & Brainard Co., 1884. (DAR)

BURNHAM – Burnham, Roderick H.
The Burnham family; or Genealogical records of the descendants of the four emigrants of the name, who were among the early settlers in America. By Roderick H. Burnham... Hartford, Press of Case, Lockwood & Brainard, 1869. (LoC)

BURRITT – Burritt, Lewis L.
The Burritt family in America, descendants of William Burritt of Stratford, Conn., 1635-1940. Compiled by Lewis L. Burritt. (n.p., 1940). (LoC)

BURRITT – Raymond, M. D.
Sketch of Rev. Blackleach Burritt and related Stratford families... By M. D. Raymond. (Bridgeport, Conn., 1892). (LI)

BURWELL –
Proceedings of the Burwell family picnic, held at Burwell's farm, Milford, Connecticut, August 18, 1870. Cleveland, G. S. Newcomb & Co., printers, 1870. (LoC)

BURWELL –
Proceedings of the Burwell family picnic, Burwell's Farm, Milford, Connecticut, August 18, 1870. Cleveland, Oh., 1870. (NGS)

BURWELL –
Proceedings of the Burwell family picnic, held at Burwell's farm, Milford, Connecticut, August 18, 1870. [S.1.:s.n., 1979?]. (LoC)

BUSHNELL – Bushnell, George Eleazer
Bushnell family genealogy; anncestry and posterity of Francis Bushnell, 1580-1646, of Horsham, England and Guilford, Connecticut, including genealogical notes of other Bushnell families, whose connections with this branch of the family tree have not been determined. By George Eleazer Bushnell. Nashville, 1945. (LoC)

BUSHNELL – Porter, G. S.
Genealogy: family of Bushnell, Francis, of Guilford, Conn. By G. S. Porter. Norwich, Conn., n.d. (FW)

BUTLER – Bloss, Meredith
John Butler of Norwalk, Connecticut, and some of his descendants. Edited by Meredith Bloss and Arline B. Campbell. Tryon, N. C.; MA Designs, c1985. (LoC)

BUTLER – Butler, Bryant Ormond
The Butler family of Lebanon, Connecticut; an account of the ancestry and descendants of Patrick Butler and Marcy Bartlett. Compiled by Bryant Ormond Butler. Rutland, Vt., The Tuttle Company, 1934. (LoC)

BUTLER – Butler, Elmer Ellsworth
Butlers and kinsfolk, Butlers of New England and Nova Scotia and related families of other names, including Durkees, descendants of Lieut. William and Sarah (Cross) Butler, of Ipswich, Mass., and of Eleazer 1st and Lydia (Durkee) Butler, of Ashford, Conn. and Yarmouth, N. S. Compiled by Elmer Ellsworth Butler... Milford, N. H., The Cabinet Press, 1944. (LoC)

BUTLER – Ravenscroft, Ruth (Thayer)
Proof of descent of Saranne Butler Geer from Rev. Samuel Stone through the Butler family of Connecticut, Ohio, and Pennsylvania. By Ruth (Thayer) Ravenscroft, 1956. (PH)

BUTLER –
Butler Family of Saybrook, Ct. (1887), 61 pgs. [1]

BYAM – Byam, Edwin C.
Descendants of George Byam (? – 1680). By Edwin C. Byam. Suffield, Conn., Byam, 1975. (FW)

BYAM – Byam, Edwin Colby
Descendants of George Byam (?-1680). By Edwin Colby Byam. Suffield, Conn.: Byam, 1975. (LoC)

C

CABLER – Cabler, William
Family records and notes. By Willilam Cabler. Book No. 2. By William C.Moore. (Stamford, Conn., 1963). (NY)

CALAWAY – Calaway, Merle L.
The descendants of the "Connecticut Calaways" and family album illustrated, photos and charts. By Merle L. Calaway. (Conneaut, Ohio): Calaway, 1976. (NY)

CALDWELL – Caldwell, Charles T.
William Coalwelll, Caldwell or Coldwell of England, Massachusetts, Connecticut and Nova Scotia. Historical sketch of the family and name and record of his descendants. By Charles T. Caldwell... Washington, D. C., Press of Judd & Detweiler, Inc., 1910. (LoC)

CALDWELL – Caldwell, Charles Tufts

William Coalwell, Caldwell or Coldwell of England, Massachusetts, Connecticut and Nova Scotia. Washington, D. C., 1910. (NGS)

CALHOUN – Calhoun, Mildred B.
The story of the Calhouns of Judea, Connecticut; in 1779 renamed Washington, Connecticut. Woodbury, Conn.: Calhoun, 1956. (DAR)

CALHOUN – Calhoun, Mildred I. (B.)
The story of the Calhouns of Judea, Connecticut (in 1799 renamed Washington, Conn.). By Mildred I. (B.) Calhoun. Stamford, Conn., 1956. (MH)

CALLAWAY – Calaway, Merle L.
Descendants of the "Connecticut Calaways" and family album illustrated. By Merle L. Calaway. (Conneaut, O.), 1976. (FW)

CALLAWAY – Calaway, Merle Leland
The descendants of the "Connecticut Calaways" and family album illustrated. Photos and charts by Merle L. Callaway. (Conneaut, Ohio), Calaway, c1976. (LoC)

CAMERON – Cameron, Kenneth Walter
Strictly personal: A teacher's reminiscences. Hartford, Ct., c1979. (NGS)

CAMP – Camp, Russell L.
Edward Camp of New Haven, Connecticut and his descendants. By Russell L. Camp. (Denver) Lamont, 1976. (DP)

CAMP – Wheeler, Nettie E.
Some data regarding the Camp family of Durham, Conn., and the Eells family of Middletown, Conn. ... By Nettie E. Wheeler. (New York, 1915). (NY)

CANTINE – Huntington, Alice Contine
The Contine family, descendants of Moses Cantine. West Hartford, Conn.: Chadwato Servicce, 1957. (DAR)

CARPENTER – Lewis, Eleanor R.
Some descendants of four pioneer families who came from Rhode Island and Conn. to Stephentown, N. Y. and Hancock, Mass. in the 18th century. By Eleanor R. Lewis. N.p., 1972. (FW)

CARPENTER – Roberts, Martin L.

Genealogy of one branch of the Carpenter family. By Martin L.
Roberts. Willimantic, Conn., Enterprise Printing Co., 1877. (LoC)

CARRIER – Carrier, E. E. P. B.
Descendants of Thomas Carrier of Colchester, Conn. By E. E. P. B.
Carrier. Longmeadow, Mass., 1969. (FW)

CARRIER – May, George S.
Some descendants of Thomas Carrier of Andover and Billerica,
Massachusetts who died in Colchester, Conn., May 16, 1735 and his
wife, Martha (Allen) Carrier, who was hanged at Salem, Mass., on
Aug. 19, 1692. Fair Oaks, Ca., 1978. (NGS)

CARRIER – May, George S.
Some descendants of Thomas Carrier of Andover and Billerica,
Massachusetts, who died in Colchester, Connecticut, May 16, 1735,
and his wife Martha (Allen) Carrier, who, as a result of the infamous
witch trials, was hung at Salem, Massachusetts on August 19, 1692.
Edited by George S. May. (LoC)

CARTER – Carter, Samuel
The descendants of Samuel Carter, of Deerfield, Mass., and Norwalk,
Conn. By Samuel Carter of Brooklyn, N. Y., of the 6th generation.
Vol. 1, No. 1. (New Canaan, Ct., "Messenger" Print, 1885). (LoC)

CARTER – DeMarce, Virginia Easley
Carter of Deerfield, Mass., and Norwalk, Conn., Chartier of Quebec
Province, Canada, and New York: a study in multilingualism and
multiculturalism in eighteenth-century America. By Virginia Easley
DeMarce. Arlington, Va.: Mrs. James L. DeMarce, 1983. (LoC)

CARTER – DeMarce, Virginia Easley
Carter of Deerfield, Mass., and Norwalk, Conn., Chartier of Quebec
Province, Canada, and New York: a study in multilingualism and
multiculturalism in eighteenth-century America. By Virginia Easley
DeMarce. Rev. ed. Arlington, Va.: V. E. DeMarce, 1985. (LoC)

CASE – Dermott, Henry Sage
Some descendants of John Case of Simsbury, Connecticut, 1656-1909.
Comp. by Henry Sage Dermott. Albany, N. Y., 1909. (LoC)

CASTO – Heywood, Jacqueline Monday
Cunningham & Crites family history: includes Casto, Fisher, Fowler,
Harrison, Price, Wolfe. Written by Jacqueline Monday Heywood.

41

Baltimore: Gateway Press; Ridgefield, Ct.: J. M. Heywood, 1986.
(LoC)

CHAFFEE –
Chaffee; dedication in devoted memory of Jerome Stuart Chaffee,
1873-1947... inscribed by his wife, G. D. K. Chaffee. (Hartford,
Conn., State Hist. Co., 1947). (FW)

CHAMPION – Trowbridge, Francis Bacon
The Champion genealogy. New Haven, Conn.: Tuttle, Morehouse &
Taylor, 1891. (DAR)

CHAMPION – Trowbridge, Francis Bacon
The Champion genealogy. A history of the descendants of Henry
Champion, of Saybrook and Lyme, Connecticut, together with some
account of other families of the name. By Francis Bacon Trowbridge.
New Haven (Conn.). Printed for the author, 1891. (LoC)

CHAPIN – Chapin, Gilbert Warren
The Chapin book of genealogical data... descendants of Deacon
Samuel Chapin. Hartford, Conn.: Chapin Family Assoc., c1924.
(DAR)

CHAPIN – Chapin, Gilbert Warren
The Chapin book of genealogical data, with brief biographical sketches,
of the descendants of Deacon Samuel Chapin. Compiled by Gilbert
Warren Chapin... Hartford, Conn., Chapin Family Association, 1924.
(LoC)

CHAPIN. See also: Bruce, 1914
                        Dixon, 1922
                        Goodwin, 1915
                        Neil, 1915

CHAPIN – Parker, Rev. Edwin P., D. D.
...Appreciation of Calvin Chapin, D.D., of Rocky Hill, Conn. By the
Rev. Edwin P. Parker, D. D. ... Providence, Snow & Farnham Co.,
Printers, 1908. (LoC)

CHAPMAN – Chapman, Edward M.
The Chapmans of Old Saybrook, Connecticut. New London, Conn.:
Bingham Press, c1941. (DAR)

CHAPMAN – Chapman, Edward M.

The Chapmans of old Saybrook, Connecticut; a family chronicle. By
Edward M. Chapman. (New London, Conn.) Priv. print. (The
Bingham Press), 1941. (LoC)

CHAPMAN – Chapman, Emilas Ravaud
Chapman genealogy, being the descendants (!) of John Chapman, the
first settler, of Stonington, Conn., who married Sarah Brown, down ten
generations from 1610-1931... Compiled and published by Emilas
Ravaud Chapman. Akron, O., 1931. (LoC)

CHAPMAN – Chapman, F. W.
The Chapman family, or the descendants of Robert Chapman, one of
the first settlers of Say-Brook, Conn., with genealogical notes of
William Chapman... Edward Chapman... John Chapman... and Rev.
Benjamin Chapman... Hartford, Conn.: Chapman, 1854. (DAR)

CHAPMAN – Chapman, Rev. F. W.
The Chapman family: or The descendants of Robert Chapman, one of
the first settlers of Say-brook, Conn., with genealogical notes of
William Chapman, who settled in New London, Conn.; Edward
Chapman, who settled in Windsor, Conn.; John Chapman, of
Stonington, Conn.; and Rev. Benjamin Chapman, of Southington,
Conn. By Rev. F. W. Chapman... Hartford, Case, Tiffany and Co.,
1854. (LoC)

CHAPMAN – Gundry, E. P.
Ichabod Chapman of Colchester, Conn. and his descendants. By E. P.
Gundry. Flint, Mich., 1962. (FW)

CHAPMAN – Hudson, Mrs. Lillian Chapman
Genealogical notes of the descendants of Edward Chapman, of
Windsor, Connecticut. Comp. by Mrs. Lillian Chapman Hudson.
Alameda, Cal., 1894. (LoC)

CHAPMAN – Saunders, Dorothy Chapman
Robert Chapman-David Thomson allied family lines: 93 allied family
lines from Robert Chapman, Sr., Saybrook, Conn., 1635, and David
Thomson, Portsmouth, N. H., 1623. C1983. (NGS)

CHATFIELD – Sharpe, William C.
The Chatfield family. Seymour, Conn.: Sharpe, 1896. (DAR

CHATFIELD – Sharpe, William C.

The Chatfield family. Principally from records in the Naugatuck Valley, Conn. Comp. by William C. Sharpe. Seymour, Conn., 1896. (LoC)

CHENEY – Cheney, William or Donald E.
Some of the descendants of William Cheney of Cambridge, Mass., and Ashford, Conn. ... By William or David E. Cheney. (Prospect, Ohio), 1975. (NY)

CHESEBROUGH – Chesebrough, Amos S.
A biographic sketch of William Chesebrough, the first white settler of Stonington, Conn. By Amos S. Chesebrough... Hartford, Conn., Press of the Case, Lockwood & Brainard Co., 1893. (FW)

CHESEBROUGH – Wildey, Anna Chesebrough
Genealogy of the descendants of William Chesebrough of Boston, Rehoboth, Mass., the founder and first white settler of Stonington, Conn., born 1594, in or near Boston, England, and died 1667, Stonington, Conn. He sailed from Cowes, England, in good ship "Arbella" (of Gov. John Winthrop's Massachusetts Bay Colony), March 29, 1630, and arrived in Salem, Mass., New England, America, June 14, 1630. By Anna Chesebrough Wildey... New York, Press of T. A. Wright, 1903. (LoC)

CHESTER –
Descendants of Leonard Chester, of Blaby, Eng., and Wethersfield, Conn. Boston, D. Clapp & Son, 1868. (LoC)

CHESTER – Chester-Waters, Robt. Edmond
Genealogical notes of the families of Chester of Blaby, Leicestershire, and Chester of Wethersfield, Conn., New England. Comp. by Robt. Edmond Chester-Waters... (Printed for the author). Leicester, Clarke and Hodgson, 1886. (LoC)

CHEVALIER – Salisbury, Edward E.
Pedigree of Chevalier-Anderson family. By (Edward E.) Salisbury. New Haven, Conn., 1885. (NY)

CHITTENDEN – Talcott, Alvan
Chittenden family. New Haven, Conn.: Tuttle, Morehouse & Taylor, 1882. (DAR)

CHITTENDEN – Talcott, Alvan

44

Chittenden family: William Chittenden of Guilford, Conn., and his descendants. Comp. by Alvan Talcott... (New Haven, Conn., Morehouse & Taylor, 1882). (LoC)

CHRISTOPHERS – Totten, John R.
Christophers genealogy. Jeffrey and Christopher. Christopher of New London, Conn., and their descendants. Comp. by John R. Totten... (New York, 1921). (LoC)

CHURCH –
Church Family of Hartford, Ct. (1878), 6 pgs.. [1]

CHURCH – Anjou, Gustave
History of the Church family: ancestors and some descendants of Richard Church of Hartford, Conn. By Gustave Anjou. (N.p., 1916?). (NY)

CHURCH – Church, Alice M.
Genealogy and history of the Church family in America, descended from Richard Church of Hartford, Connecticut and South Hadley, Mass. By Alice M. Church. Hollywood, Calif. (1949). (FW)

CHURCH – Church, Charles Washburn
Simeon Church of Chester, Connecticut, 1708-1792, and his descendants. Waterbury, Conn.: Mattatuck Press, c1914. (DAR)

CHURCH – Church, Charles Washburn
Simeon Church of Chester, Connecticut, 1708-1792, and his descendants. Comp. by Charles Washburn Church... Waterbury, Conn. (The Mattatuck Press, Inc.), 1914. (LoC)

CHURCH – Lyman, Frinda B.
Ancestors and descendants of Henry (Shutts) Church. New Haven, Conn.: Press of Lyman Printing Co., 1921. (DAR)

CLAPP –
Ancestral records of Colonel John B. Clapp... (Hartford, R. S. De Lamater, photographer, 1874?). (LoC)

CLARK –
Clark Family of Milford, Ct. (1870), 11 pgs. [1]
Clark Family of Connecticut (1877) [1]
Clark Family of Haddam, Ct. (1880), 11 pgs. [1]
Clark Family of Farmington, Ct. (1882), 94 pgs. [1]

CLARK –
Deacon Theodosius Clark, Hon. William J. Clark; biography and
genealogy. A reprint from the "Commemorative biographical record of
New Haven County." (Chicago, J. H. Beers & Co.), 1902. (LoC)

CLARK –
The direct Clark ancestry of Edmund Clark, Jr. (1815-1902) of Russell,
St. Lawrence County, New York; a descendant of Daniel Clark of
Windsor, Connecticut (1622-1710). Scarsdale, N. Y., 1966. (LoC)

CLARK – Bryant, George Clarke
Deacon George Clark(e) of Milford, Connecticut and some of his
descendants. Portland, Me.: Anthoensen Press, 1949. (DAR)

CLARK – Bryant, George Clarke
Deacon George Clark(e) of Milford, Connecticut, and some of his
descendants. Prepared for publication by Donald Lines Jacobus. By
George Clarke Bryant. Ansonia, Conn., 1949. (LoC)

CLARK – Clark, Salter S.
Few genealogical items connected with the family descended from
William Clark, one of the original settlers of Haddam, Conn. ... By
Salter S. Clark. (N. Y., 1880). (FW)

CLARK – Clark, Salter Storrs
A few genealogical items connected with the family descended from
William Clark, one of the original settlers of Haddam, Conn.,
especially in the line of Ebenezer Clark, who from 1753 to 1800, lived
in Washington, Conn. (By Salter Storrs Clark). (New York, 1880).
(LoC)

CLARK – Floyd, Elizabeth A.
Clues for finding your Vermont Clarks: a master index & four cross
indexes, 1770s-1800s: references to ancestors in Massachusetts,
Connecticut & New Hampshire, and to emigration to other states.
Compiled by Elizabeth A. Floyd; pesented to Connecticut State Library
by the Connecticut Society of Genealogists, Inc. [Connecticut]: The
Society, 1979. (LoC)

CLARK – Gay, Julius
A record of the descendants of John Clark, of Farmington, Conn.
Hartford, Conn.: Press of the Case, Lockwood & Braindard Co., 1882.
(DAR)

CLARK – Gay, Julius
A record of the descendants of John Clark, of Farmington, Conn. The many branches brought down to 1882. the female branches one generation after the Clark name is lost in marriage. By Julius Gay. Hartford, Conn., The Case, Lockwood & Brainard Company, 1882. (LoC)

CLARK – Glazier, Prentiss
Clark-Clarke families of early Connecticut and Massachusetts. By Prentiss Glazier. (Sarasota, Fla., 1973). (FW)

CLARK – Hoagland, Lloyd Walter Clark
Descendants of John Clark of New Haven, Connecticut: who came on the ship Elizabeth in 1634 from Ipswich, County Suffolk, England. Compiled by Lloyd Walter (Clark) Hoagland. Watsonville, Calif.: L. W. Hoagland, 1990. (LoC)

CLARK – Jones, Henry A.
The Clark genealogy, embracing a full account of the Clark reunion. Compiled and arranged by Henry A. Jones, Southington, Conn., July 17, 1890. Hartford, Conn., Press of the Case, Lockwood & Brainard Company, 1890. (LoC)

CLARK – Kyes, Helen Myers
John Clarke of Hartford and Saybrook, Conn., and some of his descendants. Comp. and published by Helen Myers Kyes. (Parker, S. D., 1912). (LoC)

CLARK – Tracy, Louise
A historic strain of blood in America. Frances Latham – mother of governors. By Louise Tracy... New Haven, Conn. (1908). (LoC)

CLARK – Wallace, Robert N.
Twelve generations of descendants of John Alden and of John Clarke of Hartford, Connecticut. Compiled and published by Robert N. Wallace. (Joliet, Ill., 1940). (LoC)

CLARK – Walton, Emma Lee
The Clark genealogy; some descendants of Daniel Clark, of Windsor, Connecticut, 1639-1913. Comp. by Emma Lee Walton. Published through Walton Clark. New York, Frank Allaben Genealogical Company, 1913. (LoC)

CLARKE – Todd, Frances Bruce

The descendants of Daniel Clarke of Windsor, Connecticut. Maple
Falls, Wash.: Todd, c1970. (DAR)

CLARKE – Todd, Frances Bruce
The descendants of Daniel Clarke of Windsor, Connecticut. By
Frances Bruce Todd. Maple Falls, Wash., 1960. (FW)

CLARKE – Todd, Frances Bruce
The descendants of Daniel Clarke of Windsor, Connecticut. By
Frances Bruce Todd. Maple Falls, Wash., 1970. (LoC)

CLASON – Eberlein, R.
Clason, Longwell, Green, Tyler, Carver, Washburn family documents,
Fairfield County, Conn., Westchester, Dutchess, Putnam Counties, N.
Y., Sussex County, N. J. By R. Eberlein. New York City, 1964. (NY)

CLASON – Lapham, William B.
...Stephen Clason of Stamford, Connecticut, in 1654 and some of his
descendants. Comp. and arranged from data chiefly collected by Oliver
B. Glason of Gardiner, Maine. By William B. Lapham. August,
Kennebec Journal Print, 1892. (LoC)

CLEVELAND – Cleveland, H. G.
An account of the lineage of General Moses Cleveland, of Canterbury
(Windham County) Conn., the founder of the city of Cleveland, Ohio
(with portrait). Comp. by his kinsman, H. G. Cleveland. Also a sketch
of his life from the January (1885) number of the magazine of western
history, by Hon. Harvey Rice. Cleveland, O., W. W. Williams, 1885.
(LoC)

CLEVELAND – Cleveland, Horace Gillette
A genealogy of Benjamin Cleveland, a great-grandson of Moses
Cleveland, of Woburn, Mass., and a native of Canterbury, Windham
County, Conn. With an appendix. Comp. by his great-grandson
Horace Gillette Cleveland... Chicago, Printed for the compiler, 1879.
(LoC)

CLOSSON –
A conspectus of a Clsson family whose intermediate generations
centered in Lebanon, Conn., and Thetford, Ver. ... With charts of the
ancestry of Carlos C. Closson and his wife Charlotte A. Holt. By Leon
M. Closson. Los Angeles, Cal., 1933. (LA)

COALDWELL – Caldwell, Charles T.

William Coaldwell, Caldwell or Coldwell of England, Massachusetts, Connecticut and Nova Scotia. Washington, D. C.: Caldwell (Judd & Detweiler), 1910. (DAR)

COCHEU – Cocheu, Lincoln Chester
The Cocheu family. By Lincoln Chester Cocheu. Hampton, Conn., 1947. (LoC)

CODDING – Warner, S. M. C.
The family record of Samuel Codding, from 1783 to 1878. (By S. M. C. Warner). Collinsville, Conn., Press of C. N. Codding, 1878. (OH)

COE –
Coe-Ward memorial and immigrant ancestors. Meriden, Conn.: Converse Publ. Co., 1897. (DAR)

COE – Coe, Levi Elmore
Coe-Ward memorial and immigrant ancestors... (By Levi Elmore Coe). Limited ed. ... Meriden, Conn., Press of the Converse Publishing Co., 1897. (LoC)

COIT –
Mehetable Chandler Coit; her book, 1714. (Norwich, Conn., Bulletin Print, 1895). (LoC)

COIT – Chapman, F. W.
The Coit family. Hartford, Conn.: Press of the Case, Lockwood & Brainard Co., 1874. (DAR)

COIT – Chapman, Rev. F. W.
The Coit family; or The descendants of John Coit, who appears among the settlers of Salem, Mass. in 1638, at Gloucester in 1664, and at New London, Conn. in 1650. Compiled at the request of Samuel Coit of Hartford, Conn. By Rev. F. W. Chapman... Hartford, Press of the Chase, Lockwood & Brainard Co., 1874. (LoC)

COLE – Cole, Frank T.
The early genealogies of the Cole family in America, including Coles and Cowles, with some account of the descendants of James Cole of Hartford, Connecticut, 1635-1652, and of Thomas Cole, of Salem, Massachusetts, 1649-1672. Columbus, Ohio: Cole (Printed by Hann & Adair, 1887). (DAR)

COLE – Paine, Gustave Swift

Daniel Cole and Ruth Chester; notes on some of their descendants.
Prepared by Gustave Swift Paine. New York and Southbury, Conn.,
1946. (LoC)

COLGATE – Abbe, Truman
Robert Colgate the immigrant. New Haven, Conn.: Tuttle, Morehouse
& Taylor Co., 1941. (DAR)

COLLIER – Collier, William Miller
Descendants of Jochem Collier... A preliminary memorandum as to
Herbert F. Seversmith's article on the Colyer family in his series now
in preparation, entitled Colonial families of Long Island, New York,
and Connecticut. By William Miller Collier. (Auburn, N. Y.), 1947.
(LoC)

COLLIN –
Cyclopedia of biography, containing a history of the family and
descendants of John Collin, a former resident of Milford, Conn., to
which is appended a notice of their kindred, near and remote, by blood
and affinity. Hudson?: M. P. Williams, Register & Gazette Office,
1872. (DAR)

COLLIN –
Cyclopedia of biography, containing a history of the family and
descendants of John Collin, a former resident of Milford, Conn., to
which is appended a notice of their kindred, near and remote, by blood
and affinity. Hudson, M. P. Williams, Register and Gazette Office,
1872. (LoC)

COLLINS –
Collins Family of Milford, Ct. (1872), 124 pgs. [1]

COLLINS – Stong, Ruth Collins
John Collin, stem and branches: the descendants of Captain John Collin
and his wife Hannah Merwin Collin, of Milford, Connecticut. By Ruth
Collin Stong. Elmira, N. Y.: R. C. Stong, 1980, c1981. (LoC)

COLT – Grant, Ellsworth S.
The Colt legacy: the Colt Armory in Hartford, 1855-1980. By
Ellsworth S. Grant. Providence, R. I.: Mowbray Co., c1982. (LoC)

COLVER – Colver, Frederic Lathrop
Colver-Culver genealogy, descendants of Edward Colver of Boston,
Dedham, and Roxbury, Massachusetts, and New London and Mystic,

Connecticut. Tenafly, N. J.: Frank Allaben Genealogical Co., c1910.
(DAR)

COLVER – Colver, Frederic Lathrop
Colver-Culver genealogy; descendants of Edward Colver of Boston,
Dedham and Roxbury, Massachusetts, and New London, and Mystic,
Connecticut. By Frederic Lathrop Colver. (New York) F. Allaben
Genealogical Company (c1910). (LoC)

COMSTOCK – Comstock, Cyrus B.
A Comstock genealogy; descendants of William Comstock of New
London, Conn., who died after 1662: ten generations. Ed. by Cyrus B.
Comstock. New York, The Knickerbocker Press, 1907. (LoC)

COMSTOCK – Comstock, Ernest Bernard
The Comstock family in America; ten generations of the descendants of
William Comstock of Wethersfield, Connecticut, 1636. Compiled by
Ernest Bernard Comstock... Dallas, Tex., 1938. (LoC)

CONANT – Conant, William Shubael
The family of Shubael Conant, of Connecticut. (by) William Shubael
Conant. Washington, D. C., 1945. (LoC)

CONANT. See also: Barrett   Dunham, 1956
                       Connet   Lleach

CONE – Cone, William Whitney
Some account of the Cone family in America, principally of the
descendants of Daniel Cone, who settled in Haddam, Connecticut, in
1662. Brandsville, Mo.: Cone, 1903. (DAR)

CONE – Cooper, Katherine F.
Account of the Albert Sidney Cone families of America: a descendant
of Daniel Cone, who settled in Haddam, Conn., in 1662. By Katherine
F. Cooper. Holland, Mich., 1970. (FW)

CONE – Cone, William Whitney
Some account of the Cone family in America, principally of the
descendants of Daniel Cone, who settled in Haddam, Connecticut, in
1662. Comp. by William Whitney Cone... Topeka, Printed by Crone
& Company, 1903. (LoC)

CONVERSE –

Some of the ancestors and descendants of Samuel Converse, Jr., of Thompson Parish, Killingly, Conn.; Maj. Jas. Convers, of Woodburn, Mass.; Hon. Heman Allen, M. C. of Milton and Burlington, Vt.; Capt. Jonathan Bixby, Sr., of Killingly, Conn. (LoC)

CONVERSE. See also:

Dixon, 1922
Haughey, 1917
Morris, 1894
Stott, 1914
Tower, 1962

CONVERSE – Converse, Charles Allen
Some of the ancestors and descendants of Samuel Converse, Jr., of Thompson Parish, Killingly, Conn., Major James Convers of Woburn, Mass., Hon. Herman Allen, M. D., of Milton and Burlington, Vermont, Captain Jonathan Bixby, Sr., of Killingly, Conn. Boston, Mass.: Eben Putnam, 1905. (DAR)

COOK –
Cooke Family of Mass. and Ct. (1882), 36 pgs. [1]

COOK – Cook, James
A genealogy of families bearing the name Cooke, or Cook. Principally in Massachusetts and Connecticut. 1665-1882. By James Cook... Lowell, Mass., Vox Populi Press: Huse, Goodwin & Co., 1882. (LoC)

COOK – Phillips, Daniel L.
Epitaphs from the Cooke burying grounds at Glasgo, town of Griswold, Connecticut. By Daniel L. Phillips. Genealogical notes by Wm. B. Cook, Jr. (Brooklyn) 1924. (NY)

CORBIN – Lawson, Harvey M.
History and genealogy of the descendants of Clement Corbin of Muddy River (Brookline), Mass. and Woodstock, Conn. with notices of other lines of Corbins. S.1.: Hartford Press (Case, Lockwood & Brainard Co.), 1905. (DAR)

CORBIN – Lawson, Rev. Harvey M.
History and genealogy of the descendants of Clement Corbin of Muddy River (Brookline), Mass. and Woodstock, Conn. with notices of other lines of Corbins. Comp. by Rev. Harvey M. Lawson... (Hartford, Conn.) Hartford Press, 1905. (LoC)

CORLISS – Corliss, Mary

Corliss-Sheldon family, genealogical, biographical. (By Mary Corliss). Hartford, Conn., States Historical Society, Inc. (1934?). (LoC)

CORNWALL – Cornwall, Edward E.
William Cornwall and his descendants. New Haven: Tuttle, Morehouse & Taylor, 1901. (DAR)

CORNWALL – Cornwall, Edward E., M. D.
William Cornwall and his descendants; a genealogical history of the family of William Cornwall, one of the Puritan founders of New England, who came to America in or before the year 1633, and died in Middletown, Connecticut, in the year 1678. By Edward E. Cornwall, M. D. New Haven, The Tuttle and Taylor Company, 1901. (LoC)

CORNWALL – Holman, Alfred L.
Assemblage of abstracts or copies of census records, pension records, etc. on the names Cornwall (Cornwell, Cornell) Barlow and Wright... in Conn. and N. Y., Massachusetts... By Alfred L. Holman. (Chicago, 1937). (FW)

CORNWELL – Fennell, Lela Brooks
Nathaniel Brooks of Ashford, Connecticut: revolutionary war pensioner, some of his ancestors and descendants, plus brief genealogies of four allied lines, Aldrich, Boothe, Cornwall, Killoran-Gurry. By Lela Brooks Fennell. Baltimore; Gateway Press; Wilmington, De: L. B. Fennell, 1989. (LoC)

COSSITT –
...The Cossitt family; a genealogical history of Rene Cossitt, a Frenchman who settled in Granby, Conn., A. D. 1717, and of his descendants. By Pearl Steele Cossitt, A. M., 1879, and continued to 1925 by Fredric Henry White and Frederic Briggs Stebbins. Pasadena, Calif., 1925. (LoC)

COSSITT – White, Frederic Henry
The Cossitt family, a genealogical history of Rene Cossitt, a Frenchman who settled in Granby, Conn. A. D. 1717, and of his descendants. Pasadena, Calif.: White, c1925. (DAR)

COTTON – Leighton, Perley M.
Ancestors and descendants of Lucius Storrs Cotton, 1843-1899: thirty Massachusetts and Connecticut families. Compiled by Perley M. Leighton. Westbrook, Me., P. M. Leighton, 1984. (LoC)

COWLES – Cowles, Calvin Duvall
Genealogy of the Cowles families in America. New Haven, Conn.:
Tuttle, Morehouse & Taylor Co., 1729. (DAR)

COWLES – Cowles, Colonel Calvin Duvall
Genealogy of the Cowles families in America... Compiled by Colonel
Calvin Duvall Cowles... historian of the Cowles Family Association.
New Haven, Conn., The Tuttle, Morehouse & Taylor Co., 1929. (LoC)

COWLES – Leighton, Perley M.
Ancestry of Lucy Cowles, 1788-1838, wife of Rev. George Colton:
twenty-five families, mainly in Connecticut. Compiled by Perley M.
Leighton. Westbrook, Me., P. M. Leighton, 1984. (LoC)

COWLES – Manchester, Irving E.
The history of Colebrook, by Iving E. Manchester, and other papers.
(Winsted, Conn., The Citizen Printing Company) 1935. (LoC)

COYNE – Fulton, Ruth Coan
Coan genealogy, 1697-1982: Peter and George of East Hampton, Long
Island and Guilford, Connecticut, with their descendants in the Coan
line as well as other allied lines. Compiled by Ruth Coan Fulton.
Portsmouth, N. H., P. E. Randall; Portland, Me., c1983. (LoC)

CRAMPTON –
Crampton family of Guilford, Conn. By (Your Ancestors). (Orchard
Park, N. Y., authors, 1948). (OS)

CRANKSHAW – Crankshaw, M. G.
Descendants of Charles and Ann (Reilly) Crankshaw, 1803-1852;
U. S. A., 1842. By M. G. Crankshaw. (Hartford, Conn., 1960). (FW)

CROSBY – Crosby, Albert Hutchings
John Crosby of Yorkshire and some of his descendants, 1440-1940.
Hartford, Conn.: Crosby, 1940. (DAR)

CULVER – Giorgi, Valerie Dyer
Colver-Culver family genealogy: as descended from Edward Colver of
Groton, Connecticut, to the thirteen generations in America. By
Valerie Dyer Giorgi. Santa Maria, Calilf., V. D. Giorgi, 1984. (LoC)

CUMMINS – Cummins, Annie Blair Titman
Cummins-Titman and allied families. Hartford, Conn.: States
Historical Co., 1946. (DAR)

CURTIS –
A genealogy of the Curtiss-Curtis family of Stratford, Connecticut; a supplement to the 1903 edition (by Frederic Haines Curtis. Stratford). Curtiss-Curtis Society (1953). (LoC)

CURTIS. See also:
Barnes, 1911	Fox
Davis, 1959	Hart, 1923
Dillon, 1927	Towne, 1927
Duval, 1931	

CURTISS. See Curtis

CURTIS –
Letters and journals. Judge William Edmond, 1755-1838, Judge Holbrook Curtis, 1787-1858, Judge William Edmond Curtis, 1823-1880, William Edmond Curtis, 1855-1923, and Dr. Holbrook Curtis, 1856-1920. (Hartford, The Case, Lockwood & Brainard Co., c1926. (LoC)

CURTIS – Bangs, Lena M. (G.)
Descendants of Thomas Curtis of Wethersfield, Conn. By Lena M. (G.) Bangs. N.p., 1939. (LA)

CURTIS – Curtis, Charles Boyd
Thomas Curtis (of) Wethersfield, Connecticut. By Charles Boyd Curtis. New York (1899). (LoC)

CURTIS – Curtis, Clarissa Baldwin
Lineal ancestors of Clifford Clarke Curtis, Clifton, N. J., Walter Stanley Curtis, Stratford, Conn. and Grace Lillingston Curtis, Stratford, Conn. 1908. (DAR)

CURTIS – Curtis, Elizabeth
Letters and journals: Judge William Edmond, 1755-1833; Judge Hollbrook Curtis, 1787-1858; Judge William Edmond Curtis, 1823-1880. Hartford, Conn.: Case, Lockwood & Brainard Co., c1926. (DAR)

CURTIS – Curtis, Harlow Dunham
A genealogy of the Curtiss-Curtis family of Stratford, Connecticut. Suppl. 1975. (NGS)

CURTIS – Curtis, Harlow Dunham

A genealogy of the Curtiss-Curtis family of Stratford, Connecticut. Stratford, Ct., 1953. (NGS)

CURTIS – Curtiss, Frederic Haines
A genealogy of the Curtiss family; being a record of the descendants of widow Elizabeth Curtiss, who settled in Stratford, Conn., 1630-40. By Frederic Haines Curtiss... Boston, Rockwell and Churchill Press, 1903. (LoC)

CURTIS – Goodwin, Rose Mary
A family named Curtis: descendants of Thomas Curtis of Wethersfield, Ct., 1598-1982. Compiled by Rose Mary Goodwin. (Sunland, Ca.), R. M. Goodwin, 1983. (LoC)

CURTIS – Johnson, Maude Horne
Thomas Curtis of Wethersfield, Connecticut and his descendants. Los Angeles, Calif.: Johnson & Johnson, 1963. (DAR)

CURTIS – Johnson, Maude H.
Thomas Curtis (Curtice) of Wethersfield, Conn. and some of his descendants. By Maude H. Johnson. (Los Angeles), 1958. (NY)

CURTISS – Curtis, Harlow Dunham
A genealogy of the Curtiss-Curtis family of Stratford, Connecticut. Stratford, Conn.: Curtiss-Curtis Society, c1953. (DAR)

D

DALTON – Samuelson, Nancy B.
The Dalton gang family: a genealogical study of the Dalton outlaws and their family connections. By Nancy B. Samuelson. Eastford, Ct.: N. B. Samuelson, c1989. (LoC)

DANIELS – Daniels, Clark E.
Genealogical record of a branch of the Daniels family beginning with John Daniels No. 1 of New London, Connecticut. By Clark E. Daniels. (Ottumwa, Iowa, 1960 or 61). (LoC)

DARROW – Darrow, Erastus
History of the Darrow family of Connecticut. By Erastus Darrow. (Rochester, N. Y.? 189-?). (MH)

DARROW – Richardson, David A.

History and genealogy of Richard Darrow of Conn. and Mary (Darrow) Richardson of N. Y. and Ut. and their descendants. Compiled by David A. Richardson. Logan, Utah, 1933. (LoC)

DART – Sharpe, William C.
Dart genealogy. By William C. Sharpe... Seymour, Conn., Record Steam Print, 1888. (LoC)

DASKAM – Daskam, Faith (Stoek)
Descendants of William Daskam, 1760-1834, of North Stratford and Darien, Connecticut. 1961. (DAR)

DAVENPORT – Davenport, Robert Ralsey
The Davenport genealogy: history and genealogy of the ancestors and descendants of the Rev. John Davenport, founder of New Haven, Connecticut, and of Yale College. By Robert Ralsey Davenport. (Cambridge, Ma.). R. R. Davenport, c1982. (LoC)

DAVENPORT – Davenport, Royal W.
The Davenport genealogy: history and genealogy of the ancestors and descendants of the Rev. John Davenport, founder of New Haven, Connecticut, and of Yale College. Cambridge, Mass., c1982. (NGS)

DAVIS –
Genealogy of the descendants of Col. John Davis of Oxford, Conn, (formerly a part of Derby, Conn.), together with a partial genealogy of his ancestors in the United States, also biographical sketches and portraits of some of his descendants and other matters of interest. Collected, arranged and comp. by his great grandson, Geo. T. Davis. New Rochelle, N. Y., 1910. (LoC)

DAVIS – Davis, Edwin
Record down to 1909 of descendants of Gaius Davis, 1749-1815 and Wilson Kies, Jr. 1774-1835, both of Killingly, Conn., with biographical data. By Edwin Davis. Larimore, N. D., H. V. Arnold, 1909. (FW)

DAVIS – Davis, George T.
Genealogy of the descendants of Col. John Davis of Oxford, Conn. (formerly a part of Derby, Conn.). New Rochelle, N. Y.: Davis, 1910. (DAR)

DAVIS – Davies, Henry Eugene

Davies memoir; a genealogical and biographical monograph on the family and descendants of John Davies of Litchfield, Connecticut. By Henry Eugene Davies. (N.p.) Priv. print. 1895. (LoC)

DAVIS – Davis, John Lawrence
The Davis homestead: a farm since 1680 in lower Pawcatuck, Connecticut: a collection of writings. By John Lawrence Davis. Stonington, Ct.: Stonington Historical Society, c1986. (LoC)

DAVIS – Hitchcock, Solomon G.
A biographical sketch of the Rev. Thomas Davies, A. M., missionary of the Society for propagating the gospel in foreign parts, in several of the towns of Litchfield County, Conn., from the year 1761 to the year 1766. By a minister of the county. By Solomon G. Hitchcock. New Haven, Printed by Stanley & Chapin, 1843. (LoC)

DAVIS – Snow, Helen
The book of Davis ancestry. By Helen Snow. (Madison, Conn., 195-?). (SP)

DAWSON – Dawson, C. C.
Record of the descendants of Robert Dawson, of East Haven,, Conn. ....
By C. C. Dawson. Albany, N. Y., J. Munsell, 1874. (FW)

DAY –
Day Family of Hartford (1840), 44 pgs. [1]
Day Family of Hartford, 2d ed. (1848), 129 pgs. [1]

DAY –
The family of the Rev. Jeremiah Day of New Preston to January 1, 1900. New Haven, Conn.: Tuttle, Morehouse & Taylor, 1900. (DAR)

DAY – Bogue, Gladys Taylor, 1899
The genealogical register of the family of Alfred Day, 1794-1886, and Lydia Calkins Day, 1796-1879. Being a continuation of the "Genealogical register of Robert Day" who died in Hartford, Conn. in 1648, through a branch of the family of Robert's son, John. St. Paul, Minn., Printed by J. Roberts Co., 1970. (LoC)

DAY – Day, George E.
A genealogical register of the descendants in the male line of Robert Day, of Hartford, Conn., who died in the year 1648. Northampton, Mass? J. & L. Metcalf, 1848. (DAR)

DAY – Day, George E.

A genealogical register of the descendants in the male line of Robert Day, of Hartford, Conn., who died in the year 1648. New Haven, Conn.: William Storer, Jun., 1840. (DAR)

DAY – Day, George Edward

A genealogical register of the descendants in the male line of Robert Day, of Hartford, Conn., who died in the year 1648. (By George Edward Day). New Haven, Printed by W. Storer, June, 1840. (LoC)

DAY – Day, Leonard F.

Copy of and additions to the genealogical register of Robert Day of Hartford, Connecticut, and his two sons, Thomas and John, as compiled by Rev. George Edward Day in the second edition of 1848. Pontiac, Mich.: Day, 1972. (DAR)

DAY – McGivney, Vivian

Third supplement to the descendants of Robert Day of Hartford, Connecticut and Captain John Day, number 194, of Sheffield, Ohio and Alfred Day of Mondovi, Wisconsin. Prepared by Vivian McGivney and Mrs. Ken (Vivian) Nogle. 1978 ed. Hartford, Ky. McDowell Publications, c1978. (LoC)

DAY – Seymour, Thomas Day

The family of the Rev. Jeremiah Day of New Preston to January 1, 1900. New Haven, Ct. 1900. (NGS)

DAY – Seymour, Thomas Day

The family of the Rev. Jeremiah Day of New Preston to January 1, 1900; a genealogical appendix to The chronicles of the Day family. (By Thomas Day Seymour). (New Haven, The Tuttle, Morehouse & Taylor Co.) 1900. (LoC)

DAYTON – Dayton, Edson C.

The record of a family descent from Ralph Dayton and Alice (Galdhatch) Tritton, married June 16, 1617, Ashford, County Kent, England; a genealogical and biographical account of one branch of the Day family in America. By Edson C. Dayton. (Hartford) Priv. print. (The Case, Lockwood & Brainard Co.), 1931. (LoC)

DAYTON – Jacobus, Donald Lines

The early Daytons and descendants of Henry, Jr. New Haven Colony Historical Society, 1959. (DAR)

DAYTON – Jacobus, Donald L.
The early Daytons and descendants of Henry, Jr. By Donald L.
Jascobus. New Haven, Conn., New Haven Colony Historical Society,
1959. (FW)

DEACON – Deacon, Edward
The descent of the family of Deacon of Elstowe and London, with
some genealogical biographical and topographical notes, and sketches
of allied families including Reynes of Clifton and Meres of Kirton.
Bridgeport, Conn.: Deacon? 1898. (DAR)

DEACON – Deacon, Edward
Preliminary sketch of the genealogy of the family of Deacon, originally
of Bedfordshire, England. By Edward Deacon. Bridgeport, Conn.,
1895. (FW)

DEAN –
Genealogy of the Dean family descended from Ezra Dean, of
Plainfield, Conn. and Cranston, R. I., preceded by a reprint of the
article on James and Walter Dean, of Taunton, Mass., and early
generations of their descendants, found in volume 3, New England
historical and genealogical register, 1849. Scranton, Printed for the
author by F. H. Gerlock, 1903. (LoC)

DEAN – Dean, B. S.
...A history of the William Dean family of Cornwall, Conn. and
Canfield, Ohio. Containing the direct descent from Thomas Dean of
Concord, Mass., together with a complete genealogy of William Dean's
descendants. By B. S. Dean... and J. E. Dean... (Cleveland, O., Press
of the F. W. Roberts Co., 1903?). (LoC)

DECHMAN – Dechman, Don A.
Dechmans in North America. By Don A. Dechman. Darien, Ct., 1973.
(NY)

DEFOREST –
DeForest and allied families of New York and Connecticut. N.p.:n.d.
(FW)

DEFOREST – DeForest, J. W.
The DeForests of Avesnes (and of New Netherland) a Huguenot thread
in American colonial history, 1494 to the present time, with three
heraldic illustrations. By J. W. DeForest... New Haven, Conn., The
Tuttle, Morehouse & Taylor Co., printers and publishers, 1900. (LoC)

DEFOREST – DeForest, J. W.
The deForests of Avesnes (and of New Netherland). New Haven,
Conn.: Tuttle, Morehouse & Taylor, 1900. (DAR)

DEFOREST – DeForest, John L. (John LeRoy)
Anthony DeForest of Stanford, Connecticut, 1739: his ancestry and
some of his descendants. By John L. DeForest. (Stamford, Conn.).
J. L. DeForest, 1983. (LoC)

DEKARAJAN – Hammer, Rosamond Swan
A daughter of Firenze: an account of my mother's childhood in Italy.
By Rosamond Swan Hammer. New Haven, The Tuttle, Morehouse &
Taylor Press, 1924. (LoC)

DELAVAN – Bennett, Elmer Milton
Cornelius Delavan of Stamford, Connecticut, and some of his
descendants. Westwood, Mass.: Bennett, 1940. (DAR)

DELAVAN – Bennett, Elmer H.
Cornelius Delavan of Stamford, Connecticut and some of his
descendants. (By Elmer H. Bennett) (Westwood, Mass., 1940).
(FW)

DEMING – Deming, Judson Keith
Genealogy of the descendants of John Deming of Wethersfield,
Connecticut. Dubuque, Iowa: Mathis-Mets, 1904. (DAR)

DEMING – Deming, Judson Keith
Genealogy of the descendants of John Deming of Wethersfield,
Connecticut, with historical notes. Comp. and ed. by Judson Keith
Deming... Dubuque, Ia., Press of Mathis-Mets Co., 1904. (LoC)

DEMING – Helligso, Martha Stuart
John Deming of Wethersfield, Connecticut: including one line of
descent and related Connecticut lines of Baldwin, Beardsley, Belcher,
Brunson, Camp, Capen, Churchill, Dickinson, Foote, Foster, Galpin,
Gaylord, Gilbert, Hawes, Harris, Moore, Norton, Phippen, Rockwell,
Smith, Stanley, St. John, Thoson, Treat, Welles. Compiled by Martha
Stuart Helligso. Omaha, Nebr., M. S. Helligso, c1985. (LoC)

DENISON –
Denison Family of Stonington, Ct. (1881), 423 pgs. [1]

DENISON –

A record of the descendants of Capt. George Denison, of Stonington, Conn. With notices of his father and brothers, and some account of other Denisons who settled in America in the colony times. Prepared by John Denison Baldwin and William Clift. Worcester, Printed by Tyler & Seagrave, 1881. (LoC)

DENISON –

Robert Denison of Milford, Conn. Addenda to: Descendants of George Denison. By Baldwin and Clift. Collated by Ervine D. York. (Flushing) 1915. (NY)

DENISON –

Denison genealogy; a record of the ancestors and descendants of James Post Denison; a revolutionary war soldier who moved with his family from Saybrook, Conn., to Burlington, Otsego County, New York in 1796. By E. Glenn Denison... and Harry Emmett Bolton... (Fredonia, N. Y., Printed by the Fredonia Censor, 1939). (LoC)

DENISON –

Denison genealogy, ancestors and descendants of Captain George Denison (by) E. Glenn Denison, Josephine Middleton Peck (and) Donald L. Jacobus. Stonington, Conn., Published for the Denison Society (by) Pequot Press (1963). (LoC)

DENISON. See also: Abbott, 1936
                               Chesebrough, 1903
                               Ellery, 1956
                               Hughes, 1879
                               James, 1912
                               Read, 1957
                               Smith, 1924

DENISON –

The George and Ann Borodell Denison society incorporated, Pequotsepos Manor. Organized 1930, Mystic, Connecticut. (Mystic, The Riverside Press), 1939. (NY)

DENISON – Cody, Edward Perrine

Genealogy of George Denison family of Stonington, Conn. By Edward Perrine Cody. (Wethersfield? Conn., 1949?). (LoC)

DENISON – Denison, E. Glenn

Denison genealogy. Stonington, Conn.: For the Denison Society, Inc. by the Pequot Press, 1963. (DAR)

DENISON – Denison, Elverton Glenn
Denison genealogy, ancestors and descendants of Captain George Denison. Also by Josephine M. Peck and Donald L. Jacobus. Stonington, Ct., 1963. (NGS)

DENISON – Haynes, William
Captain George and Lady Ann, the Denisons of Pequotsepos Manor. By William Haynes. (Stonington, Conn., Pequot Press, 1963). (FW)

DENISON – York, Ervine D.
Denison book; the ancestry and family connections of the Denisons of Brookfield, N. Y., descendants of Capt. George Denison of Stonington, Conn. Supplementing the genealogy works of Baldwin and Clift, Wheeler, Burlingame and others, with numerous collateral lineages… By Ervine D. York. Flushing, N. Y. (1920). (NY)

DEVEREAUX –
A genealogy of the family of Deveraux of the line of Jonathan Devereaux, born in Wethersfield, Connecticut, November 7, 1716. With some additions. Compiled by Cyril Allyn Herrick and Charles F. Haight. Lansing, Mich., C. F. Haight, 1929. (LoC)

DEWEY –
Our birthright of kinship with distinguished descendants of the immigrant Thomas Dewey who settled in Windsor, Connecticut, in 1633, and many notable non-Dewey ancestors. Containing an abstract of ancestry for the founder of this legacy. The whole vitalized by instantaneous keys to all relationships… Philadelphia, Pa., W. E. Dewey (c1913). (LoC)

DEWOLF – DeWolf, Oratia J.
DeWolf genealogy. Ascendants and descendants of Joseph DeWolf of Granby, Conn. later Vernon, O. By Oratia J. DeWolf. (Corapolis, Pa., 1902). (LI)

DEWOLF – Perry, Calbraith B., D. D.
Charles D'Wolf of Guadaloupe, his ancestors and descendants. Being a complete genealogy of the "Rhode Island D'Wolfs," the descendants of Simon De Wolf, with their common descent from Balthasar de Wolf, of Lyme, Conn. (1668). With a biographical introduction and appendices on the Nova Scotia de Wolfs and other allied families, with

a preface by Bradford Colt de Wolf. By Rev. Calbraith B. Perry, D. D.
New York, Press of T. A. Wright, 1902. (LoC)

DIAMOND – Sheftall, John McKay
The Dimons of Fairfield, Connecticut: a family history. By John
McKay Sheftall. 1st ed. Roswell, Ga., W. H. Wolfe Associates.
Atlanta, Ga., c1983. (LoC)

DICKERMAN – Dickerman, Edward Dwight
Dickerman genealogy. New Haven, Conn.: Tuttle, Morehouse &
Taylor, 1922. (DAR)

DICKINSON –
Descendants of Nathaniel Dickinson. By Addie M. Dickinson and the
Dickinson Association. (Windsor, Conn., M. F. Dickinson), 1955.
(FW)

DICKINSON – Dickinson, Frederick
To the descendants of Thomas Dickinson, son of Nathaniel and Anna
Gull Dickinson, of Wethersfield, Connecticut, and Hadley,
Massachusetts. (Comp. by Frederick Dickinson) (Chicago, W. D.
Grant, stationer and printer), 1897. (LoC)

DICKINSON – Gesner, Anthon Temple
The Dickinson family of Milton and Litchfield. By Anthon Temple
Gesner. 1913. Middletown, Conn., Pelton & King, printers and
bookbinders, 1913. (LoC)

DIMAN – Dimond, Edwin R.
The genealogy of the Dimond or Dimon family, of Fairfield, Conn.,
together with records of the Dimon or Dymont family of East
Hampton, Long Island, and of the Dimond family of New Hampshire.
By Edwin R. Dimond... Albany, N. Y., Pub. for the comp. by J.
Munsell's Sons, 1891. (LoC)

DIMOND – Dimond, Edwin R.
The genealogy of the Dimond or Dimon family of Fairfield, Conn.
Albany, N. Y.: for the compiler by Joel Munsell's Sons, 1891. (DAR)

DIMOND – Dimond, Edwin R.
The genealogy of the Dimond or Dimon family of Fairfield, Conn.,
with records of the Dimon or Dymont family of East Hampton, L. I.
and of New Hampshire. By Edwin R. Dimond. Albany, N. Y., 1891.
(LI)

DIMONS – Sheftall, John McKay
The Dimons of Fairfield, Connecticut: a family history. Roswell, Ga.,
1983. (NGS)

DIODATE –
Mr. William Diodate (of New Haven from 1717 to 1751) and his Italian
ancestry, read before the New Haven colony historical society, June 28,
1875, by Edward E. Salisbury. Taken from the Society's archives, by
permission, for private circulation, and printed, after revision, in April,
1876. (New Haven, printed by Tuttle, Morehouse & Taylor, 1876).
(LoC)

-    Supplement to the Diodate genealogy by Prof. Edward E. Salisbury...
(New Haven? 1878?) (LoC)

DIXON –
The ancestors of Courtlandt Palmer Dixon, and his wife Hannah
Elizabeth Williams of Stonington, Connecticut, containing also a list
of their descendants. Compiled by Evalena Dixon Stevens and
Louise Dixon Du Bois. (New York). Printed for the members of the
Dixon Association, 1927. (LoC)

DIXON – Dewey, Emily (McKay)
Dickson, Scotch-Irish: Connecticut, 1719, Nova Scotia, 1761,
California, 1865; descendants of Charles and Amelia Bishop Dickson
on Onslow, Nova Scotia: Dickson, Archibald, Campbell, Davison,
Foss, Henderson, McKay, Mackenzie, Purves, Patterson, Roach. By
Emily (McKay) Dewey. (Boston), 1953. (LoC)

DIXON – Stevens, Evalena Dixon
The ancestors of Courtlandt Palmer Dixon and his wife Hannah
Elizabeth Williams of Stonington, Conn. 1927. (DAR)

DODD –
Genealogies of the male descendants of Daniel Dodd, of Branford,
Conn., a native of England. 1646 to 1863. By Bethuel L. Dodd, M. D.,
and John R. Burney... Newark, N. J., Printed at the Daily Advertiser
Office, 1864. (LoC)

DOMMERICH –
Dommerich, Hall and allied families. Edited by Louis Effingham de
Forest... Privately published by Alexander Louis Dommerich. (New
Haven, Conn., The Tuttle, Morehouse & Taylor Company), 1924.
(LoC)

DORRANCE – Welch, Emma Finney
Dorrance inscriptions. By Emma Finney Welch. Old Sterling
township burying ground, Oneco, Connecticut. (By) Emma Finney
Welch (n.p.), 1909. (LoC)

DOTY – Doty, Harrison
Lines of descent: from Edward Doty, Mayflower passenger, 1620, John
Parmelee, New Haven Colony, 1639, William Leete, Guilford Colony,
1639: to and from Harrison Parmelee Doty, born 1910, Leete Parmelee
Doty, born 1917, Carol Parmelee Doty Wilson, born 1918, plus notes
on kssing kin & divers others: an adventure in genealogy begun in 1925
and concluded in 1985. 1st ed. Brattleboro, Vt.: H. Doty, c1985.
(LoC)

DOUDE – Dowd, W. W.
The descendants of Henry Doude who came from England in 1639.
Hartford, Conn.: Press of the Case, Lockwood & Brainard Co., 1885.
(DAR)

DOWD –
The first reunion of the descendants of Henry Doude at Madison, Conn.
1885. (LI)

DRAKE –
The descendants of John Drake of Windsor, Connecticut. Compiled by
the direction of Frank B. Gay, trustee of the Timothy Drake fund, and
includes the manuscript of the late Harrie Beekman Drake. Rutland,
Vt., The Tuttle Company, 1933. (LoC)

DRAKE –
Pedigree of Drake including Gilbert, Grenville, Prideaux and Dennis.
Ancestry of John Drake of Wiscombe who was in New England in
1630; afterwards in Windsor, Conn. (NY)

DRAKE – Gay, Frank B.
The descendants of John Drake of Windsor, Connecticut. Rutland, Vt.:
Tuttle, 1933. (DAR)

DRIGGS – Driggs, Alfred W.
A genealogical and family survey of the ancestors and descendants of
Alfred Waldo Driggs and Alice May Williams, both of East Hartford,
Connecticut. S.1.: Driggs, c1963. (DAR)

DUNCAN –

Charles and Hazle (Bartram) Duncan: their ancestors and descendents [sic]. Dale and Maxene Duncan. [Stamford, Conn.]: D. and M. Duncan, 1985. (LoC)

DUNHAM – Dunham, Isaac Watson
Dunham genealogy. Norwich, Conn.: Bulletin Print, 1907. (DAR)

DUNHAM – Dunham, Isaac Watson
Dunham genealogy. English and American branches of the Dunham family. Compiled by Isaac Watson Dunham... Norwich, Conn., Bulletin Print (c1907). (LoC)

DUNHAM – Moore, Sophie Dunham
Jacob Dunham (1727-1779) of Lebanon, Conn. and Mayfiield, N. J. Kalamazoo, Mich.: Moore, 1933. (DAR)

DUNN – Duedemann, Judith M. H.
The ancestry of Harvey Dunn. By Judith M. H. Duedemann. Chester, Conn., Pequot Press (1972). (FW)

DUNNAM – Dunnam, Frances C.
A short history of the Dunnam family. 1942. (DAR)

DUNNING – Haskell, Alice (D.)
Ebenezer Dunning (1761-1838) of Norfield parish, Fairfield, Connecticut, Stillwater, Champlain and Milton, New York, Bennington, Vermont, and some of his descendants. By Alice (D.) Haskell. (Amherst, Mass.), 1940. (DP)

DUNNING – Dunning, Miles M.
Descendants of Rev. Benjamin Dunning of Saybrook, Conn. By Miles M. Dunning, 1954. (SU)

DURAND – Durand, Samuel R.
Durand genealogy, descendants of Dr. John Durand (1664-1727) of Derby, Connecticut. By Samuel R. Durand. (Palo Alto, Calif., 1972?). (FW)

DURANT – Durant, William
The Durant genealogy; a history of the descendants of George and Elizabeth (----) Durant of Malden, Mass. and Middletown, Conn. Compiled to 1890 by William Durant and continued in part to 1966 by his great nephew Alexander G. Rose, III. Baltimore (1966-68). (LoC)

E

EAMES – Eames, Edward Harris
One Eames family: a short history of my family. By Edward Harris
Eames. (Norwalk? Conn.); Eames, c1980. (LoC)

EASTON – Easton, William Starr
Descendants of Joseph Easton, Hartford, Conn., 1636-1899. St. Paul,
Minn.: Easton, 1899. (DAR)

EASTON – Easton, William Starr
Descendants of Joseph Easton, Hartford, Conn., 1636-1899. Compiled
by William Starr Easton... St. Paul, Minn., 1899. (LoC)

EATON –
Report of the ---- annual reunion of the Eaton Family Assoc. New
Haven, Tuttle, Morehouse & Taylor, Printers, 18--. (FW)

EATON – Eaton, Daniel C.
To all persons in the United States bearing the name of Eaton... (by
Daniel C. Eaton), New Haven, Conn., 1881. (LI)

EDGECOMB – Converse, Charles Allen
Edgecomb of Devonshire, England, and Connecticut, New England;
reprinted from the Converse family and allied families. By Charles
Allen Converse, 1905. (Boston) Priv. print., 1907. (LoC)

EDSON – Wells, Harriette Hyde
Several ancestral lines of Josiah Edson and his wife,Sarah Pinney;
married at Stafford, Conn.., July 1, 1779, with a full genealogical
history of their descendants to the end of the nineteenth century...
Albany, N. Y.: Joel Munsell's Sons, Printers, 1901. (DAR)

EDSON – Wells, Harriette Hyde
Several lines of Josiah Edson and his wife, Sarah Pinney, married at
Stafford, Conn., July 1, 1779. With a full genealogical history of their
descendants to the end of the nineteenth century. Covering three
hundred years and embracing ten generations. By Harriette Hyde
Wells, assisted by Harry Weston Van Dyke. Albany, N. Y. J.
Munsell's Sons, Printers, 1901. (LoC)

EDWARDS –
Edwards Family of Cromwell, Ct. (1891), 12 pgs. [1]

EDWARDS – Andrews, Frank D.
Richard Edwards (Sheriff's Deputy) of Hartford, Colony of
Connecticut. Vineland, N. J.: Andrews? 1924. (DAR)

EDWARDS – Edwards, William Hopple
Ancestors of William Lemly Edwards and Stella Lee Edwards.
Meriden, Conn.: Edwards, 1962. (DAR)

EDWARDS – Riley, Margarete R. (S.)
Hon. Bulkeley Edwardrs, Cromwell, Middlesex Co., Conn, 1891. (By
Margarete R. (S.) Riley) (Middletown, Conn., 1891). (LI)

EDWARDS – Smith, Captain Elizur Yale
The descendants of William Edwards, Colonist to Connecticut, 1639...
By Captain Elizur Yale Smith. (N.p., 1941). (LoC)

EGGLESTON – Burlingame, Evelyn E. (O.)
Eggleston history and genealogy: allied families: Sloat, Wickrich-
Widrig of Connecticut, Massachusetts, New York, and Minnesota. By
Evelyn E. (O.) Burlingame. Minneapolis, 1969. (MH)

ELDREDGE – Eldredge, Charles C. Q.
Story of a Connecticut life. By Charles C. Q. Eldredge. Troy, N. Y.,
Allen Print, 1919. (FW)

ELDRIDGE –
Eldredge-Story and allied families: genealogical, biographical.
Hartford, Conn., States Historical Co., 1943. (FW)

ELDRIDGE –
The Captain's daughter of Martha's Vineyard. As recalled by the
Eldridge sisters – Nina, Mary, Ruth, Gratia; edited by Eliot Eldridge
Macy. Old Greenwich, Conn.: Chatham Press: distributed by the
Devin-Adair Co., c1978. (LoC)

ELIOT –
Proceedings at the reunion of the descendants of John Eliot, "the
apostle to the Indians," at Guilford, Conn., Sept. 15th, 1875. Second
meeting of South Natick, Mass., July 3rd, 1901; and the two hundred
and fiftieth anniversary of the founding of South Natick by John Eliot
and his praying Indians, July 4th, 1901. (Historical, natural history, and
library society of South Natick, Mass. South Natick, Mass., The
Society, 1901). (LoC)

ELIOT – Eliot, William H.
Genealogy of the Eliot family. New Haven, Conn.: George B. Bassett
& Co., 1854. (DAR)

ELIOT – Eliot, William Horace, Jr.
Genealogy of the Eliot family. New Haven, Ct., 1854. (NGS)

ELIOT – Emerson, Wilimena H.
Genealogy of the descendants of John Eliot. New Haven, Conn.:
Tuttle, Morehouse & Taylor, 1905. (DAR)

ELLER – Hook, James W.
George Michael Eller and descendants of his in America, related
families Vannoy and Van Noy, McNeil, Stoker, Welker, Graybill,
Colvard, Whittington, Hook, and others. New Haven, Ct., 1957.
(NGS)

ELLER – Hook, James W.
George Michael Eller and descendants of his in America. New Haven,
Conn.: Hook, 1957. (DAR)

ELLIOTT – Indiana DAR, G. R. C.
Family history of families from Connecticut, Delaware, New Jersey,
Virginia, Kentucky. 1949. (DAR)

ELLIS – Porter, G. S.
Genealogy: family of Richard Ellis, Stonington, Conn. By G. S. Porter.
Norwich, Conn., n.d. (FW)

ELLIS – Porter, George S.
James Ellis of Stonington, Conn. By George S. Porter. Norwich,
Conn., n.d. (FW)

ELMER –
Elmer Family of Connecticut (1899), 96 pgs. [1]

ELMER – Johnson, Rev. William W.
Elmer-Elmore genealogy. Records of the descendants of Edward
Elmer, of Braintree, Eng., and Hartford, Conn., through his son
Edward. 1632-1899. Comp. by Rev. William W. Johnson... North
Greenfield, Wis., The compiler, 1899. (LoC)

ELSEVIER – Davies, Davis William

The world of the Elseviers, 1580-1712 [by] David W. Davies.
Westport, Conn., Greenwood Press [1971]. (LoC)

EMMONS – Emmons, Corwin J.
An Emmons genealogy. (Compiled by Corwin J. Emmons: updated by
Wilbur D. Emmons). Southington, Conn.: W. D. Emmons, c1983.
(LoC)

ENO – Richardson, Douglas
The Eno and Enos family in America: descendants of James Eno of
Windsor, Connecticut. By Douglas Richardson. Rev. and republished
1985. [Bethany, Okla.] [Richardson Reprints], 1985. (LoC)

ENO – Richardson, Douglas C.
The Eno and Enos family in America... descendants of James Eno of
Windsor, Conn. By Douglas C. Richardson. (Sacramento, Calif.),
1973. (FW)

EUCHNER – Kaufholz, C. Frederick
The Euchner ancestry; the ancestors and some of the descendants of
Christopher and Dorothea (Brandstetter) Euchner. Lakeville, Ct., 1976.
(NGS)

EYMANN – Eyman, Carl E.
Members of the Eyman family enjoy a high privilege and a proud
heritage. (By Carl E. Eyman, Stamford, Conn., 1969). (LoC)

F

FAIRMAN – Allen, Orrin Peer
Descendants of John Fairman of Enfield, Conn., 1683-1898. Palmer,
Mass.: C. B. Fiske & Co., Printers, 1898. (DAR)

FAIRMAN – Allen, Orrin Peer
Descendants of John Fairman of Enfield, Conn., 1683-1898. By Orrin
Peer Allen... (Palmer, Mass., C. B. Fiske and Company, Printers,
1898. (LoC)

FAREWELL – Holton, David Parsons
Farwell ancestral memorial. Henry Farwell, of Concord and Chelsford,
Massachusetts, and all his descendants to the fifth generation: to which
are added three branches – the families of Daniel[5], of Groton and
Fitchburg, Mass., 1740-1815; Bethiah[5], of Mansfield, Conn., and

Westminster, Vt., 1747-1813; Elizabeth[5], of North Charlestown, N. H., 1751-1840, and their descendants to 1879. By David Parsons[7] Holton... and his wife Frances-K[7]. (Forward) Holton... New York, D. P.[7] Holton, 1879. (LoC)

FELT – Morris, John E.
The Felt genealogy. Hartford, Conn.: Case, Lockwood & Brainard Co., 1893. (DAR)

FELT – Morris, John E.
The Felt genealogy. A record of the descendants of George Felt of Casco Bay. Comp. by John E. Morris. Hartford, Conn., Press of the Case, Lockwood & Brainard Company, 1893. (LoC)

FENN – Balduc, Mrs. Edward
Some of the descendants of Edward Fenn of Wallingford, Conn. By Mrs. Edward Balduc. (Virginia, Minn., 1970?). (GF)

FENN – Griggs, Leverett Stearns
Reminiscences of the life and character of Elam Fenn, and Lydia, his wife, with a brief survey of the times in which they lived. By Leverett Stearns Griggs. (Hartford, Conn., Press of the Case, Lockwood & Brainard Company, 1884). (LoC)

FENN – Walker, Ara Fenn
The descendants of Edward Fenn of Wallingford, Conn., 1688. (DAR)

FENN – Walker, Ara F., S. J.
The descendants of Edward Fenn of Wallingford, Conn., 1688. By Ara F. Walker, S. J. Virginia, Minn., 1972. (SP)

FENTON – Weaver, William L.
A genealogy of the Fenton family, descendants of Robert Fenton, an early settler of ancient Windham, Conn. (now Mansfield). Willimantic, Conn.: Weaver, 1867. (DAR)

FENTON – Weaver, William L.
A genealogy of the Fenton family, descendants of Robert Fenton, an early settler of ancient Windham, Conn. (now Mansfield). Compiled by William L. Weaver... Willimantic, Conn., 1867. (LoC)

FENWICK – Gates, Gilman C.

Saybrook at the mouth of the Connecticut, the first one hundred years.
By Gilman C. Gates. (Orange and New Haven, Press of the Wilson H.
Lee Company), 1935. (LoC)

FIELD – Hobart, Helen Elizabeth
Proof of services in War of the Revolution of Dr. Simeon Field from
Enfield, Connecticut. 1951. (DAR)

FIFIELD – Sheppard, Walter L., Jr.
The descendants of William Fifield. By Walter L. Sheppard, Jr. (New
Haven, Conn., The Tuttle, Morehouse & Taylor Co.), 1940. (FW)

FISH –
A discourse commemorative of the Rev. Joseph Fish, for fifty years
(from 1732 to 1781), pastor of the Congregational Church in North
Stonington, Conn. Delivered at that place, Lord's day, August 16th,
1863, by Rev. Stephen Hubbell... with an Appendix. Norwich,
Bulletin Job Office, 1863. (LoC)

FISH –
Genealogy of one line of the Fish family whose ancestors settled in the
state of Connecticut about 1651, or possibly earlier. Compiled by
descendants of the family. Typed by Miss Jennie M. Ames.
Cleveland, O., 1941. (LoC)

FITCH – Fitch, Edward
The descendants of Seymour Fitch and Elizabeth Hoyt of New Canaan,
Connecticut; a contribution to the early history of Walton, New York.
Clinton, New York: Fitch, 1939. (DAR)

FITCH – Fitch, Edward
The descendants of Seymour Fitch and Elizabeth Hoyt of New Canaan,
Connecticut; a contribution to the early history of Walton, New York.
By Edward Fitch. Clinton, N. Y., 1939. (LoC)

FITCH – Porter, G. S.
Fitch family of Conn.: Rev. James Fitch. By G. S. Porter. Norwich,
Conn., n.d. (FW)

FITCH – Fitch, John T. (John Townsend)
A Fitch family history: English ancestors of the Fitches of Colonial
Connecticut. By John T. Fitch. 1st ed. Camden, Me.: Picton Press,
1990. (LoC)

FLYER – Flyer, Wadsworth Gray

A history and geneology [sic] of the Flyer family. West Simsbury, Conn. and Babson Park, Fla.: (Filer) Flyer Family Association, c1967. (DAR)

FOOT – Brainard, Lucy A.

A supplement to the Foote genealogy, comp. by Nathaniel Goodwin of Hartford, Conn., in 1849. Giving the descendants of Nathaniel Foote, of the seventh generation from Nathaniel Foote, one of the first settlers in Wethersfield, Conn. By Lucy A. Brainard... Morrisville, N. Y., Spooner & Stillman, Printers, 1886. (LoC)

FOOT – Foote, Abram W.

Foote family, comprising the genealogy and history of Nathaniel Foote, of Wethersfield, Conn., and his descendants; also a partial record of descendants of Pasco Foote of Salem, Mass., Richard Foote of Stafford County, Va., and John Foote of New York City. By Abram W. Foote... Rutland, Vt., Marble City Press, The Tuttle Company, 1907-32. (LoC)

FOOT – Goodwin, Nathaniel

The Foote family: or, The descendants of Nathaniel Foote, one of the first settlers of Wethersfield, Conn., with genealogical notes of Pasco Foote, who settled in Salem, Mass., and John Foote and others of the name, who settled more recently in New York. By Nathaniel Goodwin... Hartford, Press of Case, Tiffany and Company, 1849. (LoC)

FOOTE –

Foote Family of Colchester, Connecticut (1886), 26 pgs. [1]

FOOTE – Foote, Abram W.

Foote family comprising the genealogy and history of Nathaniel Foote of Wethersfield, Conn. and his descendants; also a partial record of descendants of Pasco Foote of Salem, Mass., Richard Foote of Stafford County, Va., and John Foote of New York City. Rutland, Vt.: Marble City Press – Tuttle, 1907, 1932. (DAR)

FOOTE – Foote, Abram William

Foote family, comprising the genealogy and history of Nathaniel Foote of Wethersfield, Conn., and his descendants... By Abram W. Foote. Baltimore: Gateway Press; Hughson Co. L. B. F. Beekman, 1981. (LoC)

FOOTE – Gaskill, Bessie Alice Shurtlieff

The maternal ancestry of Ellerton Flinders Gaskill, 10th generation of the Foote family, Wethersfield, Conn., Burhans – Pawling – Morey families of New York, Flinders – Gaskill ancestries. 1966. (DAR)

FOOTE – Goodwin, Nathaniel

The Foote family. Hartford, Conn.: Press of Case, Tiffany & Co., 1849. (DAR)

FORBES – Porter, G. S.

John Forbes in America, 1636. By G. S. Porter. Norwich, Conn., n..d. (FW)

FOWLER –

Fowler Family of Windsor, Connecticut (1857), 27 pgs. [1]
Fowler Family of Milford, Connecticut (1867), 12 pgs. [1]
Fowler Family of New Haven, Connecticut (1870), 42 pgs. [1]

FOWLER –

A genealogical memoir of the descendants of Ambrose Fowler of Windsor, and Capt. Wm. Fowler of New Haven, Connecticut. Boston: H. W. Dutton and Son Printers, 1857. (DAR)

FOWLER –

A genealogical memoir of the descendants of Ambrose Fowler of Windsor, and Capt. Wm. Fowler of New Haven, Connecticut. Reprinted with additions, from the New England historical and genealogical register for July, 1857. Boston, H. W. Dutton and Son, Printers, 1857. (Loc)

FOWLER –

Golden wedding exercises at the fiftieth anniversary of Mr. and Mrs. John W. Fowler, Milford (Conn.)... 1887. New Haven, 1887. (FW)

FOWLER – Fowler, James

A genealogical memoir of the descendants of Capt. William Fowler of New Haven, Conn. Reprinted with additions... By James Fowler. Milwaukee, Starr & Son, 1870. (FW)

FOWLER – Fowler, John W.

An historical sketch and genealogical record of the Fowlers of Milford, Conn. By John W. Fowler. New Haven, Conn., 1887. (FW)

FOWLER – Sweet, Ruth Perkins

The Fowlers: forgotten Indians of Preston, Connecticut. [Lebanon, Conn.]: R. P. Sweet [198-]. (LoC)

FOX –
Fox Family of Haddam, Connecticut (1890), 31 pgs. [1]

FOX –
Daniel Fox of East Haddam, Ct., and some of his descendants. Albany (Brandow Printing Company) 1890. (LoC)

FOX –
Daniel Fox of East Haddam, Connecticut. (n.p.: n.d.) (FW)

FOX – Fox, George Henry
Descendants of... Samuel Fox... of New London, Conn. Third son of Thomas Fox of Concord, Mass. (Five generations). (By George Henry Fox) (New York?), 1931. (LoC)

FOX – Fox, George Henry
Descendants of John Fox of New London, Ct. (Fourth son of Thomas Fox). Compiled by George Henry Fox... (New York, 1931?). (LoC)

FOX – Fox, George Henry
Descendants of... Isaac Fox... of Medford, Mass. & New Canaan, Ct., sixth son of Thomas Fox of Concord, Mass. (Five generations). (By George Henry Fox). (New York?), 1931. (LoC)

FRANCIS –
Francis, Goodrich, Boardman, (mainly reprinted from the Boardman genealogy by William F. J. Boardman, a descendant in the Boardman-Francis-Goodrich lines. For private circulation... Hartford, Conn., Press of the Case, Lockwood & Brainard Company, 1898. (LoC)

FRANCIS – Chatfield, Mrs. Carrie Eastman (Secombe)
Family records of some of the descendants of Robert Francis of Wethersfield, Conn. (By Mrs. Carrie Eastman (Secombe) Chatfield. (Minneapolis), 1900. (LoC)

FRANCIS – Francis, Charles E.
Francis. New Haven: Tuttle, Morehouse & Taylor Co., 1906. (DAR)

FRANCIS – Francis, Charles E.
Francis; descendants of Robert Francis of Wethersfield, Conn. Genealogical records and fragments of history of the various branches

of the Francis families of Connecticut origin, also records of some other Francis families. Comp. by Charles E. Francis. New Haven, The Tuttle, Morehouse & Taylor Company, 1906. (LoC)

FRANKLIN –
Franklin Family, Woodbury, Connecticut (1839), 103 pgs. [1]

FRENCH –
French Family of Milford (1890), 8 pgs. [1]

FRENCH –
Ancestors of Sarah Jane French; the French family of Huntington, Connecticut, 1690-1922. (N. Y., 1922). (FW)

FRENCH – French, Rev. Hollis Myron
A genealogy of the French family of Hartland, Ct. By Rev. Hollis Myron French... (n.p.) Priv. print., 1927. (LoC)

FRENCH – French, Mansfield Joseph
Ancestors and descendants of Samuel French the joiner of Stratford, Connecticut. Ann Arbor, Mich.: Edwards Bros., Inc., 1940. (DAR)

FRENCH – French, Mansfield Joseph
Ancestors and descendants of Samuel French, the joiner, of Stratford, Connecticut. By Mansfield Joseph French... biographies, illustrations, maps and charts. Ann Arbor, Mich., Edwards Brothers, Inc., 1940. (LoC)

FRISBIE – Frisbie, Nora G.
Third Frisbie supplement; descendants of Edward Frisbie of Branford, Connecticut in the female line. 1973. (NGS)

FULLER –
Early Fuller families of Lebanon, Connecticut. (n.p.:n.d.). (FW)

FYLER – Fyler, Wadsworth George
Fyler, history and genealogy. By Wadsworth George Fyler. (West Simsbury, Conn., Fyler Family Association, 1967). (LoC)

G

GAGER – Gager, Edmund R.
The Gager family; the descendants of Dr. William Gager, of Suffolk County, England, and Charlestown, Mass., through his only surviving

son, John Gager, who later settled in Norwich, Connecticut. By
Edmund R. Gager. Baltimore: Gateway Press: Vincentown, N. J.:
E. R. Gager, 1985. (LoC)

GALLUP – Gallup, John Douglass
The genealogical history of the Gallup family in the United States.
Hartford, Conn.: Hartford Printing Co., 1893. (DAR)

GALLUP – Williams, Charles Fish
Genealogical notes of the Williams and Gallup families, especially
relating to the children of Caleb M. and Sabra Gallup Williams,
descendants of Robert Williams of Roxbury, and Capt. John Gallup,
Sr., of Boston, Mass. ... (by) Charles Fish Williams... Hartford,
Conn. Press of the Case, Lockwood & Brainard Company, 1897.
(LoC)

GANNETT – Gannett, Michael R.
Gannetts in America. By Michael R. Gannett. (Wilton, Conn., 1954).
(FW)

GARLICK – Walton, Nettie (F.)
Garlick genealogy. Henry Garlick of Milford, Conn., to seventh
generation. By Nettie (F.) Walton. (New York) 1937. (NY)

GARRISON – Garrison, Harry C.
Ancestors and descendants of Charles Cleveland Garrison and Mary
Virreoner Rasor. Westport, Conn.: Garrison, 1955. (DAR)

GARRISON – Garrison, Harry Cleveland
Ancestors and descendants of Charles Cleveland Garrison and Mary
Virreaner Rasor.. By Harry Cleveland Garrison. (Westport? Conn.),
1955. (LoC)

GATES –
Complete list of births, marriages and deaths under the name Gates,
Gate; (see alsoo Cates and Gatte) as found in the general index of
Connecticut vital records July 14, 1932. (Hartford) Barbour
Collections, Conn. State Lib., 1932. (FW)

GEE – Benjamin, Charles E. (Charles Evert)
Descendants of Solomon Gee of Lyme, Connecticut. Compiled by
Charles E. Benjamin. (New Haven? Ind.): C. E. Benjamin, 1981.
(LoC)

GEER – Geer, James
Historical sketch and genealogy of George and Thomas Geer, from
1621 to 1856. By James Geer. Hartford, Conn., E. Geer, 1856. (FW)

GIDDINGS – Giddings, Minot S.
The Giddings family. Hartford, Conn.: Case, Lockwood & Brainard
Co., 1882. (DAR)

GILBERT –
One of the Gilbert family of New England; ancestry of Sarah Rebecca
(Gilbert) Bloss, (wife of John B. Bloss, of Washington, D. C.), eighth
in descent from Johnathan Gilbert, of Hartford, Conn. The larger part
of the following information was obtained by Mr. Homer W. Brainard,
of Hartford, Conn., after a search through the early records of Hartford,
Hebron, Bolton, and Colchester, Conn. Washington, D. C., Judd &
Detweiler, Printers, 1902. (LoC)

GILBERT – Brainard, Homer Worthington
The Gilbert family. New Haven, Conn.: A. C. Gilbert, 1953. (DAR)

GILBERT – Brainard, Homer W.
The Gilbert family; descendants of Thomas Gilbert, 1582(?)-1659, of
Mt. Wollaston (Braintree), Windsor and Wethersfield, Conn. By
Homer W. Brainard. New Haven, Connn., 1953. (SP)

GILBERT – Brainard, Homer Worthington
The Gilbert family: descendants of Thomas Gilbert, 1582(?)-1659, of
Mt. Wollaston (Braintree), Windsor, and Wethersfield. By Homer
Worthington Brainard, Harold Simeon Gilbert, and Clarence Almon
Torrey; edited with a foreward by Donald Lines Jacobus. Weston, Ct.
A. J. Hoe (1984), c1953. (LoC)

GILDERSLEEVE – Gildersleeve, Willard Harvey
Gildersleeve of Gildersleeve, Conn. and the descendants of Philip
Gildersleeve. Meriden, Conn.: The Journal Publishing Co., 1914.
(DAR)

GILDERSLEEVE – Gildersleeve, Willard Harvey
Gildersleeve of Gildersleeve, Conn. and the descendants of Philip
Gildersleeve. By Willard Harvey Gildersleeve. Meriden, Conn., Press
of the Journal Publishing Co., 1914. (LoC)

GILLESPIE – Prindle, Paul Wesley

Descendants of John and Mary Jane (Cunningham) Gillespie. North Haven, Ct., 1973. (NGS)

GILLLESPIE – Prindle, Paul Wesley
Descendants of John and Mary Jane (Cunningham) Gillespie. North Haven, Conn.: Printed by Van Dyck Print Co., c1973. (DAR)

GILLETT –
Descendants of Jonathan Gillet, of Dorchester, Mass., and Windsor, Conn. By the late Salmon Cone Gillette, of Colchester, Conn. Arranged and enlarged by the Rev. Henry Clay Alvord... Ilion, N. Y., Citizen Publishing Co., printers, 1898. (LoC)

GILLETT –
Genealogical data concerning the families of Gillet, Gillett, Gillette, chiefly pertaining to the descendants of Jonathan Gillet, who came from Chafcombe, Somersetshire, England, to Dorchester, Massachusetts, in 1630 and removed to Windsor, Connecticut, in 1636; also the descendants of his brothers, Nathan and Jeremiah, with mention of a number of intermarried families. Compiled and edited with additions by Esther Gillett Latham from material collected over a period of many years by her father Charles Homer Gillett. (Somerville? Mass.), 1953. (LoC)

GILLETT – Coddington, John Insley
Jonathan Gillett of Dorchester, Mass., and Windsor, Conn., and Mary Dolbere or Dolbiar, his wife. By John Insley Coddington... (New Haven, Conn., 1939). (LoC)

GILLETT – Thomas, Wilma G.
The Joseph Gillet/Gillette family of Connecticut, Ohio and Kansas. By Wilma G. Thomas. Chicago. Adams Press (1970). (NY)

GILMAN – Gilman, Lloyd
The Gilmans of Connecticut. Compiled by Lloyd Gilman, Willmar, Minn. L. Gilman (1984). (LoC)

GODDARD – Goddard, Winfred Rawdon
The Goddards of Granby, Connecticut. San Diego, Ca., 1985. (NGS)

GODDARD – Goddard, Winfred R. (Winfred Rawdon)
The Goddards of Granby, Connecticut. By Winfred B. [sic] Goddard, Jr. San Diego, Calif. Goddard Enterprises, 1985. (LoC)

GOLDTHWAITE – Goldthwaite, Charlotte
Goldthwaite genealogy. Hartford, Conn.: Goldthwaite, 1899. (DAR)

GOODFELLOW – Fellows, Erwin W. (Erwin Wilcox)
Goodfellow families: a genealogical study of Goodfellow families in
New York State before 1800 with their descendants and their possible
relationship to Thomas Goodfellow of Connecticut. Compiled and
published by Erwin W. Fellows. Zephyrhills, Fla.: E. W. Fellows,
1987. (LoC)

GOODRICH – Case, Lafayette Wallace, M. D.
The Goodrich family in America. A genealogy of the descendants of
John and William Goodrich of Wethersfield, Conn., Richard Goodrich
of Guilford, Conn., and William Goodridge of Watertown, Mass.,
together with a short historical account of the family in England, the
origin of the name, a description of Goodrich castle, etc. Edited for the
Goodrich – family – Memorial Association, by Lafayette Wallace Case,
M. D. Chicago, Fergus Printing Company, 1889. (LoC)

GOODSELL – Goodsell, Percy Hamilton
The Goodsell family of Connecticut. By Percy Hamilton Goodsell, Jr.
Cheshire, Conn.: P. H. Goodsell, c1986. (LoC)

GOODWIN –
Goodwin Family of Connecticut (1891), 798 pgs. [1]
Goodwin Family Notes of Connecticut. [1]

GOODWIN –
The Goodwins of Hartford, Connecticut, descendants of William and
Ozias Goodwin. Comp. for James Junius Goodwin. Hartford, Conn.,
Brown and Gross, 1891 (LoC)

GOODWIN –
English Goodwin family papers; being material collected in the search
for the ancestry of William and Ozias Goodwin, immigrants of 1632
and residents of Hartford, Connecticut... Hartford, Conn., 1921. (LoC)

GOODWIN – Jessop, Augustus
The Goodwins of East Anglia. By Augustus Jessopp [sic]. (Hartford,
Conn?) Priv. print, 1890. (FW)

GOODWIN – Starr, Frank Farnsworth
The Goodwins of Hartford, Connecticut. Hartford, Conn.: Brown and
Gross, 1891. (DAR)

GOODWIN – Starr, Frank Farnsworth
Various ancestral lines of James Goodwin and Lucy (Morgan)
Goodwin of Hartford, Connecticut. Hartford, Conn.: Goodwin, 1915.
(DAR)

GOODWIN – Starr, Frank Farnsworth
Various ancestral lines of James Goodwin and Lucy (Morgan)
Goodwin of Hartford, Connecticut. Comp. by Frank Farnsworth Starr
for James J. Goodwin... Hartford, Conn. (New Haven, The Tuttle,
Morehouse & Taylor Press), 1915. (LoC)

GORDON –
List of birth (!), marriages and deaths, under the name Gorden, as found
in the general index of Connecticut church records, Nov. 28, 1933.
(Hartford) Connecticut State Library, 1933. (LoC)

GORDON –
List of births, marriages and deaths, under the name, Gordon, Gaordon,
Gordan, Gorden, Gordien, Gordins, Gordton, Gorndon (see also
Gorton) as found in the general index of Connecticut vital records,
Nov. 27, 1933. (Hartford) Barbour Collection. Connecticut State
Library, 1933. (LoC)

GORHAM –
Gorham Family of Ct. and Vt. (1903), 6 pgs.[1]

GORHAM – Parsons, Gerald J.
The Gorham family; ancestors and descendants of Ephraim Gorham
(1753-1830), Revolutionary soldier of Canterbury,Conn. and Elbridge,
N. Y. By Gerald J. Parsons. Rochester, N. Y., 1955. (FW)

GORHAM – Sprague, Frank William
The Gorham family in Connecticut and Vermont. By Frank William
Sprague. Boston. Press of D. Clapp & Son, 1903. (LoC)

GOULDEN – Whitmore, Harriet E. (G.)
A memorial of the kindred and ancestry of Harriet L. Sturges Goulden,
of Fairfield, Conn. By Harriet E. (G.) Whitmore. (Hartford). Print. for
private circulation, 1899. (PH)

GOWDY – Gowdy, Allen C.
Gowdys of Connecticut: an addendum to Gowdy family in Connecticut
by Mahlon M. Gowdy/ Allen C. Gowdy. [S.1.]: Gowdy, c1976. (LoC)

GRAHAM – Steele, Mrs. E. G.
Henry and Mary Graham, or Grimes, Hartford, Conn., 1661 to 1685 and their descendants. By Mrs. E. G. Steele. (Winsted, Conn., 1911). (FW)

GRANBERRY –
(The Granberry family and allied families, including the ancestry of Helen (Woodward) Granberry, based on data collected by and for Edgar Francis Waterman and compiled by Donald Lines Jacobus. Hartford, Conn., E. F. Waterman, 1945. (FW)

GRANBERRY – Jacobus, Donald Lines
The Granberry family and allied families including the ancestry of Helen (Woodward) Granberry. Hartford, Conn.: Edgar F. Waterman, 1945. (DAR)

GRANGER – Granger, James N.
Launcelot Granger of Newbury, Mass., and Suffield, Conn. Hartford, Conn.: The Case, Lockwood & Brainard Co., 1893. (DAR)

GRANGER – Granger, James N.
Launcelot Granger of Newbury, Mass., and Suffield, Conn. A genealogical history. By James N. Granger... Hartford, Conn., Press of the Case, Lockwood & Brainard Company, 1893. (LoC)

GRANNIS – Strong, Frederick Augustus
The descendants of Edward Grannis. Bridgeport, Conn.: Strong, 1927. (DAR)

GRANNIS – Strong, Frederick Augustus
The descendants of Edward Grannis who was in New Haven, Connecticut as early as 1649 and died there December 10th, 1719. Compiled by Frederick Augustus Strong... (New Haven, Conn., The Tuttle, Morehouse & Taylor Company), 1927. (LoC)

GRAVES – Graves, Gemont
Graves genealogy traced from Thomas Graves, of Hartford, Ct., and Hatfield, Mass., one of the family founders in America, before and after the year 1645, down to George Graves and family of Rutland, Vt., in 1879 and later, together with some English ancestors. Also Collins genealogy as connected with the Graves family per Joseph Collins of Ira, Vt., and North Granville, N. Y., since the year 1826, and as traced down from ancestors of about the year 1600. (By Germont Graves). Burlington, Vt., Free Press Printing Company, 1911. (LoC)

GRAY –
A history of one branch of the Fairfield, Connecticut, Gray family;
compiled by Mary Sibyl Gray May, Grace Gray Hoch, and Richard
Holman May. Middletown, Conn., Godfrey Memorial Library, 1953.
(LoC)

- Index compiled in 1964 by Richard Holman May. (Washington,
1965). (LoC)

GRAY –
Genealogy of the Right Reverend Walter Henry Gray, eighth Bishop,
Diocese of Connecticut, Protestant Episcopal Church in the U. S. A.
(Hartford? Conn.), 1960. (LoC)

GRAY – May, Mary Sibyl (Gray)
A history of one branch of the Fairfield, Connecticut, Gray family.
Also by Grace G. Hock and Richard H. May. Middletown, Ct., 1953.
(NGS)

GRAY – May, Mary Sibyl Gray
A history of one branch of the Fairfield, Connecticut, Gray family.
Middletown, Conn.: Godfrey Memorial Library, 1953. (DAR)

GREEN –
Green Family of Bethlehem, Connecticut (1893), 100 pgs.[1]

GREEN – Green, Charles R.
Genealogy of Ezra Green, born in Litchfield County, Conn., 1754. By
Charles R. Green... Lyndon, Kan., 1897-(99). (LoC)

GREEN – Green, Charles R.
Family of Ezra Green... By Charles R. Green. Bethlehem, Litchfield
Co., Conn., 1754. Remsen, Oneida Co., N. Y., 1824... Pub. 1893.
(SU)

GREENLEAF – Boardman, William F. J.
The ancestry of Jane Greenleaf, wife of William Francis Joseph
Boardman. Hartford, Conn.: Boardman, 1906. (DAR)

GRIFFING – Stone, Clara J.
Genealogy of the descendants of Jasper Griffing. Guilford, Conn.:
Stone? 1881. (DAR)

GRISWOLD –

GRISWOLD –
Griswold Family of Connecticut (1856), 6 pgs.[1]
Griswold Family of Connecticut (1884), 85 pgs.[1]

GRISWOLD –
Record of Griswolds; collated by Sylvanus C. Griswold from old
records and papers. (New Haven, Mo., Author? 1896). (FW)

GRISWOLD –
The Griswold family bulletin. (Wethersfield, Conn., 1944-54). (MH)

GRISWOLD –
Black Hall traditions and reminiscences, collected by Adeline Bartlett
Allyn, granddaughter of Col. Charles Griswold. Hartford, Conn., The
Case, Lockwood & Brainard Company, 1908. (LoC)

GRISWOLD – Allyn, Adeline Bartlett
Black Hall. Hartford, Conn.: Case, Lockwood & Brainard Co., 1908.
(DAR)

GRISWOLD –
Descendants of Matthew Griswold. (Chicago, Rand, n.d.). (FW)

GRISWOLD – Griswold, Ruth Lee
A narrative of the Griswold family from Thomas Griswold, esqre. of
Weathersfield and Guilford 1695 (by) Ruth Lee Griswold. Rutland,
Vt., Printed for the compiler by the Tuttle Company, 1931. (LoC)

GRISWOLD – Salisbury, Edward E.
Griswold family of Connecticut. By Edward E. Salisbury. N.p.
(1884?). (FW)

GROSVENOR – Gluck, James F.
The Grosvenor family in Connecticut. By James F. Gluck. Buffalo,
Grosvenor Lib., 1919. (NY)

GROSVENOR – Grosvenor, Jeannette
Descendants of Nathan E. Grosvenor and Laura Fuller, 1794-1973
(with his ancestry) removed from Mansfield, Conn. to Claridon, O. in
1854/55. By Jeannette Grosvenor. Chesterland, O., Baker Print, 1973.
(FW)

GUERNSEY – Card, Eva Louise Garnsey

The Garnsey-Guernsey genealogy: an account of thirteen generations
of descendants from Henry Garnsey (-1692) of Dorchester, Mass.,
and Joseph Guernsie-Garnsey (-1688) of Stamford, Conn. Originally
compiled by Eva Garnsey Card and Howard Abram Guernsey, 1963.
2d ed. Rev. with additions and corrections by Judith L. Young –
Thayer, 1979. Baltimore: Gateway Press, 1979. (LoC)

GUILD –
Guild Family of Connecticut (1878), 40 pgs.[1]
Guild Family of Lebanon, Connecticut (1886), 20 pgs.[1]

GUILD –
Lebanon branch of the Guild family in Connecticut, and some of its
descendants. Woodbury, Conn.: W. W. Wisegarver, 1886. (DAR)

GUILD – Guild, L. A. and T.
Genealogy of a part of the Guild family, in the United States and
Canada, and an enumeration of the descendants of Jeremiah Guild, of
the fifth generation. By L. A. and T. Guild. Waterbury, Conn., Press
of F. P. Steele, 1878. (LoC)

GUILD – Guild, L. A. and G. S.
Lebanon branch of the Guild family in Connecticut, and some of its
descendants. Supplement to a genealogy published by L. A. & T.
Guild in 1877. By L. A. and G. S. Guild. Woodbury, Conn., Press of
W. W. Wisegarver, 1886. (LoC)

GUTHRIE – Guthrie, Laurence R. (Laurence Rawlin)
American Guthrie and allied families: lineal representations of the
colonial Guthries of Pennnsylvania, Connecticut, Maryland, Delaware,
Virginia, North and South Carolina, some post-revolutionary
emigrants, and of some allied families. Compiled by Laurence R.
Guthrie. Baltimore: Gateway Press; Las Vegas, Nv. 1985. (LoC)

H

HAIGHT – Mackenzie, Grenville C
Early records of the Haight family of Mount Pleasant and New Castle.
By Grenville C. Mackenzie. Westport, Conn., 1946. (NY)

HALE –
Hale Family of Conn. (1907), 13 pgs.[1]

HALE –
Hale, House, and related familes, mainly of the Connecticut River
Valley. By Donald Lines Jacobus and Edgar Francis Waterman.
Hartford, Connecticut Historical Society, 1952. (LoC)

HALE – Hale, Oscar Fitzalan
Ancestry and descendants of Josiah Hale, fifth in descent from Samuel
Hale of Hartford, Conn., 1637, to which is added an epistolary
appendix showing other lines of descent. Comp. by Oscar Fitzalan
Hale. Rutland, Vt., The Tuttle Company, Printers, 1909. (LoC)

HALE – Hale, Oscar Fitzalan
Ancestry and descendants of Josiah Hale, fifth in decent from Samuel
Hale of Hartford, Conn., 1637. Rutland, Vt.: Tuttle Co., Printers, 1909.
(DAR)

HALE – Jacobus, Donald Lines
Hale, House and related families, mainly of the Connecticut River
Valley. Hartford, Connecticut: Connecticut Historical Society, 1952.
(DAR)

HALE – Morris, Seymour
The Hale family of Connecticut. Boston: David Clapp & Son, 1907.
(DAR)

HALE – Morris, Seymour
The Hale family of Connecticut. By Seymour Morris. Boston, Press of
D. Clapp & Son, 1907. (LoC)

HALE – Stuart, I. W.
Life of Captain Nathan Hale, the martyr-spy of the American
revolution. By I. W. Stuart... Hartford, F. A. Brown, 1856. (LoC)

HALE – Stuart, I. W.
Life of Captain Nathan Hale, the martyr-spy of the American
revolution. By I. W. Stuart... 2d ed., enl. and improved. Hartford,
F. A. Brown; New York, D. Appleton & Co., (etc.) 1856. (LoC)

HALE – Stuart, I. W.
Life of Captain Hale. Hartford: F. A. Brown, 1856. (DAR)

HALL –
Hall Family of Connecticut (1882), 31 pgs.[1]

HALL –

Revolutionary services of Lieutenant Nathaniel Hall and his son Nathaniel Hall, Jr. (drummer) of Stonington, Conn., with names of some of their descendants (!), the Daniel Hubbard Halls, the Ellwoods, Heths, Bartletts, Osterhouts and other allied families. Compiled by Nellie Allen Bartlett, Mrs. James Ellwood Bartlett. Winter Park, Fla., 1931. (LoC)

HALL – Coe, Sophia Fidelia Hall

Memoranda relating to the ancestry and family of Sophia Fidelia Hall. Meriden, Conn.: Curtiss-Way Co., 1902. (DAR)

HALL – Hall, J. D., Jr.

The genealogy of the Hall family; or, Ancestors and descendants of Noah Hall. By J. D. Hall, Jr. Danielsonville, Conn., Press of F. U. Scofield, 1882. (LoC)

HALL – Hall, Lawrence P.

Origins of my branch of Halls; study of a Hall line from John Hall of New Haven and Wallingford. Effingham, N. H., 1980. (NGS)

HALL – Hall, Lawrence P.

Pioneers and performers, in three parts, biographical accounts about the first eight generations of my Hall line. Effingham, N. H., 1982. (NGS)

HALL – Hall, Lawrence P. (Lawrence Percival)

Origins of my branch of Halls: study of a Hall line from John Hall of New Haven and Wallingford. By Lawrence P. Hall. Effingham, N. H. L. P. Hall, 1980. (LoC)

HALL – Hall, William M.

The Halls of Lyme, Ct., and ancestry. By William M. Hall. (Weston, Conn., 1967). (NY)

HALL – Putnam, Agnes Hall

Records of the Halls of Wallingford and the Buckinghams of Milford. Compiled by Agnes Hall Putnam... (Jersey City, N. J., Jersey City Printing Co.), 1901. (LoC)

HALL – Shepard, James

John Hall of Wallingford, Conn., a monograph. New Britain, Conn.: Record Press, 1902. (DAR)

HALL – Shepard, James

John Hall of Wallingford, Conn. A monograph. By James Shepard.
New Britain, Conn., Record Press, 1902. (LoC)

HALLOCK – Hallock, Wm. A.
The Hallock ancestry. For the memoir of Rev. Jeremiah Hallock of
Connecticut and Rev. Moses Hallock of Massachusetts, 1863. By
(Wm. A. Hallock). (N. Y., 1863). (LA)

HALSTED – Wheeler, W. Ogden
Descendants of Rebecca Ogden, 1729-1806 and Caleb Halsted, 1721-
1784. Sharon, Conn.: Wheeler, Morristown, N. J.: Halsey, 1892?
(DAR)

HAMLIN – Jones, Robert C. (Robert Clarence)
Supplement to "The book." The Hamlin family, a genealogy of Capt.
Giles Hamlin of Middletown, Connecticut, 1654-1900, by Hon. H.
Franklin Andrews. Supplement by Robert C. Jones. [United States]:
R. C. Jones, 1985. (LoC)

HAND – Oedel, Howard T.
Daniel Hand of Madison, Conn., 1801-1891. By Howard T. Oedel,
1973. (FW)

HANDY –
Some descendants of Richard Handy and Anna Parmelee of Guilford,
Connecticut and ancestral lines of related families. Arlington, Va.,
1963. (LoC)

HANDY – Jacobs, Esther Handy
Some descendants of Richard Handy and Anna Parmelee of Guilford,
Connecticut and ancestral lines of related families. 1963. (DAR)

HANFORD – Golding, Augustus C.
Descendants of Rev. Thomas Hanford. Norwalk, Conn.: Ruth Golding,
1936. (DAR)

HANFORD – Golding, Augustus C.
Descendants of Rev. Thomas Hanford... Compiled by Augustus C.
Golding. Norwalk, Conn., 1936. (LoC)

HANKS – Hanks, Edgar Freeman
Hanks and other ancestors of mine. By Edgar Freeman Hanks. (Essex,
Conn., 1968). (LoC)

HARRIS –
Harris Family of New London, Connecticut (1878), 239 pgs.[1]

HARRIS – Harris, Gale I.
Descendants of Joseph Harris of Connecticut and New York. By Gale
I. Harris. (Alva, Okla?), n. d. (FW)

HARRIS – Haskell, Edythe L.
Capt. Seers Harris of Plainfield in Connecticut. By Edythe L. and
David C. Haskell. [Connecticut]: E. L. Haskell, c1987. (LoC)

HARRIS – Hindman, Mrs. Laura (Unger)
Genealogy of the Harris and allied families, being a continuation of the
"Harris genealogy. A history of James Harris of New London, Conn.,
and his descendants, from 1640 to 1878... By Nath'l Harris Morgan...
Hartford, 1878." By Mrs. Laura (Unger) Hindman. (n. p., 1940).
(LoC)

HARRIS – Morgan, Nathaniel Harris
Harris genealogy. Hartford: Case, Lockwood & Brainard Co. Print,
1878. (DAR)

HARRIS – Morgan, Nath'l Harris
Harris genealogy. A history of James Harris, of New London, Conn.,
and his descendants; from 1640 to 1878... With an appendix
containing brief notices of several other early settlers of New England
of the name Harris... By Nath'l Harris Morgan... Hartford, The Case,
Lockwood & Brainard Co. Print, 1878. (LoC)

HARRIS – Stover, Margaret Harris
Ely Harris and Lucretia Ransom of Connecticut, New York, and
Ontario. By Margaret Harris Stover. Decorah, Iowa: Anundsen
Pub.Co., 1990. (LoC)

HARRISON – Corbin, Mrs. Frances Harrison
Five generations of Connecticut Harrisons. By Mrs. Frances Harrison
Corbin. (Reprinted from the New England historical and genealogical
register for January, 1916). Boston, New England Historic
Genealogical Society, 1916). (LoC)

HARRISON – Fellows, Maxwell Henry
Thirteen generations of the Harrison family, 1638-1980: the Harrison
line beginning with Richard in 1638, history and descendants from
Connecticut, Massachusetts, New York, and Pennsylvania. By

Maxwell Henry Fellows. (Farmington, Mass.): M. H. Fellows, 1980.
(LoC)

HART –
Hart Family of Connecticut (1875), 606 pgs.[1]

HART –
William A. Hart and family, Durham, Middlesex County, Connecticut.
S.1.: s. n., 1903. (DAR)

HART – Andrews, Alfred
Genealogical history of Deacon Stephen Hart, and his descendants,
1632, 1875... New Britain, Conn., Austin Hart, 1875. (DAR)

HART – Grant, Marion H.
The Hart dynasty of Saybrook. By Marion Hepburn Grant. West
Hartford, Conn.: Fenwick Productions for the Old Saybrook Historical
Society, 1981. (LoC)

HARTWELL – Densmore, L. W.
The Hartwell familly. Hartford, Conn.: Fowler & Miller Co., Printers,
1895. (DAR)

HATCH –
Hatch Family of Hartford (1879), 36 pgs.[1]

HATCH – Fletcher, Edward Hatch
Major Timothy Hatch of Hartford, Ct., and his descendants. New
York: Thaddeus B. Mead, 1879. (DAR)

HATCH – Fletcher, Edward Hatch
Major Timothy Hatch of Hartford, Ct., and his descendants. By
Edward Hatch Fletcher... New York, Printed for the author by T. B.
Mead, 1879. (LoC)

HAWK – Lane, Imogene Hawks
John Hawks, a founder of Hadley, Massachusetts: after a sojourn of
twenty-four years at Windsor, Connecticut: thirteen generations in
America. By Imogene Hawks Lane. Baltimore: Gateway Press, 1989.
(LoC)

HAWLEY – Huftalen, Sarah L. (G.)

...Hawley family; direct lineage from Joseph Hawley, the 1st, Stratford, Ct., 1603-1690. (By Sarah L. (G.) Huftalen. Manchester, Ia., 1941?). (OH)

HAYDEN –
Hayden Family of Connecticut (1859), 15 pgs.[1]
Hayden Family of Connecticut (1885), 20 pgs.[1]
Hayden Family of Connecticut (1888), 329 pgs.[1]

HAYDEN – Hayden, Jabez Haskell
Records of the Connecticut line of the Hayden family. Windsor Locks, Conn.: Hayden (Case, Lockwood & Brainard Co.), 1888. (DAR)

HAYDEN – Hayden, Jabez H.
Sketch and genealogy of the first three generations of the Connecticut Haydens, with a map showing the locality in which they settled, by Jabez H. Hayden... Hartford, Conn., Press of the Case, Lockwood & Brainard Company, 1885. (LoC)

HAYDEN – Hayden, Jabex Haskell
Records of the Connecticut line of the Hayden family. By Jabez Haskell Hayden... (Windsor Locks, Conn., The Case, Lockwood & Brainard Company, Printers) 1888. (LoC)

HAYES –
Hayes Family of Lyme, Ct. (1904), 192 pgs.[1]

HAYES –
Descendants of Richard Hayes, of Lyme, Connecticut, through his son, Titus Hayes. By Harriet Morse Weeks... Ed. by Rollin Hillyer Cook... Pittsfield, Mass., Press of the Eagle Publishing Co., 1904. (LoC)

HAYES –
Descendants of George Hayes of Salmon Brook, Conn. Los Angeles Public Library for W. P. A., n. d. (LA)

HAYES – Weeks, Harriet Morse
Descendants of Richard Hayes, of Lyme, Connecticut, through his son, Titus Hayes. Pittsfield, Mass.: Eagle Pub. Co., 1904. (DAR)

HAYNES –
Pedigree of Mabel Harlakenden (wife of Gov. John Haynes of New England), traced back to William the Conqueror, by Rev. Henry Jones of Bridgeport, Conn. 2d ed., with added information by Henry Evans

of New York). (New York, Ottman Lithographic Company, 1897).
(LoC)

HAYNES – Burch, George W.
Ancestry and descendants of John Russell Haynes. Hartford, Conn.:
Burch, 1924. (DAR)

HECOX – Hecox, Leon C.
The Hecox genealogy; descendants of William Hickok of Farmington,
Conn. ... By Leon C. Hecox. Carroll, O., E. H. Melvin, 1969. (OH)

HEMPSTEAD –
Hempstead Family Association. Report. New London, Conn. (1910).
(FW)

HEMPSTEAD – Benn, Bertha (H.)
Nine generations of the Hempstead family and allied lines of New
London, Conn. By Bertha (H.) Benn. N.p., n. d. (LA)

HERRICK –
Herrick genealogy; one line of descent from James Herrick, who settled
at Southampton, Long Island about 1653, with particular attention paid
to the descendants (both male and female) of Rev. Claudius Herrick, of
New Haven, Connecticut, and his wife Hannah Pierpont. Oakland,
Calif., Priv. Print., Pacific Rotaprinting Co., 1950. (LoC)

HICKCOX – Hickcox, Howard Miner
Record of one line of the Hickcox family in Connecticut from 1640.
By Howard Miner Hickcox. (Princeton) Printed at Princeton
University Press, 1937. (LoC)

HICKCOX – Harmon, Edith Andrews
A history of William Hickok, a first settler of Farmington, Connecticut,
and William Andrews, a first settler of New Haven, Connecticut, and of
their descendants from 1635 to 1972; pioneer settlers of Troy Grove,
Illinois. Compiled by Edith Andrews Harmon. (Mendota, Ill., 1973).
(LoC)

HICKOK – Hickok, Charles Nelson
The Hickok genealogy; descendants of William Hickocks of
Farmington, Connecticut, with ancestry of Charles Nelson Hickok.
Compiled by Charles Nelson Hickok... Rutland, Vt., The Tuttle
Publishing Company, Inc., 1938. (LoC)

HIGBY – Patterson, David W.
Genealogy of the Higbe family: Edward of New London, 1647-1899.
By David W. Patterson. N.p., n. d. (FW)

HILL –
Hill Family of Fairfield, Connecticut (1879), 29 pgs.[1]
Hill Family of Connecticut (1895), 22 pgs.[1]

HILL – Hill, Edwin A.
Notes on the family of John Hill of Guilford, Conn. By Edwin A.
Hill... Boston, Press of D. Clapp & Son, 1903. (LoC)

HILL – Hill, Francis C.
Biographical sketch and genealogical record of the descendants of
Melanchthon Hill, of Connecticut, 1610 to 1895. New York: T. A.
Wright, Printer & Publisher, 1895. (DAR)

HILL – Hill, Francis C.
Biographical sketch and genealogical record of the descendants of
Malanchthon Hill, of Connecticut. 1610 to 1895. By Francis C. Hill.
New York: T. A. Wright, 1895. (LoC)

HILL – Hosley, Eva Loesa Hill
Descendants of William Hill, of Fairfield, Conn., who came from
Exeter, England, June 5, 1632, in ship William and Frances...
Meriden. Conn.: Horton Press, 1909. (DAR)

HILL – Hosley, Eva Loesa Hill
Descendants of William Hill, of Fairfield, Conn., who came from
Exeter, England, June 5, 1632, in ship William and Frances. With
genealogical notes and biographical sketches of his descendants as far
as can be obtained including notes on collateral branches. Comp. by
Eva Loesa Hill Hosley... Meriden, Conn., Horton Press, 1909. (LoC)

HILLIS – Bruce, Helen M.
The descendants of Adam Hillis, 1789-1875. By Helen M. Bruce.
Bethel, Conn., B. & W. Services, 1963. (FW)

HILLS – Salven, Zola Covell
William Hills of Roxbury, Massachusetts and Hartford, Connecticut.
Santa Barbara, Calif.: Salven, 1970. (DAR)

HILLYER – Heck, Pearl Leona

The Hillyer family of Connecticut, Ohio and Florida, from 1640 to 1933. By Pearl Leona Heck. 1933. (DAR)

HINE – Hine, Robert C.
Hine genealogy and history of the descendants of Thomas Hine of Milford, Conn., 1639. (DAR)

HINMAN – Hinman, R. R.
A family record of the descendants of Sergt. Edward Hinman, who first appeared at Stratford in Connecticut about 1650. Hartford: Case, Tiffany and Co., 1856. (DAR)

HINMAN – Hinman, R. R., Esq.
A family record of the descendants of Sergt. Edward Hinman, who first appeared at Stratford in Connecticut, about 1650. Collected from state, colony, town and church records; also from old Bibles and aged people. By R. R. Hinman, Esq. ... (In his catalogue of the names of the first Puritan settlers of the colony of Connecticut. Hartford, 1852-56). (LoC)

HINMAN – Hoagland, Edward Coolbaugh
Some brief notes on the Hinman and Burrows families, giving a possible clue to the identity of Hannah, wife of Edward Hinman, Jr., of Stratford, Conn. By Edward Coolbaugh Hoagland. Wysox, Pa., Colportage Publishers, 1946. (LoC)

HINMAN – Wright, Gertrude B.
Ancestors and descendants of Havilah Burritt Hinman of Stratford, New Hampshire, with lineage back to Edward Hinman, the youngest son of Sergt. Edward Hinman of Stratford, Connecticut, with Barrett family notes. Compiled by Gertrude B. Wright. Hanover, N. H., 1966. (LoC)

HITCHCOCK –
Genealogy of one direct line of the Hitchcock family, who are descended from Luke Hitchcock of Withersfield, Conn., U. S. A., and some related families. Compiled and published by Clarence H. Hitchcock and his sister, Grace Helen Hitchcock. Toronto, Northern Miner Press (1958). (LoC)

HITCHCOCK – Hitchcock, Mrs. Edward, Sr.
The genealogy of the Hitchcock family, who are descended from Matthias Hitchcock of East Haven, Conn., and Luke Hitchcock of Wethersfield, Conn. Compiled... by Mrs. Edward Hitchcock, Sr. ...

Arranged for the press by Rev. Dwight W. Marsh, D. D. ... Amherst, Mass., Press of Carpenter & Morehouse, 1894. (LoC)

HITCHCOCK – Hitchcock, Mary L.
The genealogy of the Hitchcock family; who are descended from Matthias Hitchcock of East Haven, Conn., and Luke Hitchcock of Wethersfield, Conn. Amherst, Mass.: Carpenter & Morehouse, 1894. (DAR)

HOADLEY – Trowbridge, Francis Bacon
The Hoadley genealogy. New Haven: Trowbridge, (Tuttle, Morehouse & Taylor), 1894. (DAR)

HOADLEY – Trowbridge, Francis Bacon
The Hoadley genealogy. A history of the descendants of William Hoadley of Branford, Connecticut, together with some account of other families of the name. By Francis Bacon Trowbridge... New Haven, Printed for the author, 1894. (LoC)

HODGKINS – Brown, Geoffrey
John Hodgkin (Hotchkin) of Guilford, Connecticut and his descendants. Compiled by Geoffrey Brown. New York, N. Y.: G. Brown, 1988. (LoC)

HOLBROOK – Holbrook, Mary Louise
The Holbrook family of Derby, Connecticut. New Haven, Conn.: Tuttle, Morehouse & Taylor, 1932. (DAR)

HOLBROOK – Holbrook, Mary Louise
The Holbrook family of Derby, Connecticut. Compiled by Mary Louise Holbrook. New Haven, Conn., The Tuttle, Morehouse & Taylor Co., 1932. (LoC)

HOLCOMB – Holcomb, Walter
Memories of Walter Holcomb of Torrington, Litchfield County, Connecticut; with a few departures in genealogy, public records, customs, etc. By Walter Holcomb. (Torrington? Conn.), 1935. (FW)

HOLLY – Holly, Charles M.
Record of the Holly family in America. (By Charles M. Holly) (Stamford, Conn., 1861). (NY)

HOLMES –
Holmes Family of Connecticut (1865), 76 pgs.[1]

HOLMES –
Holmes family of East Haddam, Connecticut. 1924. (DAR)

HOLMES –
The descendants of George Holmes of Roxbury. 1594-1908.
Compiled by George Arthur Gray... To which is added the
descendants of John Holmes of Woodstock, Conn. (By E. Holmes
Bugbee). Boston, Press of D. Clapp & Son, 1908. (LoC)

HOLT – Tatum, V. Holt
The Holt family in Europe and America, 1248-1971, a brief account of
the genealogy, history, and armory in England and Germany in Europe:
also in the State of Massachusetts, Connecticut, Virginia, North
Carolina, Tennessee, Mississippi, and Utah in America. Compiled by
V. Holt Tatum from notes provided by Maudie Holt Black and others.
Cincinnati (1971). (LoC)

HOLTON –
Some of the descendants of William Holton, early settler of Hartford,
Conn., particularly the children of Joel Holton, of Westminster, Vt.,
together with all the descendants of William of the sixth to the ninth
generation. New York, 1866. (LoC)

HOLTON – Holton, David Parsons
Radial chart of the descendants of Dea. William Holton of Hartford,
Conn., 1636, (in line of Joel of Westminster, Vt.). By David Parsons
Holton. New York, 1872. (LoC)

HOLTON – Holton, David Parsons
Radial chart of the Sheldon-Holton families, being the descendants of
Amasa Sheldon of Rockingham, Vt., 1771, and his wife's ancestry
back to William Holton of Hartford. By David Parsons Holton. New
York, 1877? (LoC)

HOLTON – Holton, Edward Payson
A genealogy of the descendants in America of William Holton, 1610-
1691, of Hartford, Conn., and Northampton, Mass. Crete, Ill.: Mrs.
Ernest A. Ewers, 1965. (DAR)

HOLTON – Holton, Edward P.
A genealogy of the descendants in America of William Holton (1610-
1691) of Hartford, Conn., and Northampton, Mass. By Edward
P.Holton... (Cleveland, O., 1935). (MH)

HOOK –
Hook family Bible records. Photostats made by Yale University
Library, F. G. Ludwig, photographer. New Haven, 1952. (LoC)

HOOK – Hook, James William
James Hook and Virginia Eller. New Haven, Conn.: Tuttle, Morehouse
& Taylor Co., 1925. (DAR)

HOOK – Todd, Frederick W.
Humphrey Hook of Bristol and his family and descendants (!) in
England and America during the seventeenth century. By Frederick W.
Todd... (New Haven? Conn., 1933). (LoC)

HOOKE – Todd, Frederick W.
Humphrey Hook of Bristol and his family and descendants in England
and America during the seventeenth century. New Haven, Conn.:
Tuttle, Morehouse & Taylor Co., 1938. (DAR)

HOOKE – Todd, Frederick W.
Humphrey Hooke of Bristol and his family and descendants in England
and America during the seventeenth century. By Frederick W. Todd.
New Haven, The Tuttle, Morehouse & Taylor Co., 1938. (FW)

HOOKER –
Paper, by Commander Edward Hooker, U. S. Navy, prepared for the
Hooker reunion, at Hartford, Conn., and in his absence read by John
Hooker, Esq. (Hartford, Conn.), 1890. (LoC)

HOOKER – Hammond, Jennie E. Seymour
Partial outline of the Hooker family. West Hartford, Conn., 1931.
(LoC)

HOOKER – Hooker, Edward
The descendants of Rev. Thomas Hooker, Hartford, Connecticut, 1586-
1908. Rochester, N. Y.: M. H. Hooker, 1909. (DAR)

HOOKER – Hooker, Edward
The descendants of Rev. Thomas Hooker, Hartford, Connecticut, 1586-
1908. By Edward Hooker... Ed. by Margaret Huntington Hooker and
printed for her at Rochester, N. Y. (Rochester, N. Y., E. R. Andrews
Printing Company), 1909. (LoC)

HOPKINS –

... Sketch of the public and private life of Samuel Miles Hopkins, of Salem, Connecticut, written by himself, and left as a token of affection to his children. Together with reminiscences by his children, and a genealogy of the Hopkins family. Rochester, N. Y., The Society, 1898. (LoC)

HOPKINS – Hopkins, Daniel F.
The descendants of James Hopkins and Jean Thompson of Voluntown, Connecticut. By Daniel F. Hopkins. Cleveland: H. Carr, 1917. (FW)

HORSFALL – Horsfall, James G. (James Gordon)
Hunting for Horsfalls. By James G. Horsfall. Hamden, Conn. J. G. Horsfall [1983]. (LoC)

HOSMER – Hosmer, James B.
Genealogy of the Hosmer family. By James B. Hosmer. Hartford, Steam Press of E. Geer, 1861. (LoC)

HOTCHKISS – Cowdell, Nellie
The Hotchkiss family: descendants of Samuel Hotchkiss (ca. 1622-1663) of New Haven, Connecticut. By Nellie Cowdell. Baltimore: Gateway Press; Prospect, Ct., 1985. (LoC)

HOUSTON –
William Huston of Voluntown, Connecticut, ca. 1720-1777, and some of his descendants. Minneapolis, Priv. reproduced, 1950. (LoC)

HOWARD –
Howard Family of Connecticut (1884), 238 pgs.[1]

HOWARD – Howard, Jarvis Cutler
Howard genealogy. A genealogical record embracing all the known descendants in this country, of Thomas and Susanna Howard, who have borne the family name of [sic] have married into the family. Collected and arranged by Jarvis Cutler Howard... (Hartford, Conn.), The compiler, 1884. (LoC)

HOWE – La Rocca, Mary Brown
A Howe family: descendants of James How: twelve generations in Massachusetts, New Hampshire, Maine, Connecticut, California. [Compiled by Mary Brown La Rocca]. Placentia, Ca.: M. B. La Rocca, c1986. (LoC)

HOYT –

The genealogy of the Linus Hoyt family, set in order by James W. Davis. (Bridgeport, Conn? 1890?). (MH)

HOYT – Hoyt, David W.
Hoyt family. A genealogical history of John Hoyt of Salisbury, and David Hoyt of Deerfield (Massachusetts) and their descendants; with some account of the earlier Connecticut Hoyts, and an appendix, containing the family record of William Barnes of Salisbury, a list of the first settlers of Salisbury and Amesbury, &c. By David W. Hoyt... (1st ed.). Boston, C. B. Richardson, 1857. (LoC)

HOYT – Hoyt, David W.
Record of the Hoyt family meeting, held at Stamford, Connecticut, June 20 and 21, 1866. Prepared for publication by David W. Hoyt... Boston, H. Hoyt, 1866. (LoC)

HOYT – Hoyt, Rev. John William
Genealogy of Charles Davenport Hoyt of Stamford, Conn. Seventh generation from Simon Hoyt. Compiled by Rev. John William Hoyt... 1938, revised 1939. (Medford? Or.), 1939. (LoC)

HOYT – Hoyt, Rev. John Wm., B. D.
...A genealogy of Samuel Hoyt and Betsey Webb (1762-1838) (1772-1819) Stamford, Conn., sixth generation from Simon Hoyt. Compiled by Rev. John Wm. Hoyt, B. D. Medford, Ore., 1939. (LoC)

HOYT – Hoyt, Stephen B.
Concerning an old house and the people who lived therein. (By Stephen B. Hoyt). (New Canaan, Conn., 1939). (NY)

HUBBARD –
Descendants of George Hubbard of Middletown, Conn. (Sandusky, O., 1918). (LoC)

HUBBARD – Hubbard, Irvin W.
Record of the descendants of George Hubbard, one of the founders of Wethersfield, Milford, and Guilford, Connecticut. Compiled by Irvin W. Hubbard. Stockton, Calif., mimeographed by H. W. Hubbard, 1961. (LoC)

HUBBARD – Tuttle, Edmund
A historical sketch of Hon. William Hubbard, and his descendants, since 1630. By Edmund Tuttle. West Meriden (Conn.): F. E. Hinman, Printer, 1859. (LoC)

HUGGINS – Holcombe, Seth B.
The descendants of James Huggins (1752-1819) of Granby,
Connecticut... North Granby, Conn.: Holcombe, 1979. (DAR)

HUGGINS – Holcombe, Seth P.
The descendants of James Huggins (1752-1819) of Granby,
Connecticut. Compiled by Seth P. Holcombe. 1st ed. of a limited
printing. North Granby, Conn.: Holcombe, 1979. (LoC)

HULL –
Hull Family of New Haven (1869), 20 pgs.[1]
Hull Family of New Haven (1894), 78 pgs.[1]

HULL – Clarke, Samuel C.
Records of some of the descendants of Richard Hull, New Haven,
1639-1662. Comp. by Samuel C. Clarke. Boston, Printed by D.Clapp
& Son, 1860. (LoC)

HULL – Hull, Oliver
Book of the Hulls: being a genealogy of the Hull family; containing
some account of the Hulls of England, Massachusetts, Connecticut, and
Rhode Island. By Oliver Hull... (New York) Printed by P.Eckler,
1863. (LoC)

HULL – Mason, Puella Follet Hull
A record of the descendants of Richard Hull of New Haven, Conn.
Milwaukee, Wis.: Swain & Tate Co., Printers, 1894. (DAR)

HULL – Mason, Puella Follett (Hull)
A record of the descendants of Richard Hull, of New Haven. Conn. ...
Comp. by Puella Follett (Hull) Mason... (Milwaukee, Swain & Tate
Co., Printers) 1894. (LoC)

HUNGERFORD – Hungerford, Stanley W.
A summary of the families Hungerford, descendants of Thomas, of
Connecticut, including the families of Thomas, of Ireland, and William,
of Maryland. By Stanley W. Hungerford. Juneau, Alaska, author,
1976. (SP)

HUNGERFORD – Leach, F. Phelps
Thomas Hungerford of Hartford and New London, Conn., and some of
his descendants with their English ancestors. S.1.: Leach, 1924.
(DAR)

HUNT – Hunt, Mitchell J.
The early Hunt family of Sharon, Connecticut and surrounding areas of
Litchfield County: where they came from and where they went.
Mitchell J. Hunt. Willow Grove, Pa.: M. J. Hunt, [1985]. (LoC)

HUNT – Hunt, Mitchell J.
The Hunt families of Halifax, Vermont: with genealogy of Thomas
Hunt (1663-1746), pioneer at Lebanon, Ct. (1700), and descendants:
from manuscript on the Hunt families of Vermont. Mitchell J. Hunt.
Willow Grove, Pa.: M. J. Junt, [1987]. (LoC)

HUNT – Whittelsey, C. B.
(Descendants of Thomas Hunt). Compiled by C. B. Whittelsey.
Hartford, Conn., 1935. (LoC)

HUNT – Whittelsey, Charles B.
(The Hunt family genealogy). By Charles B. Whittelsey. Hartford,
Conn. (1935). (NY)

HUNTINGTON –
The Huntington family in America; a genealogical memoir of the
known descendants of Simon Huntington from 1633 to 1915, including
those who have retained the family name, and many bearing other
surnames. Hartford, Conn., Huntington family association, 1915.
(LoC)

HUNTINGTON –
Supplement to the genealogical memoir of the Huntington family, pub.
in 1863. Supplement: Norwich, Conn., 1962. (SP)

HUNTINGTON –
Huntington family in America, supplement to the Genealogical Memoir
pub. in 1915; and including those know descendants... since that time.
Huntington Family Assoc., Norwich, Conn., 1962. (FW)

HUNTINGTON – Huntington, E. B.
A genealogical memoir of the Huntington family in this country.
Stamford, Conn.: Huntington, 1863. (DAR)

HUNTINGTON – Huntington, Rev. E. B., A. M.
A genealogical memoir of the Huntington family in this country:
embracing all the known descendants of Simon and Margaret
Huntington, who have retained the family name, and the first

generation of the descendants of other names. By Rev. E. B.
Huntington, A. M. Stamford, Conn., The author, 1863. (LoC)

HUNTINGTON – Huntington, Elijah Baldwin
A genealogical memoir of the Huntington family. Stamford, Ct., 1863.
(NGS)

HUNTINGTON – Huntington Family Association
Huntington family in America, a supplement to the genealogical
memoir published in 1915. Norwich, Ct., 1962. (NGS)

HUNTINGTON – Huntington, Richard Thomas
The Huntington family in America. Hartford, Conn.: Huntington
Family Association, 1915. (DAR)

HUNTLEY – Horn, Ivy Huntley
John Huntley of Lyme, Connecticut. Herndon, Va,: Horn, 1953.
(DAR)

HUNTLEY – Horn, Ivy Elizabeth (Huntley)
John Huntley of Lyme, Connecticut (sic) and his descendants. By Ivy
Elizabeth (Huntley) Horn. (Herndon? Va.), 1953. (LoC)

HUNTLEY – Huntley, Virgil W.
John Huntley, immigrant of Boston & Roxbury, Massachusetts and
Lyme, Connecticut, 1647-1977, and some of his descendants. Mystic,
Conn.: Huntley, c1978. (DAR)

HUNTLEY – Huntley, Virgil W.
John Huntley, immigrant of Boston & Roxbury, Massachusetts and
Lyme, Connecticut, 1647-1977, and some of his descendants.
Compiled by Virgil W. Huntley. Mystic, Conn.: Huntley, c1978.
(LoC)

HURD – Kilbourn, James
How to live; a discourse, 1855, at the funeral of Mrs. Rebecca Bowers
of Middle Haddam, Con.. By James Kilbourn (with Hurd family
appendix). Hartford, 1856. (LI)

HURLBURT – Hurlburt, Henry H.
The Hurlburt genealogy; or, Record of the descendants of Thomas
Hurlburt, of Saybrook and Wethersfield, Conn., who came to America
as early as the year 1637. With notices of others not identified as his

descendants. By Henry H. Hurlburt... Albany, N. Y., J. Munsell's
Sons, 1888. (LoC)

HUSTON – Eck, Aimee Huston
William Huston of Voluntown, Connecticut. Minneapolis, Minn.: Eck,
1950. (DAR)

HUSTON – Eck, Aimee M. (H.)
William Huston of Voluntown, Conn. and some of his descendants.
(By Aimee M. (H.) Eck). (Minneapolis, 1947). (MH)

HUTCHINS – Hutchins, Isaac T.
Sketches. S.l.: Killingly, Conn., 1878. (DAR)

HYDE – Cummings, Dorothy Hyde Tallman
The Hydes of Connecticut, 1611-1982. (Syracuse, N. Y.? D. H. T.
Cummings, 1981). (LoC)

HYDE – Hyde, Edith Drake
The descendants (!) of Andrew Hyde of Lenox, Massachusetts, sixth in
descent from William Hyde of Norwich, Connecticut, including the
descendants (!) of Rebecca Hyde Aye, of Morrow County, Ohio. By
Edith Drake Hyde. Ann Arbor, Mich., Edwards Brothers, Inc., 1937.
(LoC)

HYDE – Hyde, Raymond S.
Record of some Rushville Hydes from Norwich, Conn., 1600 to 1975.
By Raymond S. Hyde. (Fort Wayne, Ind.), 1975. (FW)

HYDE – Morse, Willard S.
Descendants of Humphrey Hide, Fairfield, Conn., 1957. (DAR)

I

INDICOTT – McIntosh, John C.
An historical record of the descendants of Dr. John Indicott, of
Hartford, Conn. By John C. McIntosh. Springfield, Mass., C. W.
Bryan & Co., 1888. (LI)

INMAN – Inman, Charles G.
Daniel Inman of Connecticut, Ontario, N. Y. and Sugar Grove, Ill. and
his descendants, ca. 1775 – ca. 1960. By Charles G. Inman. (Fort
Edward, N. Y.), 1961. (FW)

INSLEY – Insley, Rebecca Ann (Mrs. Louis Casper)
William Quinn Insley, M. D., descendants Andrew Insley, emigrant,
Dorchester County, Maryland, and Celia Ann Whitmore Insley,
descendant John Whitmore, emigrant, Wethersfield, Connecticut.
Allied families: Griswold, Sage, Stafford, Webb (and) Wright. By
Rebecca Ann Insley (Mrs. Louis Casper). Drawings by Robert Mark
Blanchard. (New York?) 1950 (i.e. 1951). (LoC)

ISBELL – Mason, Edna Warren
The descendants of Robert Isbell in America. New Haven, Conn.:
Tuttle, Morehouse & Taylor, 1944. (DAR)

ISBELL – Mason, Edna Warren
The descendants of Robert Isbell in America. By Edna Warren
Mason... New Haven, Conn.: The Tuttle, Morehouse & Taylor
Company, 1944. (LoC)

ISHAM – Phinney, Mary Allen
Isham genealogy. A brief history of Jirah Isham (of New London,
Connecticut) and his descendants from 1670 to 1940, by his great-
granddaughter Mary Allen Phinney. Rutland, Vt., The Tuttle
Publishing Company, Inc. (1940). (LoC)

J

JACKSON –
The Edward Jackson family of Newton, Massachusetts, in the line of
Commodore Charles Hunter Jackson, United States Navy, Middletown,
Conn. Comp. by Frank Farnsworth Starr for James J. Goodwin.
Hartford, Conn. (Cambridge, U. S. A., University Press, J. Wilson and
Son) 1895. (LoC)

JACKSON – Forbes, Mary R.
Descendants of Joseph and Esther Jackson who settled in Canterbury,
Conn. in 1733. Covina, Calif.: Forbes, 1959? (DAR)

JACKSON – Forbes, Mary R.
Descendants of Joseph and Esther Jackson, who settled in Canterbury,
Conn. in 1733. By Mary R. Forbes. Covin, Calif. (1959). (LA)

JACKSON – Jackson, Charles E.
Jackson family genealogy, 1602-1910... also some Fenwick genealogy.
By Charles E. Jackson. Middletown, Conn. (1962). (LA)

JACKSON – Jackson, Horace Mortimer
The family history of Michael Jackson, emigrant from Ireland, citizen of Hartford County, Connecticut, his descendants, and collateral families with whom they were connected. By Horace Mortimer Jackson, Atchison, Kansas. 1906-1908. Kansas City, Mo., F. Hudson Publishing Co., 1909. (LoC)

JACOBS – Reeves, Nell W.
The New England ancestry of John Clark Jacobs. By Nell W. Reeves. Madison, Conn., 1959. (FW)

JAGGER – Gager, Edmund R.
The Gager family: the descendants of Dr. William Gager, of Suffolk County, England and Charlestown, Mass., through his only surviving son, John Gager, who later settled in Norwich, Connecticut. By Edmund R. Gager. Baltimore: Gateway Press; Vincentown, N. J.: E. R. Gager, 1985. (LoC)

JAMES – Maher, Jane
Biography of broken fortunes: Wilkie and Bob, brothers of William, Henry, and Alice James. By Jane Maher. Hamden, Conn. Archon Books, 1986. (LoC)

JAMES – Ohler, Clara Paine
Ancestors and descendants of Captain John James and Esther Denison of Preston, Connecticut. Lima, Ohio: Ohler, 1912. (DAR)

JARVIS – Jarvis, George A.
The Jarvis family. Hartford, Conn.: Case. Lockwood & Brainard, 1879. (DAR)

JENNINGS – Jennings, John T. W.
Descendants of Jonathan Jennings, 1st settler of Windham, Conn. through Nathan Tilleston Jennings and Maria Miller. By John T. W. Jennings. (Chicago) 1927. (FW)

JENNINGS – Snow, Helen F.
Notes on the Gershon Jennings family of Fairchild, Connecticut, with related lines of Seeley, Sanford, Gregory, etc. By Helen F. Snow. Madison, Conn. (FW)

JEPSON – Coddington, John Insley
Additions and corrections to the Jepson genealogy. New Haven, Ct. 1944. (NGS)

JEROME – Garrison, Emily Olcott
Ancestors and descendants of Eugene Murray Jerome and Paulina Von Schneidau. Westport, Conn.: Garrison, 1957. (DAR)

JEWELL – Jewell, Pliny
The Jewell register. Hartford, Conn.: Press of Case, Lockwood and Co., 1860. (DAR)

JOHNSON – Adams, Arthur
Charles Frederick Johnson (by) Arthur Adams... (Hartford, 1928). (LoC)

JOHNSON – Clarkson, A. E.
Family record of Elisha Johnson (also spelled Johnston) who married Lydia Griffin about 1803 or 1804; they lived in East Haddon, Conn. By A. E. Clarkson. Houston, Tex., 1938. (FW)

JOHNSON – Farrand, Max
...The papers of the Johnson family of Connecticut. By Max Farrand. Reprinted from the Proceedings of the American antiquarian society for October, 1913. Worcester, Mass., The Society, 1913. (LoC)

JOHNSON – Johnson, F. C.
Rev. Jacob Johnson of Wallingford, (Conn.) and Wilkes-Barre, (Pa.) By F. C. Johnson... (Wilkesbarre?) 1904. (LoC)

JOHNSON – Johnson, Frederick C.
Wallingford (Conn.) Johnsons. By Frederick C. Johnson. (N.p., 1901). (LoC)

JOHNSON – Shepard, James
The New Haven and Wallingford, (Conn.) Johnsons. By James Sherpard... Reprinted for the author from the New England historical and genealogical register for April, 1902. Boston, Press of D. Clapp & Son, 1902. (LoC)

JOHNSON – Spain, Eula Miller
Johnson families of Seneca County, New York; Harris family of Somerset County, New Jersey; Deming families of Connecticut; Van Tuyl families of Somerset County, New Jersey; Sebring families of Somerset County, New Jersey and allied families. 1963. (DAR)

JOHNSON – Stivers, Mable P.
Lineage of Albert L. Johnson. Ansonia, Conn., Stivers, 1926. (DAR)

JONES – Parker, L. N.

...History and genealogy of the ancestors and descendants of Captain Israel Jones who removed from Enfield to Barkhamsted, Conn., in the year 1759. Comp. for the Hon. Asahel W. Jones by L. N. Parker. (Norwalk, O. Laning Co.) 1902. (LoC)

JONES – Jones, Howard Linden

The path of destiny; a history of events which shaped the destinies of our forefathers and a genealogy of the descendants our (sic) Benjamin Jones of Connecticut and the Wyoming Valley, Pennsylvania. By Howard Linden Jones. (Orlando? Fla., 1953?). (LoC)

JONES – Jones, Richard F.

A Jones family history. By Richard F. Jones. (Bloomfield? Conn., 1962). (LoC)

JOY – Lee, Helen Bourne Joy

The Joy genealogy. Essex, Conn.: Pequot Press, 1968. (DAR)

JOY – Lee, Helen Bourne Joy

The Joy genealogy. By Helen Bourne Joy Lee. Essex, Conn.: Pequot Press (1968). (LoC)

-      Supplement. Essex, Conn., Pequot Press (1970). (LoC)

JUDSON – Weeks, Dr. F. E.

Biography of Deacon Benjamin Judson of Woodbury, Connecticut, with names of his descendants. By Dr. F. E. Weeks. (Norwalk, O.) The author, 1914. (LoC)

K

KEELER – Keeler, Wesley B.

Keeler family: Ralph Keeler of Norwalk, Ct., and some of his descendants. Compiled by Wesley B. Keeler. Baltimore: Gateway Press; Castleton, N. Y., 1985. (LoC)

KEELER – Keeler, Wesley B.

Ralph Keeler of Norwalk, Conn., and his descendants. Compiled by Wesley B. Keeler. Albany, N. Y. W. B. Keeler, 1980. (LoC)

KELLEY –

Kelley Family of Norwich, Connecticut (1897), 137 pgs.[1]

KELLEY – Kalley, James G. (James Gorham)
Genealogical data, the Cape Cod Kelleys and associated families.
Compiled by James G. Kalley. Newtown, Conn. J. G. Kalley. (1981).
(LoC)

KELLEY – Kalley, James G. (James Gorham)
One man's family: genealogy of the Kelley and associated families.
Compiled by James G. Kalley. (Newton, Conn.). J. G. Kalley (1982).
(LoC)

KELLEY – Kelley, Hermon Alfred
A genealogical history of the Kelley family descended from Joseph
Kelley of Norwich, Connecticut, with much biographical matter
concerning the first four generations and notes of inflowing female
lines. Comp. by Hermon Alfred Kelley. Cleveland, O., Priv. print.,
1897. (LoC)

KELLEY – Porter, George S.
Joseph Kelley family (1690-1801). By George S. Porter. (Norwich,
Conn., n. d.). (FW)

KELSEY –
A genealogy of the descendants of William Kelsey who settled at
Cambridge, Mass., in 1632, at Hartford, Conn., in 1636, and at
Killingworth, Conn., in 1663. By Edward A. Claypool and Azalea
Clizbee and concluded by Earl Leland Kelsey from data collected by
Leroy Huron Kelsey... and many others. (New Haven, Tuttle,
Morehouse & Taylor Co.) 1928-47. (LoC)

KELSEY – Claypool, Edward A.
A genealogy of the descendants of William Kelsey who settled at
Cambridge, Mass., in 1632; at Hartford, Conn., in 1636; and at
Killingworth, Conn., in 1663. S.1.: Chester Caulfield Kelsey, 1928-
1947. (DAR)

KELSEY – Hiday, Nellie E. (C.)
(Notes on the William Kelsey family of Connecticut). By Nellie E.
(C.) Hiday. (Author, n. d.). (OS)

KEMP – Kemp, Thomas Jay
Kemp family passport records. By Thomas Jay Kemp. Stamford,
Conn.: T. J. Kemp, c1986. (LoC)

KENDALL – Hayward, Kendall P.

The Kendalls of Connecticut. By Kendall P. Hayward. West Hartford, Conn., Chedwato Service, 1956. (FW)

KENDALL – Hayward, Kendall Payne
The Kendalls of Connecticut. West Hartford, Conn.: Chedwato Services, 1956. (DAR)

KENDALL – Laughlin, Kendall
Descendants of William Kendall of Ashford, Connecticut and Caledonia County, Vermont. S.1.: s. n.; 1955. (DAR)

KENDALL – Laughlin, Kendall
Descendants of William Kendall of Ashford, Conn., a genealogy. By Kendall Laughlin. (N. p.), 1953. (LoC)

KENDALL – Laughlin, Kendall
Descendants of William Kendall of Ashford, Connecticut, and Caldonia County, Vermont; a genealogy. By Kendall Laughlin. 2d ed. (Chicago?) 1955. (LoC)

KENNEDY – Kennedy, Melville T.
A family chronicle. By Melville T. Kennedy. Norwich Town, Conn., 1963. (LoC)

KENNEY – Kenney, Roland W.
Ancestors of General George C. Kenney, USAF (ret.)... By Roland W. Kenney. Farmington, Conn., Kenney, 1973. (FW)

KENT – Gannett, Arthur C.
Ancestors and descendants of Benjamin Kent and Chauncey Warner, both of Suffield, Connecticut. By Arthur C. Gannett. W. Hyattsville, Md. Gannett [1979]. (LoC)

KERCHAL – Kerchal, D. Ray (David Ray)
The history of the Kerchal family in the U. S. A. 1st ed. [Stamford, Ct.]: Kerchal, 1978. (LoC)

KILBOURN – Kilbourne, Payne Kenyon
The history and antiquities of the name and family of Kilbourn. New Haven: Durrie & Peck, 1856. (DAR)

KILBOURN – Kilbourne, Payne Kenyon

The history and antiquities of the name and family of Kilbourn (in its varied orthography). By Payne Kenyon Kilbourne... New Haven, Durrie & Peck, 1856. (LoC)

KIMBERLY –

Thomas Kimberly, New Havenn, Conn. 1638. (New Haven, The Tuttle, Morehouse & Taylor Press, 1896). (LoC)

KING –

King Family of Suffield, Connecticut (1892), 7 pgs.[1]

KING – Cleveland, Edmund James

The King family of Suffield, Conn. By Edmund James Cleveland. Boston, D. Clapp & Son, Printers, 1892. (LoC)

KING – King, Cameron Haight

The King family of Suffield, Connecticut, its English ancestry, A. D. 1389-1662, and American descendants, A. D. 1662-1908, comprising numerous branches in many states of the United States, also appendices containing information concerning some of its maternal ancestors. Comp. by Cameron Haight King. San Francisco (Press of the Walter N. Brunt Co.), 1908. (LoC)

KING – King, Harvey James

The genealogy of the New York branch of the King family of Suffield, Connecticut, beginning with William King of Ugborough, Devonshire, England, the father of James King, the founder of the Suffield family, and extending to and including the descendants... of Roger King who removed from Suffield to Troy, N. Y., in the year 1795; to which is added an appendix containing historical information concerning the family, and also genealogies of some of the maternal ancestors. Comp. by Harvey James King. Troy, N. Y. (Saratoga Spring, N. Y., Printed by E. P. Howe & Son) 1897. (LoC)

KING – King, Harvey J.

The genealogy of the New York branch of the King family of Suffield, Conn., beginning with William King of Ugborough, Devonshire, England. By Harvey J. King. (Saratoga Spring, N. Y.) 1897. (LI)

KINGSBURY –

Kingsbury, Scovill, Davies and allied families, genealogical, biographical. Hartford, Conn., States Historical Society, Inc., 1937. (LoC)

KIRBY – Dwight, Melatish Everett

The Kirbys of New England; a history of the descendants of John Kirby of Middletown, Conn. and of Jospeh Kirby of Hartford, Conn., and of Richard Kirby of Sandwich, Mass., together with genealogies of the Burgis, White and Maclaren families, and the ancestry of John Drake, of Windsor, Conn. By Melatsih Everett Dwight. New York, The Trow Print, 1898. (LoC)

KNAPP – Knapp, A. A.

Roger Knapp (of New Haven, Conn., 1638/47) and some of his descendants. By A. A. Knapp. Winter Park, Fla., 1952. (FW)

KNAPP – Knapp, Alfred Averill

Roger Knapp of New Haven, Conn., 1638-1647, and some of his descendants; a genealogy founded upon research of, and material collected by, Charles Ruggles Knapp (and others). By Alfred Averill Knapp. Winter Park, Fla., 1959. (LoC)

KNAPP – Neff, Tilla (H.)

The Knapp family, Connecticut, New York, Ohio. By Tilla (H.) Neff. (Lakewood, Ohio, 1952). (FW)

KNOWLTON –

Statue of Colonel Thomas Knowlton: ceremonies at the unveiling. Hartford, Conn., Press of the Case, Lockwood & Brainard Co., 1895. (LoC)

KNOWLTON – Morse, Frank L.

...Genealogy of Thomas Knowlton (Ipswich, Mass., 1756), Deborah Tracy Adams, (Windham, Conn., 1771); Sewell Knowlton, (Wales Center, N. Y., 1800) and Deborah Tracy Pettis, (Canterbury, Conn., 1805). By Frank L. Morse. New York City, 1929. (NY)

KNOWLTON – Porter, G. S.

Richard Knowlton of England, 1553, and American descendants. By G. S. Porter. Norwich, Conn., n. d. (FW)

KNOX –

Knox Family of Hartford (1873), 107 pgs.[1]

KNOX – Griffiths, Thomas M.

Major General Henry Knox and the last heirs to Montepelier. By Thomas M. Griffiths. Monmouth, Me., Monmouth Press, 1965. (NY)

L

LACKEY – Pratt, Harriett I.
Lackey, Stratton, and allied families. Glastonbury, Conn.: Charles S.
Nutt: Marjorie P. Nutt, 1971. (DAR)

LACY – Lacy, Philip S.
The Lacy family from Fairfield, Connecticut. S.1.: Lacy, 1973. (DAR)

LACY – Lacy, Philip S.
The Lacy family from Fairfield, Conn. By Philip S. Lacy. (New York)
1973. (LA)

LAKE –
Descendants of Thomas Lake of Stratford, Connecticut. By David
Minor Lake... Albert Edward Lake and Arthur Crawford Lake...
Chicago (Fergus Printing Company) 1908. (LoC)

LAKE – Gibson, Helen M.
The Lake family of Derby, Conn. and Greene County, N. Y. By Helen
M. Gibson. Montclair, N. J. (1932). (MH)

LAMB –
Lamb Family of Conn. (1903), 7 pgs.[1]

LAMB – Lamb, Truxton G.
The family record... By Truxton G. Lamb. West Hartford, Conn.,
Chedwato Service, 1957. (FW)

LAMB – Lamb, Truxton German
The Lamb family record. West Hartford, Conn.: Chedwato Service,
1957? (DAR)

LAMBERT – Lambert, Edward R.
History of the colony of New Haven, before and after the union with
Connecticut... By Edward R. Lambert. New Haven, Hitchcock &
Stafford, 1838. (LoC)

LANE –
Lane Family of Wolcott, Connecticut (1899), 64 pgs.[1]

LANE –
Genealogical notes on the families of Daniel Lane 2d and Mary
Griswold Lane, of Killingworth and Wolcott, in Connecticut, (married

at Killingworth, July 14th, A. D. 1763). Comp. by four of their descendants (Hiram W. Lane, Mrs. Elisha R. Newell, Mrs. Joseph F. Smith, Albert C. Beckwith). Elkhorn, Wis. (The Independent Print) 1899. (LoC)

LANE – Smith, Mirian Lane
Genealogical notes on the families of Daniel Lane 2d and Mary Griswold Lane of Killingworth and Wolcott in Connecticut. Elkhorn, Wis.: H. W. Lane: A. C. Beckwith (Independent Print), 1899. (DAR)

LATHROP –
Anniversary record of the golden wedding of Mr. and Mrs. Thomas Lathrop… 1880. Plainfield, Conn., 1881. (LI)

LATHROP – Huntington, E. B.
A genealogical memoir of the Lo-Lathrop family in this country. Hartford, Conn.: Case, Lockwood & Brainard, 1884. (DAR)

LATHROP – Lathrop, Charles L.
In this place; a personal perspective of 500 years. By Charles L. Lathrop. Lebanon, Conn. (1976). (NY)

LATHROP – Lathrop, Daniel S.
Lathrop genealogy (the author's line of descendants of Samuel Lathrop of Norwich, Conn., 1648). By Daniel S. Lathrop. (Albany, N. Y., 1882). (LI)

LAW – Jenkins, Philomene
Consider Law of Lebanon, Conn., and Oneida Co., N. Y. Lincoln, Neb.: Keystone Press, 1928. (DAR)

LAWRENCE –
Lawrence Family of Canaan, Connecticut (1848), 20 pgs.[1]
Lawrence Family of Canaan, 2d Ed. (1853), 76 pgs.[1]

LAWRENCE – Jinks, Mrs. A. Lawrence
Rosman Lawrence family; embracing the descendants as far as known of Rosman Lawrence of Middletown, Connecticut, and his descendants of other names. By Mrs. A. Lawrence Jinks. Dalton, N. Y., Burt's Print. Service (1965). (LoC)

LAWRENCE. See also:

Benedict	Daniel, 1959	Goodchild
Collier, 195/a	Doty, 1942	page, 1953

Starkey, 1892	Tallman, 190-	Townley, 1883
Starkey, 1910	Thomas, 1878	Townley, 1888
Stuart, 1961	Thomas, 1883	Wetherill, 1882
		No. 3939-Colebrook

LAWSON – Lawson, Harvey M.
History and genealogy of the descendants of John Lawson of Scotland and Union, Connecticut. Southbridge, Mass.: Central Massachusetts Printing Co., 1930? (DAR)

LAWSON – Lawson, Rev. Harvey M.
History and genealogy of the descendants of John Lawson, of Scotland and Union, Connecticut. By Rev. Harvey M. Lawson, M. A. Southbridge, Mass., Central Massachusetts Printing Co. (1931). (LoC)

LAY –
Descendants of John Lay, Sr. who settled at Lyme, Conn. prior to 1648. N.p.:n.d. (PH)

LAY – Hill, Edwin A.
The descendants of Robert Lay of Saybrook, Conn. By Edwin A. Hill. Boston, New England Historic Genealogical Society, 1908. (LoC)

LAY – Parkhurst, Charles Dyer
The Lay family of Lyme, Connecticut. Hartford, Conn.: Connecticut State Library, 1928. (DAR)

LEDYARD – Ivy, Frances Ledyard
The Ledyard family of Connecticut, New York, Alabama, and Mississippi and allied families, including the Heards of Virginia, Georgia, and Mississippi. By Frances Ledyard Ivy. Columbus, Ms. Lowndes County Dept. of Archives and History, c1979. (LoC)

LEE –
Lee Family of Watertown (1893), 16 pgs.[1]

LEE –
Lee Family of Saybrook, Connecticut (1851), 31 pgs.[1]
Lee Family of Farmington, Connecticut (1874), 8 pgs.[1]
Lee Family of Farmington, Connecticut (1878), 180 pgs.[1]
Lee of Farmington, Reunion (1885), 116 pgs.[1]
Lee of Farmington, Reunion (1896), 67 pgs.[1]
Lee Family of Farrmington, 2nd Ed. (1897), 527 pgs.[1]
Lee Family of Farmington, Supp. (1900), 176 pgs.[1]

LEE –

John Lee of Farmington, Hartford Co., Conn., and his descendants.
Containing over 4,000 names. 1634. 2d. Ed. 1897. 1st Ed. by Sarah
March Lee, of Norwich, Conn., 1878. With much miscellaneous
history of the family – brief notes of other Lee families of New
England – biographical notices – valuable data collected by William
Wallace Lee – military records – to which is added a "roll of honor," of
two hundred who have served in the various wars of the country.
Comp. by Leonard Lee and Sarah Fishe Lee. Pub. by the "Lee
Association." Meriden, Conn., Republican-Record Book Print, 1897.
(LoC)

LEE –

Stratford on the Potomac, by Ethel Armes, an address on Robert E.
Lee, by Sidney Lanier; maps and line drawings by Catherine Claiborne
Armes. Greenwich, Conn., William Alexander, Jr. Chapter, United
Daughters of the Confederacy. 1928. (LoC)

LEE –

The Lee family, relating especially to Thomas Lee of Lyme,
Connecticut, and some of his descendants... (New York, Printed by
B. H. Tyrrel, 1933). (LoC)

LEE – Black, Ruth A. H.

1973 supplement to the 1897 edition of John Lee of Farmington, Conn.
and his descendants. By Ruth A. H. Black. (Chicago, Adams Press,
1974). (FW)

LEE – Black, Ruth Ann Heisey

1973 supplement to the 1897 edition of John Lee of Farmington, Conn.,
and his descendants. Mountain View, Calif.: Black, c1974. (DAR)

LEE – Black, Ruth A. H.

1975 supplement to the 1973 supplement to John Lee of Farmington,
Conn. and his descendants (1634-1897). By Ruth A. H. Black.
(Mountain View, Calif., 1975). (FW)

LEE – Clemens, William Montgomery

Lee marriages in Connecticut. (By William Montgomery Clemens).
(LoC)

LEE – Lee, Frank T.

Characteristic traits of the Lee family; address delivered at Lee family reunion, Farmington, Conn., 1896. By Frank T. Lee. Meriden, Conn., 1896. (LI)

LEE – Lee, Leonard
John Lee of Farmington, Hartford Co., Conn.; and his descendants. Meriden, Conn.: Lee Association, Republican Record Book print, 1897. (DAR)

LEE – Lee, Leonard
Re-union of the descendants of John Lee, of Farmington. Held at Farmington... August 12 and 13, 1896. Ed. from minutes of the meeting by Leonard Lee. Pub. by Lee Association. Meriden, Republican Pub. Co., 1896. (LoC)

LEE – Lee, Percy M.
Family reunion: an incomplete account of the Maxim-Lee family history. By Percy M. Lee. (Hartford, Conn. Print) n. d. (FW)

LEE – Lee, Robert Edward
Colonel Noah Lee of Salisbury, Conn., and Castleton, Vt., and his descendants. Compiled by Robert Edward Lee. [Silver Spring, Md.]: R. E. Lee, c1990. (LoC)

LEE – Lee, Sarah Marsh
John Lee, of Farmington, Hartford County, Conn., and his descendants. Norwich, Conn.: Press of the Bulletin Co., 1878. (DAR)

LEE – Lee, Sarah Marsh
John Lee, of Farmington, Hartford County, Conn., and his descendants, arranged by Sarah Marsh Lee... Norwich, Press of the Bulletin Company, 1878. (LoC)

LEE – Lee, W. W.
Lee family quarter-millennial gathering of the descendants and kinsmen of John Lee, one of the early settlers of Farmington, Conn., held in Hartford, Conn., Tues. & Wed., August 5th and 6th, 1884. (Comp. by W. W. Lee). Meriden, Republican Steam Print, 1885. (LoC)

LEE – Lee, William Wallace
Lee family. Meriden, Conn.: Republican Steam Print, 1885. (DAR)

LEEKE – Coles, H. R.

The descendants (!) of Philip Leeke. From Dover, Kent County,
England, to New England, about the year 1638. One of the first settlers
of New Haven, Ct. Compiled by H. R. Coles... (N.p., 1936?). (LoC)

LEET – Doty, Harrison
Lines of descent: from Edward Doty, Mayflower passenger, 1620, John
Parmelee, New Haven Colony, 1639, William Leet, Guilford Colony,
1639, to and from Harrison Parmelee Doty, born 1910, Leete Parmelee
Doty, born 1917, Carol Parmelee Doty Wilson, born 1918, plus notes
on kissing kin & divers others; an adventure in genealogy begun in
1925 and concluded in 1985. 1st Ed. Brattleboro, Vt.: H. Doty, c1985.
(LoC)

LEET – Helander, Joel Eliot
Leete's Island legacy. Joel E. Helander. Guilford, Conn.: J. E.
Helander, c1981. (LoC)

LEETE – Leete, Edward L.
The descendants of William Leete. New Haven: Tuttle, Morehouose &
Taylor, 1934. (DAR)

LEETE – Leete, Edward L.
The family of William Leete, one of the first settlers of Guilford, Conn.
and governor of New Haven and Connecticut colonies. Compiled by
Edward L. Leete... New Haven, Tuttle, Morehouse & Taylor, printers,
1884. (LoC)

LEETE – Leete, Edward L.
The descendants of William Leete, one of the founders of Guilford,
Conn., president of the Federation of colonies and governor of New
Haven and Connecticut colonies. Compiled by Edward L. Leete...
2d Ed. New Haven, The Tuttle, Morehouse & Taylor Co., printers
(c1934). (LoC)

LEFFINGWELL – Leffingwell, Albert
1637-1897. The Leffingwell record. A genealogy of the descendants
of Lieut. Thomas Leffingwell, one of the founders of Norwich, Conn.
By Albert Leffingwell... and Charles Wesley Leffingwell... Aurora,
N. Y., Leffingwell Pub. Co., 1897. (LoC)

LEPAK – Lepak, Anne Frary
The Lepak family of Connecticut. Anne Frary Lepak, compiler. Port
Richey, Fl.: A. F. Lepak, 1988. (LoC)

LEWIS – Dickinson, Addie M.
Descendants of William Lewis of Hartford, Conn. 1956? (DAR)

LEWIS – Shea, Thomas William
Our story, the family of William Isaac Lewis and Mary Ann Wolf
Lewis, both antecedants and descendants. Edited by Thomas William
Shea and Patricia Lewis Hovorka. Hartford, Conn.: Ace Printery,
1980. (LoC)

L'HOMMEDIEU - Gesser, Florence E.
L'Hommedieu genealogy. Norwich, Conn. 1965. (NGS)

LINDEMAN – Munsell, Claude G.
Lindeman genealogy. By Claude G. Munsell. South Norwalk, Conn.,
J. Munsell's Sons, 1949. (FW)

LINES – Jacobus, Donald Lines
The Lines family. By Donald Lines Jacobus of New Haven,
Connecticut. (Hartford, Conn., 1905). (LoC)

LINK – Prindle, Paul W.
Vital records of descendants of Helmus and Esther (Betts) Link.
Noroton Heights, Conn.: Prindle, 1956. (DAR)

LINSLEY – Linsley, Ray Keyes
Connecticut Linsleys, the six Johns, being the history, so far as known,
of the descendants of the first of the name in Connecticut. By Ray
Keyes Linsley. (Bristol? Conn., 1949). (LoC)

LOBDELL – Lobdell, Julia Harrison
Simon Lodbell (sic), 1646, of Milford, Conn. and his descendants;
Nicholas Lobden (Lobdell), 1635, of Hingham, Mass. and some of his
descendants. Chicago, Ill?: Lobdell, 1907. (DAR)

LOBDELL – Lobdell, Julia Harrison
...Simon Lobdell – 1646 of Milford, Conn., and his descendants.
Compiled and published by Julia Harrison Lobdell. Nicholas Lobden
(Lobdell) – 1635 of Hingham, Mass., and some of his descendants.
Chicago, The Windermere Press (1907?). (LoC)

LOCKWOOD – Hodge, Harriet Woodbury
Some descendants of Edmund Lockwood (1594-1635) of Cambridge,
Massachusetts, and his son Edmund Lockwood (c.1625-1693) of
Stamford, Connecticut. New York: P. V. Lockwood, 1978. (DAR)

LOCKWOOD – Hodge, Harriet Woodbury
Some descendants of Edmund Lockwood (1594-1635) of Cambridge,
Massachusetts, and his son Edmund Lockwood (c1625-1693) of
Stamford, Connecticut. New York, N. Y. 1978. (NGS)

LOCKWOOD – Hodge, Harriet Woodbury
Some descendants of Edmund Lockwood (1594-1635) of Cambridge,
Mass., and his son Edmund Lockwood (c1625-1693) of Stamford,
Conn. N. Y.:Lockwood, 1978. (LoC)

LOOMER – Shepard, Addie Eugenia (Loomer)
The descendants of Stephen Loomer of New London, Connecticut,
comprising the first to and including the ninth generation. By Addie
Eugenia (Loomer) Shepard. Allison, Iowa (1960 or 61). (LoC)

LOOMIS -
The Loomis family in America, a brochure. Addresses delivered at the
reunion of the Loomis family association, at Hartford, Connecticut,
September twenty-seventh, nineteen hundred and five, and including
the official record of the business transacted. (Hartford) Press of the
Connecticut Magazine, 1906. (LoC)

LOOMIS – Loomis, Elias
The descendants by the female branches of Joseph Loomis. New
Haven, Conn.: Tuttle, Morehouse & Taylor, 1880. (DAR)

LOOMIS – Loomis, Elias
The descendants of Jospeh Loomis. New Haven: Tuttle, Morehouse &
Taylor, 1875. (DAR)

LOOMIS – Loomis, Elias
The descendants of Joseph Loomis. New Haven, Conn.: Tuttle,
Morehouse and Taylor, 1870. (DAR)

LOOMIS – Loomis, Elias
The descendants of Joseph Loomis, who came from Braintree,
England, in the year 1638, and settled in Windsor, Connecticut, in
1639. By Elias Loomis... New Haven, Tuttle, Morehouse & Taylor,
1870. (LoC)

LOOMIS – Loomis, Elias
The descendants of Joseph Loomis, who came from Braintree,
England, in the year 1638, and settled in Windsor, Connecticut, in

1639. By Elias Loomis... 2d Ed., rev. and enl. New Haven, Tuttle, Morehouse and Taylor, 1875. (LoC)

LOOMIS – Loomis, Elias
The descendants (by the female branches) of Joseph Loomis, who came from Braintree, England, in the year 1638, and settled in Windsor, Connecticut, in 1639. By Elias Loomis... New Haven, Tuttle, Morehouse & Taylor, 1880. (LoC)

LOOMIS – Loomis, Elisha S.
Descendants of Joseph Loomis in America. 1909. (DAR)

LORD – Lord, Rev. John M.
Genealogy of the Lord family which removed from Colchester, Conn., to Hanover, N. H., and then to Norwich, Vt. By Rev. John M. Lord. Concord, N. H., I. C. Evans Co., printers, 1903. (LoC)

LORD – Lord, Kenneth
Genealogy of the descendants of Thomas Lord. New York: Lord (New Haven, Conn.: Tuttle, Morehouse & Taylor) 1946. (DAR)

LORD – Lord, Kenneth
Certain members of the Lord family who settled in New York City in the early 1800s, descendants of Thomas Lord of Hartford, Connecticut. By Kenneth Lord. (Concord) Priv. print. (Rumford Press) 1945. (LoC)

LORD – Lord, Kenneth
Genealogy of the descendants of Thomas Lord, an original proprietor and founder of Hartford, Conn., in 1636. Compiled by Kenneth Lord. New York, 1946. (LoC)

LOVELAND – Loveland, J. B.
Genealogy of the Loveland family in the United States of America, from 1635 to 1892, containing the descendants of Thomas Loveland, of Wethersfield, now Glastonbury, Conn. ... By J. B. Loveland... and George Loveland... (Fremont, O., I. M. Keeler & Son, printers, 1892-95). (LoC)

LOWE – Braunsdorff, Otto-William
...Some account of the family of Lowe, formerly of Hartford, and elsewhere in the County of Chester, subsequently of Highfield in the County of Nottingham, and now Shirenewton Hall in the County of Monmouth. Compiled from the papers left by the late Lieutenant-

colonel Alfred Edward Lawson Lowe... by Otto-Willliam
Braunsdorff... Dresden, 1896. (LoC)

LOWREY –
50th Anniversary of the descendants of Thomas Lowrey and Mary
Lowrey held at Plainville, Connecticut... 1926. (Plainville? 1926?)
(NY)

LUDINGTON – Cory, H. T.
Genealogical record of William Luddington, of Malden, Mass., and
East Haven, Conn., and his descendants. Comp. by H. T. Cory. May
1916. (N.p., 1916). (LoC)

LUDINGTON – de Forest, Louis Effingham
Ludington-Saltus records. New Haven, Conn.: Tuttle, Morehouse &
Taylor, 1925, c1926. (DAR)

LUDINGTON – de Forest, Louis Effingham
Ludington-Saltus records, originally collected by Ethel Saltus
Lundington. Edited by Louis Effingham de Forest... (New Haven,
The Tuttle, Morehouse & Taylor Company) 1925. (LoC)

LUDINGTON – Shepard, James
William Luddington of Malden, Mass., and East Haven, Conn., and his
descendants. By James Shepard. Boston, Press of D. Clapp & Son,
1904. (LoC)

LYON –
Lyon memorial. Families of Connecticut and New Jersey, including
records of the descendants of the immigrants, Richard Lyon, of
Fairfield, Henry Lyon, of Fairfield, with a sketch of "Lyons farms," by
S. R. Winans, Jr. Illustrated with maps. Editor: Sidney Elizabeth
Lyon... associate editors, Louise Lyon Johnson... A. B. Lyons...
Detroit, Mich., W. Graham Printing Co., 1907. (LoC)

MC

MCCURDY –
Family histories and genealogies. A series of genealogical and
biographical monographs on the families of MacCurdy, Mitchell, Lord,
Lynde, Digby, Newdigate, Hoo, Willoughby, Griswold, Wolcott,
Pitkin, Ogden, Johnson, Diodati, Lee and Marvin, and notes on the
families of Buchanan, Parmelee, Boardman, Lay, Locke, Cole,

DeWolf, Drake, Bond and Swayne, Dunbar and Clarke, and a notice of Chief Justice Morrison Remick Waite. With twenty-nine pedigree charts and two charts of combined descent... By Edward Elbridge Salisbury and Evelyn McCurdy Salisbury. Privately printed. (New Haven, Press of Tuttle, Morehouse & Taylor) 1892. (LoC)

MCDONALD – MacDonald, Herbert S.
One small branch of the old MacDonald tree. By Herbert S. MacDonald. [North Haven? Conn.] 1968. (LoC)

MCEWAN – Coleman, Ruth McEwen
George McEwen, 1755-1813: pioneer, New Milford, Ct. to Hinesburg, Vt., his ancestors and many descendants, some in allied families, Landon, Post, Partch, Pierce, Day. Compiled and edited by Ruth McEwen Coleman. Peterborough, N. H.: R. M. Coleman, 1980. (LoC)

MCGILLLIVRAY – Waters, Marjory McGillivray
Ne'er forgot shall be: a genealogy of Clan McGillivray of Glenelg & Skye, Inverness-shire, 1761-1979. By Marjory McGillivray Waters. (Darien, Conn.): Waters, c1980. (LoC)

MCGUIRE –
Lineage of Elisha Whipple McGuire. (Windham, Conn., Printed at Hawthorn house, 1938). (LoC)

MCINTOSH – McIntosh, Andrew
A genealogical record of the descendants of Andrew McIntosh of Willington, Conn., who was the second in name as he was in generation from Robert McIntosh of Scotland. Springfield, Mass.: Clarke W. Bryan & Co., 1888. (DAR)

MCLEAN – McLean, Allen
A genealogical memorail of the Connecticut McLean family. Edited from the manuscript volume of the Reverend Allen McLean by George McLean Milne and Janet Odell Milne. Hebron, Conn. G. M. Milne (1984). (LoC)

MCNAIR – MacNair – Mary Wilson
The clan MacFarlane, the division of the clan. Hartford, Conn.: Case, Lockwood & Brainard Co., 1914. (DAR)

MCNAIR – MacNair – Mary Wilson

The clan MacFarlane; the division of the clan. Ancestry of David D. McNair. By Mary Wilson MacNair. Hartford, Conn., The Case, Lockwood & Brainard Co., Printers, 1914. (LoC)

M

MACDONALD –
Genealogy of the MacDonald family. Ed. B. Comprising all names obtained up to February, 1876. (New Haven, Conn., Press Tuttle, Morehouse & Taylor, 1876). (LoC)

MACDONALD – MacDonald, Herbert S.
One small branch of the old MacDonald tree. ?North Haven, Ct. 1968. (NGS)

MACDONALD – MacDonald, Herbert S.
One small branch of the old MacDonald tree. By Herbert S. MacDonald. (North Haven? Conn.), 1968. (LoC)

MACFARLANE – MacNair, Mary W.
The clan MacFarlane. The division of the clan. Ancestry of David D. McNair. By Mary W. MacNair. Hartford, Conn., Case, Lockwood... 1914. (NY)

MACK – Martin, Mrs. Sophia (Smith)
The descendants of John Mack of Lyme, Conn., with appendix containing genealogy of allied families, etc. By Mrs. Sophia (Smith) Martin... Rutland, Vt., The Tuttle Company, Printers, 1903-04. (LoC)

MACLEAN – Hardy, Mary McLean
A brief history of the ancestry and posterity of Allan MacLean, 1715-1786, Vernon, Colony of Connecticut... By Mary McLean Hardy. Berkeley, Cal., Marquand Printing Co., 1905. (LoC)

MACLEAN – McLean, John J.
A brief history of the ancestry and posterity of Doctor Neil McLean, of Hartford, Conn., U. S. A. (By) John J. McLean. Palmyra, N. Y., 1900. (LoC)

MAIN – Aspinwall, Algernon Aikin
The descendants of Ezekiel Maine of Stonington, Connn. By Algernon Aikin Aspinwall. Washington, 1905. (LoC)

MAINE – Aspinwall, Algernon Aikin
The descendants of Ezekiel Maine of Stonington, Conn. Delaware,
Ohio: Frances Main and Cleveland, Ohio: Florence Maine, 1954.
(DAR)

MALTBY –
Family record of the Maltby-Morehouse family. A list of pedigrees
with genealogical notes, arranged for the convenience of the children of
George Ellsworth Maltby and Georgia Lord (Morehouse) Maltby by
their mother. (New Haven, Conn., The Tuttle, Morehouse & Taylor
Press, c1895). (LoC)

MALTBY – Maltby, Georgia Lord Morehouse
Family record of the Maltby-Morehouse family. New Haven, Conn.:
Tuttle, Morehouse & Taylor Press, 1895. (DAR)

MANN – Ammerman, Charles Richard
Man – Peters – Mann: ancestors and descendants of John Man and his
wife Margaret Peters of Hebron, Connecticut. By Charles Richard
Ammerman. St. Petersburg, Fla., 1958. (LoC)

MANSFIELD – Mansfield, H.
The descendants of Richard and Gillian Mansfield who settled in New
Haven, 1639; with sketches of some of the most distinguished. Also,
of connections of other names. Comp. and pub. by H. Mansfield. New
Haven, 1885. (LoC)

MANSFIELD – Mansfield, Horace
The descendants of Richard and Gillian Mansfield. New Haven:
Mansfield, 1885. (DAR)

MANY –
41first cousins, a history of some descendants of Jean Many, French
Huguenot. West Hartford, Conn., 1961. (LoC)

MANY – Many, Dorothy Jones
41 first cousins. West Hartford, Conn.: Many, 1961. (DAR)

MAPES – Ham, Frank Mapes
The Mapes family in America. Bridgeport, Conn.: Ham, 1962. (DAR)

MARCY – Marcy, Charles Edney

History and genealogy of John Marcy, 1662-1724, Wooodstock, Conn., and many of his descendants; eleven generations. S.1.: Marcy? c1980. (DAR)

MARKS – Lines, Eliza J.
Marks-Platt ancestry. Comp. by Eliza J. Lines... Sound Beach, Conn. Pub. by request of A. A. Marks, 1902. (LoC)

MARKS – Lines, Eliza J. Marks
Marks-Platt ancestry. Sound Beach, Conn.: Lines, 1902. (DAR)

MARSH -
Marsh Family of Hartford (1895), 584 pgs.[1]

MARSH –
Genealogy of the Marsh family. Outline for five generations of the families of John of Salem, 1633. John of Hartford, 1636. Samuel of New Haven, 1646. Alexander of Braintree, 1654. John of Boston, 1669, and William of Plainfield, 1675. With accounts of the Third family reunion at Lake Pleasant in 1886. Edited by D. W. Marsh, of the gen. com., and printed, for additions and corrections, by the Marsh Family Association. Amherst, Press of J. E. Williams, 1886. (LoC)

MARTIN – Martin, Albert P.
Martin and Pray families. By Albert P. Martin. Glastonbury, Conn., 1976. (FW)

MARTIN – Martin, Albert Pray
The Martin and Pray families: showing the ancestors, descendants, and relatives of Ira Jay Martin and Verina Leonora Pray, together with 235 other early colonial and European families connected with them. Compiled by Albert Pray Martin. Glastonbury, Conn.: Martin, c1976. (LoC)

MARVIN –
Descendants of Reinold and Matthew Marvin of Hartford, Ct., 1638 and 1635, sons of Edward Marvin, of Great Bentley, England. By George Franklin Marvin... and William T. R. Marvin... Boston, T. R. Marvin & Son, 1904. (LoC)

MARVIN – Marvin, George Franklin
Descendants of Reinold and Matthew Marvin of Hartford, Ct., 1638 and 1635. Boston: T. R. Marvin & Son, 1904. (DAR)

MARVIN – Marvin, William T. R.
The English ancestry of Reinold and Matthew Marvin, of Hartford, Ct.,
1638; their homes and parish churches. By William T. R. Marvin...
Boston, Priv. print. (T. R. Marvin & Son, Printers) 1900. (LoC)

MASKELL – Andrews, Frank D.
Thomas Maskell of Simsbury, Connecticut. Vineland, N. J.: s. n.,
1927. (DAR)

MASKELL – Andrews, Frank D.
Thomas Maskell of Simsbury, Connecticut; his son Thomas Maskell of
Greenwich, New Jersey and some of their descendants. Compiled by
Frank D. Andrews... Vineland, N. J., 1927. (LoC)

MASON – Allyn, James H.
Major John Mason's Great Island. By James H. Allyn. Mystic, Conn.:
R. N. Bohlander, c1976. (LoC)

MASON – Bulkley, Caroline (Kemper)
A double Mason line from Major John Mason, deputy-governor of
Connecticut to new cadet John Mason Kemper, West Point, 1931. (By
Caroline (Kemper) Bulkley, n. p., 1932). (LoC)

MASON – Mason, Edna Warren
Descendants of Capt. Hugh Mason in America. New Haven, Conn.:
Tuttle, Morehouse & Taylor, 1937. (DAR)

MASON – Mason, Edna Warren (Mrs. Mason Pfizenmayer)
Descendants of Capt. Hugh Mason in America. By Edna Warren
Mason (Mrs. Mason Pfizenmayer). New Haven, Conn., The Tuttle,
Morehouse & Taylor Company, 1937. (LoC)

MASON – Mason, George W.
Ancestors and descendants of Elisha Mason, Litchfield, Conn., 1759-
1858, and his wife Lucretia Webster, 1766-1853. By George W.
Mason. Litchfield, Conn. (1911) (Mattatuck Press). (FW)

MASON – Mason, Theodore West
Family record in our line of descent from Major John Mason of
Norwich, Connecticut. New York: Grafton Press, 1909. (DAR)

MASON – Mason, Theodore West

Family record in our line of descent from Major John Mason of Norwich, Connecticut. By Theodore West Mason... New York, The Grofton Press, 1909. (LoC)

MATHER –
Genealogy of the Mather family, from about 1500 to 1847; with sundry biographical notices... Hartford, Press of E. Geer, 1848. (LoC)

MATHER – Mather, Horace E.
Lineage of Rev. Richard Mather. Hartford, Conn.: Case, Lockwood & Brainard Co., 1890. (DAR)

MATHER – Mather, Horace E.
Lineage of Rev. Richard Mather. By Horace E. Mather... Hartford, Conn., Press of the Case, Lockwood & Brainard Company, 1890. (LoC)

MATHER – Mather, John
Genealogy of the Mather family from about 1500 to 1847. Hartford; Elihu Geer, 1848. (DAR)

MATTINGLY – Mattingly, Joseph F.
Descendants of Jospeh Mattingly & Hessina Hinton. By Joseph F. Mattingly & Eliza Mattingly Kelly. Hartford: McDonald Publications, 1978. (LoC)

MAUGHAM – Maugham, Robin
Somerset and all the Maughams. By Robin Maugham. Westport, Conn.: Greenwood Press, 1977, c1966. (LoC)

MAXIM – Lee, Percy M.
Family reunion, an incomplete account of the Maxim-Lee family history. By Percy M. Lee. Hartford, Conn.: Conn. Printers. (1971). (OH)

MAXWELL – Burpee, Col. Charles W.
The Maxwell family from the Story of Connecticut, by Col. Charles W. Burpee. Rockville, Conn. Priv. print. (at the sign of the Stone book, by the Case, Lockwood & Brainard Co., Hartford), 1939. (LoC)

MEACHAM – Doran, Kenneth T. (Kenneth Thompson)
A lineal account of the American ancestry of Charles Meacham (1837-1896) of Tolland, Connecticut, and a limited account of his

descendants. By Kenneth T. Doran. Albany, N. Y.: K. T. Doran, 1978. (LoC)

MEAD –
Mead Family of Connecticut (1882), 1007 pgs.[1]

MEAD – DeMille, John H.
History of the Mead family of (Horseneck). Greenwich, Conn. By John H. DeMillle. (DP)

MEAD – Draper, Cecil Mead
Jonathan Mead of Rensselaerwyck and some of his descendants, with a shorter sketch of a single line of Williams, Massachusetts, Connecticut, New York. By Cecil Mead Draper. Denver, 1972. (LoC)

MEAD – Feltus, Louise Celestia (Mead)
Our two centuries in North Greenwich, Connecticut, 1728-1924. By Louise Celestia (Mead) Feltus. (N.p.) 1945. (LoC)

-    A supplement of addenda and corrigenda. (Troy, N. Y., R. H. Prout Co.), 1948. (LoC)

MEAD – Mead, Spencer P.
History and genealogy of the Mead family of Fairfield County, Connecticut, easter New York, westerner Vermont, and western Pennsylvania. New York: Knickerbocker Press, 1901. (DAR)

MEAD – Paprker, C. E.
The Mead family of Connecticut. Compiled by C. E. Parker. Santa Ana, Calif., 1968. (LoC)

MEAD. See also:
Benedict	Pocahontas, 1887
Buck, 1917 suppl.	Pool, 1958
Funsten, 1926	Smith, 1939
Manley, 1938	No. 1459-Early
	families of… Ky.

MEAD – Sawers, Mary Beeler
Lineage of Jeremiah Mead, Jr., of Greenwich, Connecticut. Middletown, Conn.: Sawers, 1958. (DAR)

MEAD – Sawers, Mary Beller

Lineage of Jeremiah Mead, Jr., of Greenwich, Connecticut, soldier of
the American Revolution. By Mary Beller Sawers. Middletown,
Conn., 1958. (LoC)

MEAD – Wicks, Mrs. C. P.
Index to persons named in the inadequately indexed History and
genealogy of the Mead family of Fairfield Co., Conn. ... By Mrs. C. P.
Wicks. Stamford, Conn., Stamford Geneal. Soc., 1975. (FW)

MEARS – Healy, Helen E. Rickley
Some descendants of John and Lucy Rockwell Mears of Windsor,
Conn. 1960. (DAR)

MECORNEY – Mecorney, George E.
Mecorney genealogy. By George E. Mecorney. (Suffield, Conn.,
1937). (NY)

MERES –
The family of Meres and some early English newspapers. A paper
read... by Edward Deacon. Bridgeport, Conn., 1891. (LI)

MERRILL – Barbour, Heman H.
My wife and my mother. Hartford: Williams, Wiley & Waterman,
1864. (DAR)

MERRILL – Barbour, Heman H.
Genealogy prepared and published in 1864, by Heman H. Barbour as
an appendix to his book entitled, My wife and my mother. Hartford,
Press of Wiley, Waterman & Eaton, 1885. (LoC)

MERRILL – Barbour, Heman Humphrey
My wife and my mother. (By Heman Humphrey Barbour). Hartford,
Press of Williams, Wiley & Waterman, 1864. (LoC)

MERRIMAN –
Reunion of descendants of Nathaniel Merriman at Wallingford, Conn.
June 4, 1913, with a Merriman genealogy for five generations. New
Haven, Conn.: D. L. Jacobus, 1914. (LoC)

MERRIMAN – Jacobus, Donald L.
Reunion of descendants of Nathaniel Merriman at Wallingford, Conn...,
June 4, 1913. New Haven, Conn.: Jacobus, 1914. (DAR)

MERRIMAN – Merriman, Mansfield

Nathaniel Merriman, one of the founders of Wallingford in the state of Connecticut. New York, N. Y. 1913. (NGS)

MERRIMAN – Merriman, Mansfield
Nathaniel Merriman, one of the founders of Wallingford in the state of Connecticut. By Mansfield Merriman... New York, 1913. (LoC)

MERRITT – Stevens, Halsey
Merritt family records: Guilford and Killingworth, Connecticut; Fair Haven, Benson and Georgia, Vermont; St. Lawrence and Allegany Counties, New York; Fort Dodge, Webster County, Iowa. Compiled by Halsey Stevens... Peoria, Ill. (1942). (LoC)

MERRITT. See also: Bartlett, 1951
                                   Crawford, 1939

MERWIN – Merwin, George H.
The Merwins of Fairfield, Conn. and the story of Merwin's Lane. By George H. Merwin. (Greenfield Hill, Conn.) priv. print. (1941). (NY)

MERWIN – Miles Merwin Association
The Merwin family in North America; a genealogy of the descendants of Miles Merwin (1623-1697) in the male line through the tenth generation. Hartford, Ct. 1978-83. (NGS)

MERWIN – Miles Merwin (1623-1697) Association, Inc.
The Merwin family in North America. Hartrford, Conn.: Connecticut Historical Society, 1978. (DAR)

MERWIN – Newton, Carolin Gaylord
Miles Merwin, 1623-1697, and one branch of his descendants. By Carolin Gaylord Newton. (Durham, Conn.), 1909. (LoC)

MESSENGER –
The paternal lineage and some of the descendants of Isaac Messenger of Connecticut. (N.p.) 1962. (LoC)

MESSENGER –
The Messenger family in the Colony of Connecticut; genealogy and narrative of the Messenger family, concentrating on descendants of Edward Messenger, Bloomfield, Connecticut, and allied families. Compiled by Nettie Post Wright and Nettie Wright Adams. Narrated & arranged by Nettie Wright Adams (Mrs. James P. Adams). West Hartford, Conn., Printed by T. B. Simonds, 1963. (LoC)

MESSENGER –
The paternal lineage and some of the descendants of Isaac Messenger of Connecticut. 2d Ed. (N.p., 1964-). (LoC)

MESSENGER . See also: Messinger

MESSENGER – Wood, Anne Farrell Higgins
The paternal lineage and some of the descendants of Isaac Messenger of Connecticut. S.1.:s.n., 1964. (DAR)

MESSENGER – Wright, Nettie Post
The Messenger family in the colony of Connecticut. West Hartford, Conn.: T. B. Simonds, Inc., 1963. (DAR)

MESSINGER – Wright, Nettie E. (P.)
The Messinger family in the Colony of Connecticut. By Nettie E. (P.) Wright. West Hartford, Conn. Pr. T. B. Simonds, 1963. (SL)

MIDDLEBROOK – Middlebrook, Louis F.
Register of the Middlebrook family. Hartford, Conn.: Middlebrook, 1909. (DAR)

MIDDLEBROOK – Middlebrook, Louis F.
Register of the Middlebrook family, descendants of Joseph Middlebrook of Fairfield, Conn. By Louis F. Middlebrook... Hartford, Conn. (C. L. & B. Co.) 1909. (LoC)

MILLER –
Millers of Bishop's Stortford, County Herts, England; ancestors of Elizabeth (Miller) Heath, Agnes or Ann (Miller) Burnap, and Margaret (Miller) Waterman, all of Roxbury, Mass. ... Joseph Miller of Newton, Mass., and Thomas Miller of Middletown, Conn. (N. Y.) 1939. (FW)

MILLER – Miller, Maynard E.
Records of the Miller family; descendants of Jacob Miller of Lyme, Conn., 1700-1953, with historical and biographical notes. By Maynard E. Miller. New Lyme, O., 1920. (OH)

MILLS – Lamb, Eunice M.
The John-Simon Mills line of Windsor and Simsbury, Connecticut. Burlington, Vt.: Chedwato Service, 1968. (DAR)

MILLS – Lamb, Eunice M.

The John-Simon Mills line of Windsor and Simsbury, Connecticut and some descendants of John and Damaris Phelps Mills of Canton, Connecticut. By Eunice M. Lamb. Burlington, Vt.: Chadwato Service, 1968. (LoC)

MILLS. See also:

Clendinen, 1923	Halsey, 1927	Maulsby, 1902
Dickerson, 1919	Hay, 1923	Rosenberger, 1958
Doubleday, 1924	Higbie, 1914	Tyssen
Espenet	Ironmonger, 1956	Vinton, 1858a
Goodlock, 1951	McKee, 1900	Wilcox, 1911a

MILLS – Mills, Samuel H.
Samuel Mills ancestry; or George Mills and the Samuel Mills line of Jamaica, Long Island, New York and Greenwich, Conn. By Samuel H. Mills. (Denver, 1958). (DP)

MINER – Miner, John A.
The Miner family. Clement of New London – 1638 (and) Clement of Northfield – 1765. By John A. Miner. Acton, Mass., 1967. (FW)

MINER – Selleck, Lillian Lounsberry Miner
One branch of the Miner family. New Haven, Conn.: Donald L. Jacobus, 1928. (DAR)

MINOR –
Volunteer service in Army of Cumberland.. Pt. first. History of the volunteers from Clarksfield, Huron Co., Ohio, in the 101st O. V. I. ... Pt. second. List of the volunteers from Wakeman, O., the whole war. And their history since... Pt. third. Sergeant Benj. T. Strong's biography, and history of the Chickamauga campaign... Pt. fourth. Descendants of Justus Minor, who moved from Conn. in 1821 to Wakeman, O. All these several pieces written up and published by C. R. Green... 1913-14. Ed. 200. (Olathe? Kan., 1914). (LoC)

MINOR –
Thomas Minor and descendants; (Thomas) Wooodmancy (of New London, Conn.). N.p.:n.d. (FW)

MINOR – Gardiner, Tiger
The Gardiner-Squires connection: an account of the Gardiner family of Gardiner's Island, Long Island, New York, and the Squires family of Squiretown, Long Island, New York and West Haven, Connecticut, their connection and allied families – Wiggins, Miner, Beer, Wines,

and Raynor, 1559-1989. By Tiger Gardiner. Baltimore: Gateway Press, 1989. (LoC)

MINOR – Green, Charles R.
Descendants of Justus Minor who was born about 1775 in Connecticut, and removed to the Firelands, Ohio, 18821. By Charles R. Green. Olathe, Kan., 1914. (LI)

MITCHELL –
Mitchell Reunion at Britain, Connecticut (1859), 28 pgs.[1]

MITCHELL – Jordan-Solari, Marilyn
Some descendants of Michael & Sarah (Catlin) Mitchell of Connecticut & Massachusetts, 1694-1988. Compiled by Marilyn Jordan-Solari. Bowie, Md.: Heritage Books, 1988. (LoC)

MIX – Blake, William Phipps
A brief account of the life and patirotic (sic) services of Jonathan Mix of New Haven, being autobiographical memoir. Ed. from the original manuscript, with notes and additions, together with copies of the United States patents for carriage springs; an account of the Max family in New Haven and of the descendants of Jonathan Mix. By William Phipps Blake. New Haven, Printed by Tuttle, Morehouse & Taylor, 1886. (LoC)

MIX – Lainson, D. A. S.
Thomas Mix, 1643, immigrant to New Haven, Conn. By D. A. S. Lainson. Huntsville, Ark., Century Enterprises, 1972. (FW)

MOFFETT – Moffitt, Doris Parker
The Moffitt family: some of the descendants of William Moffitt as he spelt his name in Killingly, Ct. By Doris Parker Moffitt. [Bennington, Vt.]: D. P. Moffitt, 1985. (LoC)

MONSON –
...Proceedings of the first (& 2d) Munson family reunion, held in the City of New Haven, Wednesday, August 17, 1887, & Aug. 19, 1896. New Haven, Tuttle, Morehouse & Taylor, Printers, 1887, 1896. (LoC)

MONSON –
...Historical address of the first Munson family reunion held in the city of New Haven, Wednesday, August 17, 1887. New Haven, Tuttle, Morehouse & Taylor, 1887. (LoC)

MONSON – Munson, Myron A.
1637-1887. The Munson record. A genealogical and biographical account of Captain Thomas Munson (a pioneer of Hartford and New Haven) and his descendants. By Myron A. Munson... New Haven, Conn., Printed for the Munson Association, 1895. (LoC)

MONSON – Munson, Myron A.
Traditions concerning the origin of the American Munsons, gathered and digested by Myron A. Munson. New Haven, The Tuttle, Morehouse & Taylor Press, 1897. (LoC)

MONSON – Munson, Myron Andrews
The Portsmouth race of Monsons-Munsons-Mansons, comprising Richard Monson (at Portsmouth, N. H., 1663) and his descendants; being a contribution to the generalogy and history of five generations... By Myron Andrews Munson... New Haven, Conn. (The Tuttle, Morehouse & Taylor Press) 1910. (LoC)

MOORE –
Moore Family of Windsor, Connecticut (1900), 11 pgs.[1]

MOORE –
Genealogy of a branch of the Moore family, dscendants of Deacon John Moore, of Windsor, Conn. (New York, 1900). (LoC)

MOORE – Moore, Ethelbert A.
Tenth generation, written for his family. By Ethelbert A. Moore. (New Britain? Conn.) Priv. Print., 1950. (FW)

MOORE – Moore, Hon. Horace L.
Andrew Moore of Poquonock and Windsor, Conn., and his descendants. By Hon. Horace L. Moore... Lawrence, Kan., Journal Publishing Company, 1903. (LoC)

MOREHOUSE –
Ancestry and descendants of Gershom Morehouse, Jr. of Redding, Connecticut, a Captain in the American revolution. (New Haven, Conn., Press of Tuttle, Morehouse & Taylor, 1894). (LoC)

MOREHOUSE – Morehouse, Cornnelius Starr
Ancestry and descendants of Gershom Morehouse, Jr., of Redding, Connecticut. S.1.: s.n., 1938? (DAR)

MOREY – Skeels, Lydia Lowndes Maury

One American family: some Maury memories, legends, and records.
By Lydia Lowndes Maury Skeels. (Storrs, Conn.): L. Skeels, c1981.
(LoC)

MORGAN -- Morgan, N. H.
Our family genealogy. Hartford: Case, Tiffany, and Co., 1851. (DAR)

MORGAN – Morgan, Nathaniel H.
Morgan genealogy. Hartford, Conn.: Press of Case, Lockwoood &
Brainard, 1869. (DAR)

MORGAN – Morgan, Nathaniel H.
Morgan genealogy. A history of James Morgan, of New London,
Conn. and his descendants; from 1607 to 1869... With an appendix,
containing the history of his brother, Miles Morgan of Springfield,
Mass.: and some of his descendants... By Nathaniel H. Morgan.
Hartford, Press of Case, Lockwood & Brainard, 1869. (LoC)

MORGAN – Starr, Frank Farnsworth
The Miles Morgan family of Springfield, Massachusetts, in the line of
Joseph Morgan of Hartford, Connecticut, 1780-1847. By Frank
Farnsworth Starr. Hartford, Conn., 1904. (LoC)

MORRELL – Morrell, Francis V.
The ancestry of Daniel Morrell of Hartford. S.1.: John Watson Morrell,
1916. (DAR)

MORRILL – Morrell, Francis V.
The ancestry of Daniel Morrell of Hartford, with his descendants and
some contemporary families. Compiled by Francis B. Morrell...
(Hartford): J. W. Morrell, 1916. (LoC)

MORRIS –
Morris Family of E. Haven (1853), 103 pgs.[1]

MORRIS –
Memoranda of the descendants of Amos Morris of East Haven, Conn.
New York, A. S. Barnes & Company, 1853. (LoC)

MORRIS –
Genealogy of the Morris family; descendants of Thomas Morris of
Connecticut. Comp. by Mrs. Lucy Ann (Morris) Carhart; ed. by
Charles Alexander Nelson, A. M. New York, The A. S. Barnes
Company, 1911. (LoC)

MORRIS –
The east side of New Haven harbor; Morris Cove (Solitary cover), the Annex (the Indian reservation), South end & Waterside, 1644 to 1868, by Marjorie F. Hayward; text and maps based on researches by Marjorie F. Hayward and Donald V. Chidsey, frontpiece & maps drawn by Don Forrer. New Haven, New Haven Colony Historical Society, 1938. (LoC)

MORRIS – Hart, E. L.
Memoranda of the descendants of Amos Morris of East Haven, Conn. New York: A. S. Barnes & Co., 1853. (DAR)

MORRIS – Morris, Jonathan Flynt
A genealogical and historical register of the descendants of Edward Morris of Roxbury, Mass., and Woodstock, Conn. Hartford, Conn.: Morris, 1887. (DAR)

MORRIS – Morris, Jonathan Flynt
A genealogical and historical register of the descendants of Edward Morris of Roxbury, Mass., and Woodstock, Conn. Comp. by Jonathan Flynt Morris... Hartford, Conn., Pub. by the compiler (Case, Lockwood & Braindard Co., Printers) 1887. (LoC)

MORRIS – Tracy, Elsie H.
Morris: an account of some descendants of Thomas Morris and his wife Elizabeth, who settled in New Haven, Conn. in 1639... including brief accounts of their relationship to Bronson, Howlett, Judson and Tracy families. By Elsie H. Tracy. La Jolla, Calif., 1973. (NY)

MORSE –
The ancestors and descendants of George Milton Morse of Putnam, Connecticut, compiled and edited by his granddaughter, Lelia Morse Wilson. (Putnam, Conn., Patriot Press, Inc., 1930?). (LoC)

MORSE – Morse, Rev. Abner
One branch of family of John Morse (Moss) of New Haven and Wallingford, Ct.., 1639-1708. From Memorial of Morses, by Rev. Abner Morse. (New York, J. C. Wait, 1930). (LoC)

MORSE – Wilson, Lelia Morse
The ancestors and descendants of George Milton Morse of Putnam, Connecticut. Putnam, Conn.: Patriot Press, 1930? (DAR)

MORTON –

William Morton of Windsor, Conn., and some of his descendants who
are also descendants of Thomas Burnham. By Ulysses Grant Morton
and Addie Le Duc Morton. Fenton, Mich., 1950. (LoC)

MOSES – Moses, Zebina
Historical sketches of John Moses, of Plymouth, a settler of 1632 to
1640; John Moses, of Windsor and Simbury, a settler prior to 1647; and
John Moses, of Portsmouth, a settler prior to 1647; and John Moses, of
Portsmouth, a settler prior to 1640. Also a genealogical record of some
of their descendants. By Zebina Moses. Hartford, Conn., Press of the
Case, Lockwood & Brainard Company, 1890-1902. (LoC)

MOULTHROP –
The Moulthrop family of Connecticut, direct line of Colonel Samuel
Moulthrop and family, of Rochester, New York. (Rochester? 1925?).
(LoC)

MOULTHROP – Rhoades, Nelson O.
Genealogy of the Moulthrop family, Connecticut. 1918. (NGS)

MOULTHROP – Rhoades, Nelson O.
Genealogy of the Moulthrop family of Connecticut. By Nelson O.
Rhoades. (Los Angeles? Calif.) 1918. (NY)

MOULTON –
Additions and corrections to Moulton annals, by H. W. Moulton, 1906.
Additions and corrections by Kenneth L. Austin. Old Greenwich,
Conn., 1944. (NY)

MUDGE – Mudge, Florence A.
John Mudge and Hannah Hutchinson, first settlers of Plymouth, Ct.
Compiled by Florence A. Mudge. (Danvers, Mass., 1930). (LoC)

MUHLENBERG –
Muhlenberg album. (New Haven, Tuttle, Morehouse & Taylor Press,
1910). (LoC)

MUHLENBERG – Schwab, J. C.
Chart of the descendants of Henry Melchoir Muhlenberg. (By J. C.
Schwab). New Haven, 1911. (OH)

MUMFORD – Perkins, Mary E.

Chronicles of a Connecticut Farm, 1769-1905. Comp. ... for Mr. and
Mrs. Alfred Mitchell... By Mary E. Perkins. Boston, priv. print.,
1905. (LI)

MUNGER –
The Munger book; something of the Mungers, 1639-1914, including
some who mistakenly write the name Monger, and Mungor, compiled
by J. B. Munger, 1894-1914, with the valued assistance of the late Jno.
E. Munger... and Francis E. Munger... (New Haven) The Tuttle,
Morehouse & Taylor Company, 1915. (LoC)

MUNGER – Munger, Jeremiah B.
Copy of an old family tree found in attic of the old Josiah Munger
house, Guilford, Conn., with some additions and corrections. By
Jeremiah B. Munger... 1848. (W. Somerville, Mass., 1899). (FW)

MUNSELL – Munsell, Claude Garfield
A genealogy of the Munsell family, with lineages of related families:
Bissell, Bogardus, Bronck, Cooke, Coonley, Drake, Houghtaling,
Loomis, Paine, Stiles, and Taylor; and a line of descent from Rolfe,
duke of Normandy, A. D. 860. By Claude Garfield Munsell. South
Norwalk, Conn., J. Munsell's Sons, 1950. (LoC)

MUNSON –
The Munson record... Munson Assoc. (New Haven, Conn., 1895).
(PH)

MUNSON –
Munson Association... Proceedings of the 2d Munson family reunion,
held in the city of New Haven. New Haven, Tuttle, 1896. (FW)

MUNSON – Munson Association
1637-1896; proceedings of the 1st Munson family reunion, held in the
City of New Haven. New Haven, Ct., 1887. (NGS)

MUNSON – Munson, Myron A. (Myron Andrews)
1637-1887, the Munson record: a genealogical and biographical
account of Captain Thomas Munson, a pioneer of Hartford and New
Haven, and his descendants. By Myron A. Munson. New Haven,
Conn.: Printed for the Munson Association, 1895, c1896. (1984
printing). (LoC)

MUNSON – Munson, Myron A.

The Munson Record, 1637-1887. New Haven, Conn.: The Munson
Assoc., c1896. (DAR)

MURDOCK –
Murdock genealogy, Robert Murdock, of Roxbury, Massachusetts, and
some of his descendants, with notes on the descendants of John Murdo
of Plymouth, Massachusetts, George Murdock of Plainfield,
Connecticut, Peter Murdock of Saybrook, Connecticut, William
Murdock of Philadelphia, Pennsylvania, and others. Compiled by
Joseph B. Murdock... Boston, C. E. Goodspeed & Co., 1925. (LoC)

MURPHY – Downes, Michael Walter
The Murphy family. Hartford, Conn.: Case, Lockwood & Brainard,
1909. (DAR)

MURPHY – Downes, Michael Walter
The Murphy family, genealogical, historical and biographical, with
official statistics of the part played by members of this numerous
family in the making and maintenance of this great American republic.
By Michael Walter Downes. Hartford, Conn., The Case, Lockwood &
Brainard Company, 1909. (LoC)

MURRAY – Murray, William Breed
The descendants of Jonathan Murray of East Guilford, Connecticut.
Peoria, Ill.: Illinois Valley Publishing co., 1950? (DAR)

MURRAY – Murray, William Breed
The descendants of Jonathan Murray of East Guilford, Connecticut. By
William Breed Murray. Peoria, Ill., Lithographed by Illinois Valley
Pub. Co. (195-). (LoC)

MURRAY – Ward, George K.
(Descendants of Jonathan Murray of Scotland and East Guilford,
Conn.). By George K. Ward. (Broxville, N. Y., 193-). (NY)

MYGATE – Mygate, Frederick T.
A historical notice of Joseph Mygate, one of the early colonists of
Cambridge, Mass., and afterward one of the first settlers of Hartford,
Conn., with a record of his descendants. By Frederick T. Mygate...
Brooklyn. Printed by the Harmonial Association, 1853. (LoC)

NASH – Nash, Elizabeth Todd
Fifty Puritan ancestors, 1628-1660; genealogical notes, 1560-1900. By their lineal descendants, Elizabeth Todd Nash. New Haven, The Tuttle, Morehouse & Taylor Company, 1902. (LoC)

NASH – Nash, Sylvester
The Nash family. Hartford: Press of Case, Tiffany and Company, 1853. (DAR)

NASH – Nash, Sylvester
The Nash family, or, Records of the descendants of Thomas Nash of New Haven, Connecticut, 1640. Collected and compiled by Sylvester Nash. (Morristown, N. J.: Compton Press, 1979). (LoC)

NETTLETON – Hollister, Julia Nettleton
Some descendants of Daniel Nettleton, 1766-1829, & his wife Eunice Baldwin, 1767-1822, of Judea Parish, now Washington, Connecticut. S.1.:s.n., 1962. (DAR)

NEUKIRK – Neikirk, Floyd Edwin
Ohio descendants of seventeenth century ancestors in Plymouth and Providence Plantations, Massachusetts Bay and Connecticut Colonies, New York, Pennsylvania, Virginia, Maryland, New Jersey, 1620-1960. By Lloyd (sic) Edwin Neikirk. (Clyde? Ohio, 1960?). (LoC)

NEWBERRY – Lee, Helen Bourne Joy
The Newberry genealogy. Chester, Ct., 1975. (NGS)

NEWBERRY – Starr, Frank Farnsworth
The Newberry family of Windsor, Connecticut. Cambridge: John Wilson and Son, 1898. (DAR)

NEWBURY –
The Newberry family of Windsor, Connecticut, in the line of Clarinda (Newberry) Goodwin, of Hartford, Connecticut, 1634-1866. Comp. by Frank Farnsworth Starr for James J. Goodwin. Hartford, Conn. (Cambridge, University Press, J. Wilson and Son) 1898. (LoC)

NEWCOMB –
Andrew Newcomb, 1618-1686, and his descendants; a revised edition of "Genealogical Memoir" of the Newcomb family, published 1874 by John Bearse Newcomb... Compiled and revised by Bethuel Merritt

Newcomb... New Haven, Conn. Priv. print. for the author by the
Tuttle, Morehouse & Taylor Co., 1923. (LoC)

NEWCOMB – Newcomb, Bethuel Merritt
Andrew Newcomb, 1618-1686, and his descendants. New Haven, Ct.
1923. (NGS)

NEWCOMB – Newcomb, Bethuel Merritt
Andrew Newcomb, 1618-1686, and his descendants. New Haven,
Conn.: Tuttle, Morehouse & Taylor Co., 1923. (DAR)

NEWELL –
Thomas Newell, who settled in Farmington, Conn., A. D. 1632. And
his descendants. A genealogical table, comp. by Mrs. Mary A.
(Newell) Hall. Southington, Conn., Cochrane Bros. Book and Job
Printers, 1878. (LoC)

NEWELL – Hall, Mary A. Newell
Thomas Newell. Southington, Conn.: Cochrane Bros., 1878. (DAR)

NEWSOM – Newsom, E. Earl
John Edward Newsom and his ancestors. By E. Earl Newsom.
(Salisbury, Conn? 1967-71). (NY)

NEWTON – Leonard, Ermina Newton
Newton genealogy, genealogical, biographical, historical; being a
record of the descendants of Richard Newton of Subury and
Marlborough, Massachusetts, 1638, with genealogies of families
descended from the immigrants, Rev. Roger Newton of Milford,
Connecticut, Thomas Newton of Fairfield, Connecticut, Matthew
Newton of Stonington, Connecticut, Newtons of Virginia, Newtons
near Boston. Compiled by Ermina Newton Leonard. DePere, Wis.,
B. A. Leonard, 1915. (LoC)

NEWTON – Lull, Newton
Genealogical notes concerning descendants of Thomas Newton of
Fairfield, Conn. Chicago: Press of Geo. E. Moshall (sic) & Co., 1896.
(DAR)

NEWTON – Lull, Newton
Genealogical notes concerning descendants of Thomas Newton, of
Fairfield, Conn. By Newton Lull. (Chicago, G. E. Marshall, Printers,
1896). (LoC)

NEWTON – Newton, Carolina G.
Abner Newton, 1764-1852. His ancestors and descendants. By
Carolina G. Newton. (Milford, Conn? 1914). (LI)

NEWTON – Newton, Caroline Gaylord
Rev. Roger Newton, deceased 1683, and one line of his descendants.
By Caroline Gaylord Newton, 1912. (Durham? Conn., 1914?). (LoC)

NEWTON – Newton, Clair Alonzo
The Colchester, Conn., Newton family. Descendants of Thomas
Newton of Fairfield, Conn., 1639. Compiled by Clair Alonzo
Newton... Naperville, Ill., 1911-49. (LoC)

NEWTON – Newton, Robert S. (Robert Sheldon)
The Newton family: the ancestry and some descendants of David
Newton of Milford, Connecticut and Hartford, Vermont (Rev. Roger
Newton, ca. 1620-1683, of Farmington and Milford, Connecticut).
Compiled by Robert S. Newton. Washington, D. C. R. S. Newton,
1984. (LoC)

NEWTON – Newton, Robert Sheldon
The Newton family; the ancestry and some descendants of David
Newton of Milford, Connecticut and Hartford, Vermont (Rev. Roger
Newton, ca. 1620-1683, of Farmington and Milford, Connecticut).
Washington, D. C. 1984. (NGS)

NICHOLS –
The descendants of Ezra Nichols, 1763-1827. By Helen M. Bruce and
Dorothy E. Bruce. Newton, Conn., Mimeographed by B&W Services,
1964. (LoC)

NICHOLS – Hall, Ormel H.
Some descendants of Sigurd the Northman. By Ormel H. Hall.
Bridgeport, Conn.: O. H. Hall, 1923. (LI)

NICHOLS – Nicholls, Walter
Sergeant Francis Nicholls of Stratford, Connecticut, 1639, and the
descendants of his son, Caleb Nicholls. By Walter Nicholls... New
York, The Grafton Press, 1909. (LoC)

NODINE – Waters, George L.
Maudin (Nodine), Tourneur, De Vaux and allied families, New York,
Connecticut, Indiana and Oregon. By George L. Waters. Lincoln,
Nebr., author, 1967. (FW)

NORTH –
Fiftieth anniversary of the marriage of James and Mary North,
Middletown, Conn. ... 1860. Hartford, 1860. (LI)

NORTH – North, Dexter
John North of Farmington, Connecticut and his descendants.
Washington, D. C.: North, 1921. (DAR)

NORTH – North, Dexter
John North of Farmington, Connecticut, and his descendants; with a
short account of other early North families. By Dexter North.
Washington, D. C., 1921. (LoC)

NORTH – North, F. A.
...An account of the celebration of the diamond wedding of Dea.
Frederick and Harriet North, including poems, programmme of
exercises, letters of congratulations from relatives and friends,
addresses, etc., with a sketch of their golden wedding in 1880; also a
short genealogical record of that branch of the family. By F. A. North.
Hartford, Conn., Press of the Case, Lockwood & Brainard Company,
1890. (LoC)

NORTH – North, Mack O.
John North of Lincolnshire, England, and his descendants. By Mack
O. North. (Hartford, Conn.?) 1966. (FW)

NORTH – Shimkin, Mary North
Descendants of John North of Farmington, Connecticut. By Mary
North Shimkin. La Jolla: University of California, San Diego, 1987.
(LoC)

NORTON –
Norton Family of Guilford (1856), 26 pgs.[1]

NORTON – Gibboney, Harold G.
The Nortons from the Norman Conquest through the settlement of
Guilford, Conn., in 1639 to the present, 1066-1965. By Harold G.
Gibboney. 2d Ed. Athens, Ohio (1966). (FW)

NORTON – Norton, Albert B.
Descendants and ancestors of Charles Norton of Guilford, Connecticut.
Washington, D. C., 1856. (NGS)

NORTON – Norton, Albert B.

Descendants and ancestors of Charles Norton of Guilford, Connecticut. Washington, D. C.: W. H. Moore, Printer, 1856. (DAR)

NORTON – Norton, Albert B.
Descendants and ancestors of Charles Norton of Guilford, Connecticut. By Albert B. Norton. Washington, W. H. Moore, Printers, 1856. (LoC)

NORTON – Norton, Vera Y.
Some descendants of James Norton, Sr. of Farmington, Conn. By Vera Y. Norton. Lake Worth, Fla., 1972. (FW)

NORTON – Norton, Walter Whittlesey
Some descendants of John Norton of Branford,, 1622-1709. Lakeville, Ct., 1909. (NGS)

NORTON – Norton, Walter Whittlesey
Some descendants of John Norton of Branford, 1622-1709. Lakeville, Conn.: Journal Press, 1909. (DAR)

NORTON – Norton, Walter Whittlesey
Some descendants of John Norton of Branford, 1622-1709, with notes and dates of other emigrant Nortons, etc. (By) Walter Whittlesey Norton. Lakesville, Conn., The Journal Press, 1909. (LoC)

NOWELL –
The Nowell and Noell families; containing the ancestry of Peter Nowell of York, Maine, Thomas Nowell of Windsor, Conn., etc., as well as the line of the Earls of Gainsborough, etc. N.p.:n.d. (NY)

O

O'DALY – O'Daly, Edmund Emmet
History of the O'Dalys; the story of the ancient Irish sept; the race of Dalach of Corca Adaimh; compiled by Edmund Emmet O'Daly... New Haven, Connn., Printed by the Tuttle, Morehouse and Taylor Company, 1937. (LoC)

OGDEN –
The Ogdens of South Jersey. The descendants of John Ogden of Fairfield, Conn., and New Fairfield, N. J. Born, 1673, died 1745. (Philadelphia, 1894). (LoC)

OGDEN – Van Alstyne, Lawrence
Chart of English Ogden ancestry. New Haven, Conn.: Tuttle,
Morehouse & Taylor, 1907? (DAR)

OGDENS – Wheeler, William Ogden
The Ogdens of South Jersey; the descendants of John Ogden of
Fairfield, Conn., and New Fairfield, N. J. Philadelphia, Pa., 1894.
(NGS)

OKIE – Stryker-Rodda, Harriet
Okie ancestry of Reginald Okie of Greenwich, Conn. By Harriet
Stryker-Rodda. Brooklyn, N. Y., 1965. (PH)

OLCOTT –
The Olcott family of Hartford, Connecticut, in the line of Eunice
(Olcott) Goodwin, 1639-1807. Compiled by Frank Farnsworth Starr
for James J. Goodwin. Hartford, Conn. (Cambridge, University Press,
J. Wilson and Son) 1899. (LoC)

OLCOTT – Goodwin, Nathaniel
Descendants of Thomas Olcott. Hartford: Press of Case, Tiggany (sic)
and Burnham, 1845. (DAR)

OLCOTT – Goodwin, Nathaniel
Descendants of Thomas Olcott, one of the first settlers of Hartford,
Connecticut. By Nathaniel Goodwin... Hartford, Press of Case,
Tiffany & Burnham, 1845. (LoC)

OLCOTT – Olcott, Henry S.
The descendants of Thomas Olcott, one of the first settlers of Hartford,
Ct. by Nathaniel Goodwin... Revised edition, with an explanatory
preface and important additions. By Henry S. Olcott... Albany, N. Y.,
J. Munsell, 1874. (LoC)

OLDS – Olds, Lizzie M. (W.)
Dedication. to the memory of Alfred Allen Olds, 1852-1925. By
Lizzie M. (W.) Olds. Hartford, Conn., National Biographical Service.
(PH)

ORMSBY – Barlow, Claude W.
Ormsby families of Connecticut, prior to 1800. Easton, Penn.:
Ormsby, 1965. (DAR)

ORMSBY – Barlow, Claude W.

Ormsby families of Connecticut prior to 1800. Worcester, Ma., 1965. (NGS)

ORMSBY – Barlow, Claude W.
Ormsby families of Connecticut prior to 1800. Compiled by Claude W. Barlow for Francis Gratacap Ormsby. (Worcester? Mass.) 1965. (LoC)

ORTON – Orton, Edward
An account of the descendants of Thomas Orton, of Windsor, Connecticut, 1641 (principally in the male line). By Edward Orton... Columbus, O., Press of Nitschke Brothers, 1896. (LoC)

OTIS –
A discourse on the life and character of Dea. Joseph Otis, delivered in the Second Congregational Church, Norwich, Conn.., March 19, 1854. With an appendix by the pastor, Alvan Bond... Norwich, A. Stark, Printer, 1855. (LoC)

OVERMAN –
Descendants of Jacob Overman, traced from Westerfield, Hartford County, Conn., in the late 1600s to Oswego, Labette County, Kansas in 1972. N.p. (1972). (KH)

OWEN –
Descendants of John Owen (1622-99) of Windsor, Conn. News letter. (Philadelphia, etc.) 1938-. (MH)

OWEN –
Descendants of John Owen (1622-99) of Windsor, Conn. (Minutes of the reunion... Windsor, Conn? 1937-41). (NY)

OWEN – Owen, Ralph Dornfield
Descendants of John Owen of Windsor, Connecticut, 1622-1699. Philadelphia: Owen, 1941. (DAR)

OWEN – Owen, Ralph Dornfeld
Descendants of John Owen of Windsor, Connecticut (1622-1699); a genealogy. Edited by Ralph Dornfeld Owen. Philadelphia, 1941. (LoC)

P

PAGE – Page, Edith Moyer
George Page of Branford, Connecticut, and some of his descendants.
Shaker Heights, Ohio: Page, c1977. (DAR)

PAGE – Page, Edith Moyer
George Page of Branford, Connecticut and some of his descendants,
with allied lines. Compiled by Edith Moyer Page. (Shaker Heights,
Ohio): Page, 1977. (LoC)

PAINE –
Ancestors and descendants of James Payne of Pomfret, Conn., and
Hauppauge, L. I. (by) Sarah C. P. Smith (and) Margretta C. Payne...
(Northport, N. Y., Printed by Northport Observer, 1932). (LoC)

PAINE – Paine, Lyman May
My ancestors; a memorial of John Paine and Mary Ann May of East
Woodstock, Conn. Lovingly compiled by their son Lyman May Paine,
of Chicago, Ill. (Chicago, Ill.) Printed for private circulation, 1914.
(LoC)

PALGRAVE –
Palgrave family memorials. Edited by Charles John Palmer and
Stephen Tucker (Rouge Croix). Norwich, Printed by Miller and
Leavins (for private distribution only), 1878. (LoC)

PALMER –
Palmer Family of Connecticut (1881), 295 pgs.[1]
Palmer Family of Connecticut, Supp. (1882), 119 pgs.[1]
Palmer Reunion Address (1884), 15 pgs.[1]

PALMER –
Palmer Family of Conn. (1901), 240 pgs.[1]
Palmer Family of Conn. (1905), 450 pgs.[1]

PALMER –
Palmer reunion; a perfect day and a large attendance... New London,
Conn., 1881. (PH)

PALMER – Buys, Doris Palmer
Walter Palmer of Charlestown and Rehoboth, Massachusetts and
Stonington, Connecticut: a 400 year (1585-1985) family history.
Compiled, edited, typed and partly researched by Doris Palmer Buys.

148

Orem, Utah: Published for the compiler by Historical Publications, c1986. (LoC)

PALMER – Johnston, Harry F.
Walter Palmer of Stonington, Conn. and descendants. By Harry F. Johnston. N.p., 1948. (FW)

PALMER – Palmer, Noyes F.
Volume No. 1 of Palmer records. Proceedings, or memorial volume of the first Palmer family reunion held at Stonington, Conn., August 10 & 11, 1881, the ancestral home of Walter Palmer, the pilgrim of 1629. Being also a part of the genealogical, biographical, and historical records of the family, as contained in the several addresses, etc. delivered on the occasion of the reunion. (Artotype illustrations). Edited by Noyes F. Palmer. (Brooklyn): Brooklyn Union-Argus, 1881. (LoC)

PALMER – Palmer, Noyes F.
Supplement to Volume 1 of Palmer records. Addresses, poems, proceedings of the second Palmer family reunion, held at Stonington, Conn., August 10, 11 & 12, 1882... Under the auspices of the Palmer reunion associatioon. Edited by Noyes F. Palmer. Jamaica, L. I., N. Y. (1882). (LoC)

PALMER – Palmer, Walter
Genealogy of that branch of the Palmers emanating from the marriage of Gershon Palmer. Plainfield, Conn.: Printed by Andrew J. Ladd, 1887. (DAR)

PALMER – Rhoades, Helen Johnson
A history of the Walter Palmer family of Stonington, Connecticut, 1968. (DAR)

PARADISE – Paradise, Clara E. C.
Paradise family in New York and Connecticut. By Clara E. C. Paradise. Potomac, Md.: J. C. Presgraves, 1967. (FW)

PARADISE – Paradise, Clara Elizabeth Corey
A Paradise family in New York and Connecticut. Potomac, Md., 1967. (NGS)

PARDEE –

Pardee's old Morris house, public museum and civic center at Morris
Cove, New Haven, Conn. Gift of William Scranton Pardee; plans and
notes by Walter Stone Pardee... (Chicago, Ill., 1923). (LoC)

PARDEE – Jacobus, Donald Lines
The Pardee genealogy. New Haven: New Haven Colony Historical
Society, 1927. (DAR)

PARDEE – Jacobus, Donald Lines, M. A.
...The Pardee genealogy. Edited by Donald Lines Jacobus, M. A.
New Haven, Printed for the Society, 1927. (LoC)

PARISH – Parish, Roswell
New England Parish families; descendants of John Parish of Groton,
Mass., and Preston, Conn. By Roswell Parish. Rutland, Vt., The Tuttle
Publishing Company, Inc. (1938). (LoC)

PARK –
Park Family, Stonington, Ct. (1876), 14 pgs.[1]

PARK – Park, Edwin H.
The Park record; containing an account of the ancestry and descendants
of Thomas Kinnie Park and Robert Park, of Groton, Conn.; and
Grafton, Vt. ... Comp. by Edwin H. Park... (Denver, Colo, Bartow &
Ray Print, 1902). (LoC)

PARK – Park, Edwin Horatio
The Park record; an account of the descendants of Thomas Kinnie Park
and Robert Park, of Groton, Conn. and Grafton, Vt. Denver, Co., 1902.
(NGS)

PARK – Parks, Frank Sylvester
Genealogy of the Parke family of Connecticut; including Robert Parke,
of New London, Edward Parks, of Guilford, and others. Also a list of
Parke, Park, Parks, etc. who fought in the Revolutionary War. By
Frank Sylvester Parks. Washington, 1906. (LoC)

PARKE –
Supplement to Genealogy of the Parke families of Conn. Washington,
D. C., F. S. Parks, 1934. (FW)

PARKE – Parks, Frank Sylvester

Genealogy of the Parke families of Connecticut, including Robert Parke, of New London, Edward Parks, of Guilford, and others. Washington, D. C. 1906. (NGS)

PARKE – Parks, Frank Sylvester
Genealogy of the Parke family of Connecticut. Washington, D. C.: Parks, 1906. (DAR)

PARKER –
...History and genealogy of the family of Deacon Lovel Parker, who emigrated from Barkhamsted, Conn., to Kinsman, Ohio, in the year 1816. Compiled by Rufus H. and L. N. Parker. (Syracuse, N. Y.: The Mason Press) 1898. (LoC)

PARKER – Jochum, Helen Parker
Recollections. Helen Parker Jochum; illustrations by Janet Konther Monteith. [Bloomfield, Conn.]: H. P. Jochum, c1988. (LoC)

PARKER – Moulthrop, Mary A.
Descendants of Samuel Parker, Revolutionary soldier of Coventry, Conn. and Byron, N. Y. Rochester, N. Y.: Moulthrop, 1927. (DAR)

PARKER – Moulthrop, Mary A.
Descendants of Samuel Parker, revolutionary soldier of Coventry, Conn., and Byron, N. Y. Compiled by Mary A. Moulthrop. Rochester, N. Y., 1927. (LoC)

PARKER – Parker, Rev. Edwin Pond
Family records. Parker – Pond – Peck. By Rev. Edwin Pond Parker... 1636-1892. Hartford, Conn., Press of the Case. Lockwood & Brainard Co., 1892. (LoC)

PARKER – Walker, Elizabeth Parcher
Elias Parcher and some of his descendants. Elizabeth Parcher Walker. [Manchester, Ct.]: E. P. Walker, [1987]. (LoC)

PARMLEY – Doty, Harrison
Lines of descent: from Edward Doty, Mayflower passenger, 1620, John Parmelee, New Haven Colony, 1639, William Leete, Guilford Colony, 1639: to and from Harrison Parmelee Doty, born 1910, Leete Parmelee Doty, born 1917, Carol Parmelee Doty Wilson, born 1918, plus notes on kissing kin and divers others: an adventure in genealogy begun in 1925 and concluded in 1985. 1st. Ed. Brattleboro, Vt.: H. Doty, c1985. (LoC)

PARSONS –
Radial chart of descendants of Cornet Parsons of Springfield, Mass.,
1635, through Thomas Parsons of New London, Conn., born 1791. By
David Parsons Holton and Frances K. _?_ . Holton. New York, 1877.
(LoC)

PARSONS – Parsons, Gerald James
The Parsons family: descendants of Cornet Joseph Parsons (c1618-
1683), Springfield, Mass., 1636, North Hampton, Mass., 1654, through
his grandson Jonathan Parsons (1693-1782) of Northampton, Mass.,
Suffield, Conn. Baltimore, Md., 1984. (NGS)

PARSONS – Parsons, John A.
Eli Parsons of Enfield, Connecticut and Columbia Township, Bradford
County, Pennsylvania. Troy, Pa.: Parsons, 1924. (DAR)

PARSONS – Parsons, John A.
Eli Parsons of Enfield, Connecticut and Columbia Township, Bradford
County, Pennsylvania, and his brother Thomas Parsons of Enfield,
Connecticut and town of Franklin, Delaware County, New York, by
John A. Parsons... (New York) Priv. print., 1924. (LoC)

PARTCH – Partch, George E.
Quinten Patch of Connecticut and descendants incluuding the Partches.
By George E. Partch. N.p., 1946. (LA)

PATCHIN – Leggett, Grace Patchen
The history and genealogy of the Patchin-Patchen family. Waterbury,
Conn.: Patchin-en Family Association, 1952. (DAR)

PATRICK – Haslam, Patricia Liddle
Richard Patrick or Partrick of Norwalk, Conn. Stowe, Vt., c1978.
(NGS)

PATRICK – Haslam, Patricia Liddle
Richard Patrick or Partrick of Norwalk, Conn. and some of his
descendants. By Patricia Liddle Haslam. (Stowe, Vt.): Haslam, c1978.
(LoC)

PATTERSON –
Patterson Family of Conn. (1892), 55 pgs.[1]

PATTERSON –

Andrew Patterson of Stratford, Conn., and the first four generations of his descendants. N.p., 1892. (FW)

PATTERSON – Getzendaner, Georgia Belle
George Washington Patterson family history. West Hartford, Conn.: Chadwato Service, 1956. (DAR)

PAYNE –
Ancestors and descendants of James Payne of Pomfret, Conn., and Hauppauge, L. I. (by) Sarah C. P. Smith (and) Margretta C. Payne... (Northport, N. Y., Printed by Northport Observer, 1932). (LoC)

PAYNE – Smith, Sarah C. P.
Ancestors and descendants of James Payne of Pomfret, Conn., and Hauppauge, N. J. Northport, N. J.: Printed by Northport Observer, 1932. (DAR)

PEABODY – Miller, Margaret Porter
Some descendants of Robert Porter, Farmington, Connecticut, 1640: with female lines... Compiled by Margaret Porter Miller. Baltimore: Gateway Press; Easton, Md.: M. Miller, 1986. (LoC)

PEALE –
The Selected papers of Charles Willson Peale and his family. Lillian B. Miller, editor; Sidney Hart, assistant editor; Toby A. Appel, research historian. New Haven, [Conn.]: Published for the National Portrait Galler, Smithsonian Institution, by Yale University Press, c1983, c1988. (LoC)

PEARSON – Pierson, Frederick Lockwood
The descendants of Stephen Pierson of Suffolk County, England, and New Haven and Derby, Conn., 1645-1739. By Frederick Lockwood Pierson... Amenia, N. Y., Walsh & Griffen, 1895. (LoC)

PEASE –
A genealogical and historical record of the descendants of John Pease, sen., last of Enfield, Conn. Compiled by Rev. David Pease and Austin S. Pease... Springfield, Mass., S. Bowles & Company, Printers, 1869. (LoC)

PEASE – Abbe, Jessie B.
Records of Revolutionary War soldiers in the Pease family of Enfield, Connecticut. 1952. (DAR)

PEASE – Duty, Allene Beaumont
The ancestors and descendants of the Honorable Calvin Pease and
Laura Grant Risley Pease, his wife, of Suffield, Ct., Rutland, Vt., and
Warren, Ohio. Cleveland, Oh., 1979. (NGS)

PEASE – Pease, David
A genealogical and historical record of the descendants of John Pease,
Sen., last of Enfield, Conn. Springfield, Mass.: Samuel Bowles & Co.,
Printers, 1869. (DAR)

PEASE – Pease, David
A genealogical and historical record of the descendants of John Pease,
Sen., last of Enfield, Conn. Compiled by David Pease and Austin S.
Peace (sic), as associate editor. Monticello, Ky.: Manor Pub. Co.
(between 1980 and 1984). (LoC)

PECK –
Peck Family of New Haven (1877), 253 pgs.[1]

PECK – Lainson, D. A. S.
William Peck, immigrant ancestor to New Haven, Conn. before 1638
and some of his descendants. By D. A. S. Lainson. Huntsville, Ark.:
Century Enterprises, 1973. (FW)

PECK – Peck, Darius
A genealogical account of the descendants in the male line of William
Peck, one of the founders in 1638 the colony of New Haven, Conn.
Hudson: Bryan & Goeltz, 1877. (DAR)

PECK – Peck, Darius
A genealogical account of the descendants in the male line of William
Peck, one of the founders in 1638 of the Colony of New Haven, Conn.
By Darius Peck. Hudson, Bryan & Goeltz, Printers, 1877. (LoC)

PECK – Peck, Hon. Darius
Apppendix by John Hudson Peck, (2628), to genealogy of the
descendants of William Peck of New Haven, Conn. By Hon. Darius
Peck, (1363). (Troy? N. Y., 1896?). (LoC)

PECK – Royce, Helen E.
Some ancestors of Mehitabel Peck, wife of Edmund Hobart; of Canaan,
Conn., and Spencer, New York. By Helen E. Royce. (Hartford, Conn.,
1925). (NY)

PEET – Peet, Terry Charles
John Peet, 1597-1684, of Stratford, Connecticut & his descendants.
Baltimore, Md., 1986. (NGS)

PEET – Peet, Terry Charles
John Peet, 1597-1684, of Stratford, Connecticut & his descendants. By
Terry Charles Peet. Baltimore: Gateway Press; Annandale, Va,: T. C.
Peet, 1986. (LoC)

PERCY – Percy, Truman
Family record of the Connecticut branch of the Percy family.
Compiled by Truman Percy... Norfolk, Va., H. C. Percy, 1873
(Boston, Mass., Reprinted by Goodspeed's Book Shop, Inc., 1941).
(LoC)

PERKINS –
Perkins Family of Connecticut (1860), 8 pgs.[1]
Perkins Ancestry (1898), 74 pgs.[1]

PERKINS – Jacobus, Donald L.
The Perkins family of New Haven, Conn. By Donald L. Jacobus.
(New Haven, Conn., 189-). (CH)

PERKINS – Perkins, Caroline Erickson
The descendants of Edward Perkins of New Haven, Conn. Rochester,
N. Y.: Perkins, 1914. (DAR)

PERKINS – Perkins, Caroline Erickson
The descendants of Edward Perkins of New Haven, Conn. (by)
Caroline Erickson Perkins. Rchester, N. Y., 1914. (LoC)

PERKINS – Perkins, (Frederick B.)
Perkins family of Connecticut. By (Frederick B.) Perkins. (Hartford,
Conn? 1860?). (LA)

PERKINS – Perkins, Paul M. (Paul Milburn)
Genealogy and history of one branch of the Perkins family in America,
originating with Edward Perkins, immigrant to America and to New
Haven, Connecticut, before 1646. By Paul M. Perkins. Minerva, Ohio:
P. M. Perkins, 1980. (LoC)

PERRIN – Perrin, Stanley Ernest
The John Perrin family of Rehobeth, Massachusetts. Compiled by
Stanley Ernest Perrin. With several appendices including the Thomas

Perrin family of Hebron, Connecticut. Compiled by Carl Leslie Perrin. Baltimore: Gateway Press (1974). (LoC)

PERRY – Perry, Mary Curtis
A Perry family history. Researched by Mary Curtis Perry; compiled and edited by Chapman Perry. South Britain, Conn.: M. C. Perry, 1983. (LoC)

PETTIBONE –
Pettibone register; descendants of John Pettibone, c1633-1713, an original proprietor of Simsbury, Connecticut. Compiled by Kathryn S. and James W. Pontius. (N.p.) 1970. (LoC)

PHELPS – Phelps, Dudley Post
A genealogical record of the descendants of Joseph and Jemima (Post) Phelps, of Hebron, Connecticut. Showing also, in brief, the several links in the genealogical chain which connect then with the old Puritan, William Phelps, who came to America in 1630; with some historical notes and data relating to the common family name. By Dudley Post Phelps... (Syracuse, N. Y.: C. W. Bardeen), 1885. (LoC)

PHELPS – Phelps, Louise (Copeland)
The Phelps family. A history of the ancestors and the descendants of Josiah Phelps of Stafford Springs, Conn., and Pittsford, N. Y. Comp. by Louise (Copeland) Phelps... Oak Park, Ill. (1918). (LoC)

PHILLIPS – Phillips, George H.
Noah Phillips of Newton County, Ga. and Litchfield, Conn.; his ancestors & descendants. Atlanta, Ga,: Phillips, 1956? (DAR)

PHILLIPS – Phillps, George H.
Noah Phillips of Newton County, Georgia, and Litchfield, Conn.,. his ancestors and descendants. By George H. Phillips. (Atlanta, Ga., author? 1957). (FW)

PICKETT – Wood, Frederick
Chart of the descendants of John and Margaret Pickett, of Salem, Mass., 1648-1660, and Stratford, Conn., 1660-1684. By Frederick Wood. 1929. (PH)

PIERCE – Boas, Norman F.
Jane M. Pierce (1806-1863): the Pierce-Aiken papers supplement. By Norman F. Boas. Mystic, Conn.: Seaport Autographs, c1989. (LoC)

PIERCE – Boas, Norman F.
 Jane M. Pierce (1806-1863): the Pierce-Aiken papers: letters of Jane M.
 Pierce, her sister Mary M. Aiken, their family and President Franklin
 Pierce, with biographies of Jane Pierce, other members of her family,
 and genealogical tables. By Norman F. Boas. Stonington, Conn.:
 Seaport Autographs, c1983. (LoC)

PIERCE – Colby, Barnard Ledward
 Thirty-one generations; a thousand years of Percys and Pierces 972-
 1969. By Barnard Ledwood Colby. (New London, Conn., 1969).
 (LoC)

PIERCE – Colby, Barnard Ledward
 Thirty-one generations; a thousand years of Percies and Pierces, 972 to
 1948. Limited Ed. By Barnard Ledward Colby. (New London, Conn.,
 1947). (LoC)

PIERPONT –
 Account of the celebration of the 100th anniversary of the wedding of
 John Pierpont and Sarah Beers... 1867. New Haven, Tuttle, 1868.
 (LI)

PIERPONT – Marks, Edward J.
 A genealogical abstract of the family of Pierrepont, from Sir Hugh de
 Pierrepont, of Picardy, France, A. D. 980. Compiled by Edward J.
 Marks. New Haven, Conn., Hoggson & Robinson, Printers, 1881.
 (LoC)

PIERPONT – Moffat, R. Burnham
 Pierrepont genealogies from Norman times to 1913, with particular
 attention paid to the line of descent from Hezekiah Pierpont, youngest
 son of Rev. James Pierpont of New Haven. By R. Burnham Moffat.
 (New York): Priv. print. (L. Middleditch Co.), 1913. (LoC)

PIERSON –
 Pierson Family of New Haven (1895), 33 pgs.[1]

PITKIN – Daniels, Bruce C.
 Connecticut's first family: William Pitkin and his connections. By
 Bruce C. Daniels. (Conn. bicentennial series 11). Pequot Press
 (1976?). (FW)

PITKIN – Pitkin, A. P.

Pitkin family of America. A genealogy of the descendants of William Pitkin, the progenitor of the family in this country, from his arrival from England in 1659 to 1886... Also, additional notes of the descendants of Martha Pitkin, who married Simon Wolcott... By A. P. Pitkin. Hartford, Conn. (Press of the Case, Lockwood & Brainard Co.), 1887. (LoC)

PLANT – Dickerman, G. S.
The House of Plant. New Haven: Tuttle, Morehouse & Taylor, 1900. (DAR)

PLATT – Coddington, J. I.
Richard Platt of Ware, County Herford, Eng. and Milford, Conn. By J. I. Coddington. (Washington, D.C.), 1955. (FW)

PLATT – Parsons, N. Vincent (Nahum Vincent)
John Webb Platt, III, 1860-1922, Blanche (Dowzer) Platt, 1872-1960: ancestors in Connecticut and Canada, descendants in California, with related lines of Moody, Southworth, Sterne, Dinsmore, Shipley. Compiled by N. Vincent Parsons and Margaret P. Parsons. (Holland, Mich.: Parsons), 1977. (LoC)

PLATT – Platt, Charles
Platt genealogy in America, from the arrival of Richard Platt in New Haven, Connecticut, in 1638. New Hope, Pa., 1963. (NGS)

PLIMPTON – Chase, Levi B.
A genealogy and historical notes of the family of Plimpton or Plympton in America. Hartford, Conn.: Plimpton Mfg. Co., 1884? (DAR)

PLIMPTON – Chase, Levi B.
A genealogy and historical notices of the family of Plimpton or Plympton in America, and of Plumpton in England. By Levi B. Chase. Hartford, Conn., Plimpton Mfg. Co., print. (1884). (LoC)

POMEROY – Allaben, Frank
A genealogical "cause celebre." An analysis of some interpretations which obscure the ancestral genesis of the American people... By Frank Allaben. (New Haven, 1917). (MH)

POMEROY – Rodman, Wm. W.
A study in heredity: the Pomeroys in America. By Wm. W. Rodman. (New Haven, 1889). (LoC)

POMEROY – Rodman, William Woodbridge
Eltweed Pomeroy of Dorchester, Mass., and Windsor, Conn., and four
generations of his decendants. By William Woodbridge Rodman...
Boston, D. Clapp and Son, 1903. (LoC)

POND –
Pond Family of Windsor (1875), 126 pgs.[1]

POND – Pond, Nathan F.
Ponds of Milford, Conn. ... 1630 to the present. By Nathan F. Pond.
(Milford, Conn.). N.d. (FW)

PORTER –
Porter Family of Windsor (1882), 125 pgs.[1]
Porter Family of Windsor (1893), 888 pgs.[1]
Porter Family of Waterbury, Connecticut (1896), 8 pgs.[1]

PORTER –
The descendants of John Porter, of Windsor, Conn., in the line of his
great grandson, Col. Joshua Porter, M. D., of Salisbury, Litchfield
County, Conn., with some account of the families into which they
married... Saratoga Springs, N. Y., Printed for the compilers by
G. W. Ball, 1882. (LoC)

PORTER –
John Porter of Windsor, Conn., and his parents: further notes, by John
Insley __?_oddington... (New Haven, 1941). (LoC)

PORTER – Andrews, Henry Porter
The descendants of John Porter of Windsor, Conn. Saratoga Springs,
N. Y.: George W. Ball, 1882. (DAR)

PORTER – Andrews, Henry Porter
The descendants of John Porter of Windsor, Conn., 1635-9. Saratoga
Springs, N. Y.: G. W. Ball Book and Job Printers, 1893. (DAR)

PORTER – Andrews, Henry Porter
The descendants of John Porter of Windsor, Conn., 1635-9. Compiled
by Henry Porter Andrews. Saratoga Springs, G. W. Ball, printer, 1893.
(LoC)

PORTER – Burton, Henry E.

Dr. Daniel Porter, the first of Farmington, Conn., 1655-1690 (with genealogical data). By Henry E. Burton. Middletown, Conn., 1897. (LI)

PORTER – Burton, H. E.
Ancestry of James Porter 3d, and his descendants to... 1896. By H. E. Burton. (Middletown, Ct., 1896). (OH)

PORTER – Burton, Henry E.
Porter family. By Henry E. Burton, (Middletown, Conn.), 1896. (FW)

PORTER – Coddington, John Insley
John Porter of Windsor, Conn., and his parents. Vessey family – New Haven, Ct., 1941. (NGS)

POTTER –
Potters of New Haven (1902), 9 pgs.[1]

POTTER – Shepard, James
The New Haven (Conn.) Potters, 1639. By James Shepard... Boston, Press of D. Clapp & Son (1902). (LoC)

PRATT –
Pratt Family of Connecticut (1864), 420 pgs.[1]
Pratt Family of Hartford (1900), 204 pgs.[1]

PRATT –
Supplement to a history entitled "The Pratt family; or, the descendants of Lieut. William Pratt, one of the first settlers of Hartford and Say-Brook;" being a continuation of the record in the line of Zadock and Hannah Pratt of Stephentown and Jewett, New York. Printed by the co-operation of many of the descendants, for private distribution among subscribing members of the family. (New York, A. F. Southcombe), 1916. (LoC)

PRATT – Chapman, F. W.
The Pratt family. Hartford: Case, Lockwood & Co., 1864. (DAR)

PRATT – Chapman, Rev. F. W.
The Pratt family; or, the descendants of Lieut. William Pratt, one of the first settlers of Hartford and Say-Brook, with genealogical notes of John Pratt, of Hartford; Peter Pratt, of Lyme; John Pratt (Taylor) of Say-Brook. By Rev. F. W. Chapman... Hartford, Printed by Case, Lockwood and Company, 1864. (LoC)

PRATT – Pratt, Kenneth Charles
Abraham, the father of us all. Oxford, Conn.: Pratt, 1968. (DAR)

PRATT – Whittelsey, Charles B.
The ancestry and descendants of John Pratt of Hartford, Conn.
Hartford, Conn.: Hartford Press, Case, Lockwood & Brainard Co.,
1900. (DAR)

PRATT – Whittelsey, Charles B.
...The ancestry and the descendants of John Pratt of Hartford, Conn.
Compiled by Charles B. Whittelsey... By authority of Walter W.
Pratt... Hartford, Conn., the Case, Lockwood & Brainard Company,
1900. (LoC)

PRENTICE –
Prentice Family of N. London, Connecticut (1875), 14 pgs.[1]

PRESTON –
Preston Family of Conn. (1899), 67 pgs.[1]

PRESTON – Preston, Edward M.
A history of Captain Roswell Preston of Hampton, Conn., his ancestry
and descendants, including ancestry in the Eaton, Knowlton, Butt,
Raymond, Witter, Killam, Hinds and other kindred families. By
Edward M. Preston. Nevada City, Calif.: E. M. Preston, 1899. (FW)

PRICHARD – Pritchard, Jacob LeRoy
A compilation of some of the descendants of Roger Prichard, c1600-
1671; a Welshman who brought his family to Massachusetts Bay
Colony in 1636; a pioneer of Springfield, Massachusetts, and of
Wethersfield, Milford, and New Haven, Connecticut. By Jacob LeRoy
Pritchard. (San Jose? Calif., 1953). (LoC)

PRIME –
Prime Family of Milford, Connecticut (1895), 45 pgs.[1]

PRINCE –
In his Genealogy of the Prince family from 1660 to 1899. Danielson,
Conn., 1899. (LoC)

PRINCE – Prince, Frank A.
The genealogy of the Prince family from 1600 to 1899. Danielson,
Conn.: Prince, 1899. (DAR)

PRINCE – Prince, Frank A.
The genealogy of the Prince family. From 1660 to 1899. Compiled, arranged, and published by Frank A. Prince… Danielson, Conn.: J. H. Briggs, Printers, 1899. (LoC)

PRINCE – Prince, Frank A.
Descendants of Daniel Prince, born May 1st, 1775. By Frank A. Prince… Danielson, Conn.: J. H. Briggs (1898). (LoC)

PRUDDEN – Prudden, Lillian E.
Peter Prudden. New Haven, Conn.: Tuttle, Morehouose & Taylor Co., 1901. (DAR)

PRUDDEN – Prudden, Lillian E.
Peter Prudden; a story of his life at New Haven and Milford, Conn., with the genealogy of some of his descendants and an appendix containing copies of old wills, records, letters, and papers. By Lillian E. Prudden. (New Haven, Conn., The Tuttle, Morehouse & Taylor Co.) 1901. (LoC)

R

RANDALL –
Genealogy of a branch of the Randall family. 1666 to 1879. Collected and arranged by a member of the family. (Norwich, Chenango Union, 1879). (LoC)

RANDALL –
Genealogy of the descendants of Stephen Randall and Elizabeth Swezey… 1624-1668, Clarkenwell, St. James' parish, London, England; 1668-1738, Rhode Island and Connecticut, 1738-1906, Long Island, New York. (New York: J. S. Ogilvie Publishing Co., 1906?). (LoC)

RANNEY – Adams, Charles Collard
Middletown Upper Houses; a history of the North society of Middletown, Connecticut, from 1650 to 1800, with genealogical and biographical chapters on early families and a full genealogy of the Ranney family. By Charles Collard Adams… New York, The Grafton Press, 1908. (LoC)

RANSOM –

Genealogical sketch of Pelatiah Ransom and his children. (Litchfield, Conn., 1898). (LoC)

READ – Reed-Wright, Ella
Reed-Read lineage. Captain Joh Reed of Providence, R. I., and Norwalk, Conn., and his descendants through his sons, John and Thomas, 1660-1909. By Ella Reed-Wright. (Waterbury,Conn.: The Mattatuck Press, Inc., 1909). (LoC)

REED – Halstead, Vera Colton
A Reed family story. By Vera Colton Halstead. (New Fairfield, Conn., 1965). (LoC)

REED – Reed-Wright, Ella
Reed-Read lineage. Waterbury, Conn.: Mattatuck Press, 1909. (DAR)

REED – Reed-Wright, Ella
Reed-Read lineage. Captain John Reed of Providence, R. I., and Norwalk, Conn., and his descendants through his sons, John and Thomas, 1660-1909. By Ella Reed-Wright. (Waterbury, Conn.: The Mattatuck Press, Inc., 1909). (LoC)

REMINGTON – Dewey, Louis Marinus
Thomas Remington of Suffield, Conn., and some of his descendants. By Louis Marinus Dewey. Boston, New England Historic Genealogical Society, 1909. (LoC)

RESSIGUIE – Morris, John E.
The Resseguie family. A historical and genealogical record of Alexander Resseguie of Norwalk, Conn., and four generations of his descendants. Compiled by John E. Morris. Hartford, Conn.: Press of the Case, Lockwood & Brainard Company, 1888. (LoC)

REXFORD – Rexford, John De Witt
Genealogical history showing the paternal line of descent from Arthur Rexford, a native of England, who married Elizabeth Stevens, of New Haven, Conn., in 1702. Compiled by John De Witt Rexford. Janesville, Wis.: Gazette Printing Company, Printers, 1891. (LoC)

REYNOLDS –
Reynolds Family of Conn. (1905), 38 pgs.[1]

REYNOLDS –

...Annual reunion, the Reynolds family associates... Middletown,
Conn.: Pelton & King, Printers and Bookbinders. (LoC)

REYNOLDS –
The Reynolds Family Association of America; eighth to fortieth annual
reunions, 1899-1931. Middletown, Conn. (etc.), 1899-1931. (LA)

REYNOLDS – Ray, Deborah Wing
Loyal to the land: the history of a Greenwich, Connecticut family. By
Deborah Wing Ray and Gloria P. Stewart. West Kennebunk, Me.:
Published for Charter Oak Publications by Phoenix Pub., c1990. (LoC)

REYNOLDS – Reynolds Family Association
Annual reunion, the Reynolds Family Association. Middletown, Ct.
(NGS)

REYNOLDS – Reynolds, Marion H.
The history and descendants of John and Sarah (Backus) Reynolds of
Saybrook, Lyme and Norwich, Conn., 1655-1928; edited and compiled
by Marion H. Reynolds... data on living generations collected by Mrs.
Anna C. Rippier... Brooklyn, N. Y.: The Reynolds Family
Association, 1928. (LoC)

REYNOLDS – Wight, Jane Adaline Eaton
A partial record of the ancestors and complete record of the
descendants of Christopher and Charissa (Huntington) Reynolds of
Mansfield, Connecticut. Springfield, Mass.: Wight, 1905. (DAR)

REYNOLDS – Wight, Mrs. Jane Adaline (Eaton)
A partial record of the ancestors and a complete record of the
descendants of Christopher and Charissa (Huntington) Reynolds of
Mansfield, Connecticut. Compiled by Mrs. Jane Adaline (Eaton)
Wight, Springfield, Mass. (Springfield? Mass., 1905). (LoC)

RICHARDSON –
Richardsons of Stonington, Ct. (1906), 147 pgs.[1]

RICHARDSON – Hanna, Doreen Potter
Some descendants of Amos Richardson of Stonington, Connecticut.
Skowhegan? Me., 1971. (LoC)

RICHARDSON – Hanna, Doreen Potter
Some descendants of Amos Richardson of Stonington, Connecticut.
Skowhegan, Maine: Hanna, 1971. (DAR)

RIDER – Rider, Fremont
Preliminary materials for a genealogy of the Rider (Ryder) families in the United States. Middletown, Conn.: Godfrey Memorial Library, 1959. (DAR)

RIDGWAY – Ridgway, Leon A.
Ridgway family. By Leon A. Ridgway. (New Haven, Conn.), 1974. (FW)

RISDON – Risdon, Daniel B. (Daniel Bond)
Descendants of Josiah Risdon and Martha Cochran. By Daniel B. Risdon and Robert E. Cook. (West Hartford, Conn.). D. B. Risdon; (Capitolla, Calif.), R. E. Cook, c1981. (LoC)

RISING – Bunner, Gale J. (Gale Joseph)
Descendants of Jonathan Rising of Suffield, Ct. Materials gathered chiefly by Justus Rising; materials supplemented by Gale J. Bunner; compiled and edited by Gale J. Bunner. Burlington, Ma. Printed for Rising Family Association by Goodway Graphics of Massachusetts, 1983. (LoC)

RISLEY –
Charter, constitution and by-laws... Descendants of Richard Risley. Hartford, Conn.: The Deming Print Co., 1906. (NY)

ROBBINS –
Chart of the descendants of John Robbins, of Wethersfield, Ct., through his great grandson, Capt. Elisha Robbins... (New York?), c1881. (LoC)

ROBBINS –
The Robbins family in England and America, Wethersfield, Conn., branch, from: the study of the Rev. William Randolph Robbins... New Haven, 1950. (FW)

ROBBINS – Miller, Janis H. Miller
John Robbins of Branford and Lyme, Connecticut and related families in descent from William. Compiled by Janis H. Miller. Washington, 1966. (LoC)

ROBENS – Miller, Janic H.
The Robens family, Connecticut, New York, Ohio and unpublished records of Carpenters and Bentley, New York. By Janic H. Miller. Washington, 1961. (FW)

ROBERTS –
Roberts Family of Simsbury, Connecticut (1888), 7 pgs.[1]
Roberts Family of Simsbury, Connecticut (1896), 54 pgs.[1]

ROBERTS –
Roberts family, Connecticut to California. By Daphne R. Hartle,
Jennie N. Weeks (and) Margaret Watkins. (Salt Lake City?), 1965.
(LoC)

ROBERTS – Roberts, Richard C. (Richard Clarke)
Genealogy of the family of William Watson and Nancy Hoyt (Bean)
Roberts. Compiled and edited by Richard C. Roberts; illustrations by
Denise B. Roberts; restorative photography by Joseph L. Roberts;
contributing editors, Edith H. Gibson... [et al.]... Centennial Ed.
[Connecticut]. Roberts Reunion Association, 1981. (LoC)

ROBERTS – Starr, Frank Farnsworth
The Roberts family of Simsbury, Connecticut, in the line of Captain
Lemuel Roberts, 1742-1789. Compiled by Frank Farnsworth Starr for
James J. Goodwin. Hartford, Conn. (Cambridg, J. Wilson & Son),
1896. (LoC)

ROBINS – Miller, Janis H.
John Robins of Branford and Lyme, Connecticut. Washington, D. C.,
1966. (NGS)

ROBINS – Miller, Janis H.
John Robins of Branford and Lyme, Connecticut. Washington, D. C.:
Miller, 1965, c1966. (DAR)

ROBINSON – Baldwin, Edwin F.
John Robinson, 1770-1867, and his descendants. By Edwin F.
Baldwin. (Winsted, Conn., author, 1946). (FW)

ROBINSON – Edwards, William Hopple
Genealogical and ancestral notes. By William Hopple Edwards.
(Meriden, Conn., 1953-62). (LoC)

ROBINSON – Robinson, edward
Memoir of the Rev. William Robinson, formerly pastor of the
Congregational Church in Southington, Conn. With some account of
his ancestors in this country. By his son, Edward Robinson... Printed
as manuscript, for private distribution. New York: J. F. Trow, Printer,
1859. (LoC)

ROBINSON – Taylor, Bertha (S.)
Descendants of Rev. William Robinson. By Bertha (S.) Taylor.
Hartford, Conn., private print., 1936. (NY)

ROBINSON – Taylor, Bertha Smith
Descendants of Rev. William Robinson. Hartford, Conn.: Taylor,
1936. (DAR)

ROCKWELL – Boughton, James
A genealogy of the families of John Rockwell, of Stamford, Conn.,
1641, and Ralph Keeler, of Hartford, Conn., 1639. Comp. by James
Boughton... New York: W. F. Jones, 1903. (LoC)

ROCKWELL – Eldridge, Joseph
A sermon preached at the funeral of Martin Rockwell, of Colebrook...
By Joseph Eldridge; with an appendix and a genealogy of the Rockwell
family. New Haven: B. L. Hamlen, 1852. (FW)

RODMAN – Rodman, William Woodbridge
Notes on Rodman genealogy. By William Woodbridge Rodman...
(New Havenn, Conn.). Printed for the author (Tuttle, Morehouse &
Taylor, Printers), 1887. (LoC)

ROE –
Brief record of certain descendants of David Roe of Flushing, Long
Island, New York, including John Martindale of Philadelphia,
Pennsylvania and Martin Tichenor of New Haven, Connecticut and
Newark, New Jersey, including Theophilus Blake of Greenbrier
County, Virginia. (New York? 1965?). (LoC)

ROGERS –
Rogers Family, Mansfield, Ct. (1901), 7 pgs.[1]
Rogers Family of Conn. (1902), 520 pgs.[1]

ROGERS – Rogers, Fred B.
David Rogers (born 1778 at Roxbury, Conn.) and some of his
descendants; genealogical data to include the fifth generation. By Fred
B. Rogers. Chicago, Ill., 1967. (FW)

ROGERS – Rogers, Homer P.
Descendants of James Rogers of New London, Conn. By Homer P.
Rogers. (194-?). (LoC)

ROGERS – Rogers, James Swift

James Rogers of New London, Ct., and his descendants. By James
Swift Rogers... Boston, the Compiler, 1902. (LoC)

ROGERS – Waller-Frye, George
Adam and Katherine Rogers of New London, Ct., James and Katherine
Merritt of Killingworth, Ct. Storss, Conn.: Spring Hill Press, 1977.
(DAR)

ROGERS – Waller-Frye, George
Adam and Katherine Rogers of New London, Ct., James and Katherine
Merritt of Killingworth, Ct. By Waller-Frye, George. Storrs, Ct.
Spring Hill Press, 1977. (LoC)

ROLLO – Rollo, John Hollenbeck
A genealogical record of the descendants of Alexander Rollo, of East
Haddam, Conn. Wilmington, Del.: Rollo, 1896. (DAR)

ROLLO – Rollo, John Hollenbeck
A genealogical record of the descendants of Alexander Rollo, of East
Haddam, Conn., 1685-1895, with biographical notes. By John
Hollenbeck Rollo. Wilmington, Del., Priv. print. for the author, 1896.
(LoC)

ROOOSEVELT – Whittelsey, Charles Barney
The Roosevelt genealogy. Hartford, Conn.: Press of J. B. Burr & Co.,
1902. (DAR)

ROOT – Messier, Betty Brook
The roots of Coventry, Connecticut. Betty Brook Messier and Janet
Sutherland Aronson. Coventry, Conn.: 275th Anniversary Committee,
c1987. (LoC)

ROSE – Rose, Christine
Descendants of Robert Rose of Wethersfield and Branford,
Connecticut, who came on the ship "Francis" in 1634 from Ipswich,
England. San Jose, Ca., 1983. (NGS)

ROSE – Rose, Christine
Descendants of Robert Rose of Wethersfield and Branford,
Connecticut, who came on the ship "Francis" in 1634 from Ipswich,
England. By Christine Rose. San Jose, Calif.: Privately published by
Rose Family Association, 1983. (LoC)

ROUSSEAU – Dennis, Inez Jane

<u>Rousseau biographies.</u> ?Cornwall Bridge, Ct., 1965. (NGS)

ROWLEY – Crankshaw, Mildred G.
<u>Some descendants of Thomas Rowley of Windsor, Connecticut.</u>
S.1.: Crankshaw, 1961. (DAR)

ROWLEY – Crankshaw, Mildred Gertrude
<u>Some descendants of Thomas Rowley of Windsor, Connecticut, with</u>
<u>lineage of families allied by marriage.</u> By Mildred Gertrude
Crankshaw. (N.p., 1961). (LoC)

ROWLEY – Russell, Nellie L.
<u>Eleazer Rowley of East Haddam, Conn., and some of his descendants.</u>
By Nellie L. Russell. Bay Shore, N. Y. (1949). (MH)

ROYCE –
<u>New England pioneers: Robert-1 & Mary Royce of Connecticut: with</u>
<u>additions on the Calkins & Lathrop families.</u> [S.1.]: Royce Family
Association, c1988. (LoC)

RUGGLES – Bailey, Franklin Ladd
<u>The genealogy of Thomas Ruggles of Roxbury, 1637, to Thomas</u>
<u>Ruggles of Pomfret, Conn., and Rutland, Vt. The genealogy of</u>
<u>Alitheah Smith, of Hampton, Conn., the wife of Thomas Ruggles, and</u>
<u>the genealogy of the descendants – in part – of Samuel Ladd of</u>
<u>Haverhill, Mass.</u> By Franklin Ladd Bailey. (Boston) 1896. (LoC)

RUSSELL – Russell, Gurdon Wadsworth
<u>An account of some of the descendants of John Russell.</u> Hartford,
Conn.: Welles, 1910. (DAR)

RUSSELL – Russell, Nellie L.
<u>Stephen Russell of East Hampton, L. I. and Haddam, Conn., and some</u>
<u>of his descendants.</u> By Nellie L. Russell. Bay Shore, N. Y. (1949?).
(MH)

S

SAFFORD –Safford, Rae Gibson
A genealogical history of Gideon Safford and Lucy Freeman, Preston, Connecticut. S.1.: s.n., 1977. (DAR)

SAGE –
The Jonathan Sage family; descendants of David Sage of Middletown, Connecticut, second branch. (Normal? Ill.) Priv. print, 1951. (LoC)

SAGE –
Genealogical record of the descendants of David Sage, a native of Wales; born 1639, and one of the first settlers of Middletown, Connecticut – 1652. Carefully prepared and rev. by the author from authentic records. Middletown, Conn.: Pelton & King, Printers, 1878.

SAGE –
Genealogical record of the descendants of David Sage, a native of Wales; born 1639, and one of the first settlers of Middletown, Connecticut – 1652. Carefully prepared and revised by 1515 Elisha L. Sage, in 1878, from authentic records. Brought to date (1919) by 232 Charles H. Sage. Ratavia, N. Y.: C. H. Sage, 1919. (LoC)

SAGE – Snow, Helen Foster
Sage family; autobiography of Parthena (Smith) Sage, 1824-1909, wife of Horatio Sage. With descendants and notes on Smith – Chaffee – Foster. Prepared by Helen Foster Snow. (Madison, Conn., 1953?). (LoC)

ST. JOHN – Alexander, Orline St. John
The St. John genealogy; descendants of Matthias St. John of Dorchester, Massachusetts, 1634, of Windsor, Connecticut, 1640, of Wethersfield, Connecticut, 1643-1645, and Norwalk, Connecticut, 1650. By Orline St. John Alexander. New York, The Grafton Press, 1907. (LoC)

ST. JOHN – Cash, Ben Le Grande
St. John and Harries, the ancestors and descendants of Theodore Edgar St. John and his wife, Jane Ceclia Harries, including extensive ancestry of Captain Thomas Yale of New Haven, Conn., and of Henry Gregory of Norwalk, Conn., a study in cousinship. By Ben Le Grande Cash. (Albuquerque? N. M., 1973). (LoC)

SALISBURY – Salisbury, Edward Elbridge

Seventeen pedigrees from "Family-Memorials." By Edward Elbridge
Salisbury. Priv. print. (New Haven, Conn.: Press of Tuttle, Morehouse &
Taylor) 1885. (LoC)

SALISBURY – Salisbury, Edward E.
Family histories and genealogies 1892. By Edward E. Salisbury. (New
Haven, Press of Tuttle, Morehouse & Taylor). (LA)

SALISBURY – Salisbury, Evelyn (M.)
Will of Evelyn MacCurdy Salisbury, 1823-1917. By Evelyn (M.)
Salisbury. New Haven, Conn., 1918. (NY)

SALISBURY – Spencer, Emma (S.)
...Genealogy of the family of Nathaniel Salisbury; a native of Swansea,
Conn., and for many years a resident of the town of Norway, N. Y. By
Emma (S.) Spencer. Herkimer, N. Y. (1905?). (NY)

SALTONSTALL –
Ancestry and descendants of Sir Richard Saltonstall, first associate of the
Massachusetts Bay Colony and patentee of Connecticut. (Cambridge)
Printed at the Riverside Press, 1897. (LoC)

SALTONSTALL. See also: Coach, 1962
Mumford, 1900
Wanton

SANFORD –
The Sanford Association of America 4th-5th reunion, 1910-1911. Milford,
Conn., 1912. (LoC)

SANFORD – Sanford, William Atwater
The Sanford family of Newtown, Conn. New York: Sanford, 1903.
(DAR)

SANFORD – Sanford, William Atwater
The Sanford family of Newton, Conn..., in old and new England.
Genealogical. By William Atwater Sanford of New York, N. Y. (New
York: Wynkoop, Hallenbeck, Crawford Co., 1905?). (LoC)

SAVAGE – Borup, Belle
John Savage of Middletown, Conn. and his descendants. By Belle Borup.
(IG)

SAVAGE – Savage, James Francis

Family of John Savage of Middletown, Conn., 1652. By James Francis
Savage. Boston, D. Clapp & Son, Printers, 1894. (LoC)

SCHOLL – Scholl, Inge [Weisse Rose, English]
The White Rose: Munich, 1942-1943. Inge Scholl; with an introduction by
Dorothee Solle; translated from the German by Arthur R. Schultz. 1st
Wesleyan pbk. ed. Middletown, Conn.: Wesleyan University Press;
Scranton, Pa. Distributed by Harper & Row, 1983. (LoC)

SCOVILLE – Brainard, Homer Worthington
A survey of the Scovils or Scovills in England and America. Hartford:
s..n., 1915. (DAR)

SCOVILLE – Brainard, Homer Worthington
A survey of the Scovils or Scovilles in England and America, seven
hundred years of history and genealogy. By Homer Worthington Brainard.
Hartford, Priv. print, 1915. (LoC)

SCRANTON – Scranton, Erastus
The descendants of John Scranton of Guilford, Conn. Hartford, Ct., 1855.
(NGS)

SCRANTON – Scranton, Erastus
A genealogical register of the descendants of John Scranton. Hartford:
Case, Tiffany & Co., 1855. (DAR)

SCRANTON – Scranton, Rev. Erastus, A. M.
A genealogical register of the descendants of John Scranton of Guilford,
Conn., who died in the year 1671. Compiled by Rev. Erastus Scranton,
A.M. ... Hartford: Press of Case, Tiffany and Company, 1855. (LoC)

SEABURY –
Seabury-Gifford families; genealogical, biographical. Hartford, Conn.:
States Historical Co., Inc., 1941. (NY)

SEAGER – Raymoure, Dorothy
Descendants of Joseph Seager and Nehitable Parsons of Connecticut. By
Dorothy Raymoure. Grand Rapids, 1957. (LoC)

SEAGER – Seager, Cordelia Thies
The Seager families of Colonial New England including descendant lines
principally from Massachusetts, Connecticut, Rhode Island, and certain
families of New York and Ohio. Researched and compiled by Cordelia

Thies Seager, Charles William Seager. Illahee Hills, Brevard, N. C.:
Seager, c1978. (LoC)

SEBOR – Beach, Helen
A study of Jacob Sebor, 1709-1793, of Middletown, Connecticut.
S.1.: Beach, 1923. (DAR)

SEBOR – Beach, Helen
The descendants of Jacob Sebor, 1709-1793, of Middletown, Connecticut.
Compiled by Helen Beach, (n.p.) 1923. (LoC)

SEDGWICK – Sedgwick, Hubert M.
A Sedgwick genealogy. New Haven, Conn.: New Haven Colony
Historical Society, 1961. (DAR)

SEDGWICK – Sedgwick, Hubert Merrill
A Sedgwick genealogy; descendants of Deacon Benjamin Sedgwick. By
Hubert Merrill Sedgwick. New Haven: New Haven Colony Historical
Society, 1961. (LoC)

SEELEY – Ault, Helen B.
Seely(e)-Seeley of Connecticut. By Helen B. Ault. Redding, Conn.
(1940-4?). (NY)

SELDEN – Eaton, Daniel C.
Calvin Selden, of Lyme, and his children. An address delivered at a
meeting of the Selden family at Fenwick Grove, Saybrook, Conn.,
August 22, 1877, by Daniel C. Eaton. New Haven, 1877. (LoC)

SEMPLE – Semple, William Alexander
Genealogical history of the family Semple from 1214 to 1888. Compiled
and arranged by William Alexander Semple... Hartford, Conn.: Press of
the Case, Lockwood & Brainard Company, 1888. (LoC)

SEVERSMITH – Seversmith, Herbert Furman
Colonial families of Long Island, New York and Connecticut. Los
Angeles, Ca., 1944. (NGS)

SEVERSMITH – Seversmith, Herbert Furman
Colonial families of Long Island, New York and Connecticut, being the
ancestry & kindred of Herbert Furman Seversmith... by Herbert Furman
Seversmith... (Los Angeles, 1944-). (LoC)

SEVERSMITH – Seversmith, Herbert F.

Colonial families of Long Island, New York and Conn.; being the ancestry
and kindred of Herbert Furman Seversmith. By Herbert F. Seversmith.
1948-58. (SL)

SEYMOUR –
A record of the Seymour family in the revolution. (Litchfield? Conn.,
1912). (LoC)

SEYMOUR –
Genealogy of the descendants of Richard Seymour from the first settlement
of Hartford, Ct., in 1635. Brockport, N. Y.: Democrat Steam Print, 1880.
(LoC)

SEYMOUR –
Richard Seymour of Hartford and Norwalk, Conn., and some of his
descendants, communicated by Seymour Morris... (Boston, 1918). (LoC)

SEYMOUR –
Seymour family, Seamer, Seamor, Seemer, Seemor, Semor, Semer,
Seymore, Samore. (Compiled by Jennie E. Seymour Hammond and
J. Boyd.) (West Hartford? Conn., 1931). (LoC)

SEYMOUR –
A history of the Seymour family; descendants of Richard Seymour of
Hartford, Connecticut, for six generations; with extensive amplification of
the lines deriving from his son John Seymour of Hartford. Compiled and
arranged for publication under the direction of George Dudley Seymour,
by Donald Lines Jacobus, based primarily on the manuscript collections of
Mary Kingsbury __?__ and of Seymour Morris, which the author has
augmented with an introduction, various memorabilia and appendices, and
a picture gallery of Seymour family portraits, houses, seals, and family
memorials. New Haven, Conn. (Printed by the Tuttle, Morehouse &
Taylor Company) 1939. (LoC)

SEYMOUR – Bartlett, J. Gardner
The English home and ancestry of Richard Semer of Hartford, Conn.,
progenitor of the Seymours of Connecticut and New York. Communicated
to the New England historical and genealogical register by George D.
Seymour from researches by J. Gardner Bartlett. Boston (Stanhope Press:
F. H. Gilson Company) 1917. (LoC)

SEYMOUR – Jacobus, Donald Lines
A history of the Seymour family. New Haven, Conn.: George Dudly
Seymour, 1939. (DAR)

SEYMOUR – Pinney, Maria Watson
Richard Seymor, Hartford, 1640. Derby, Conn.:Pinney, 1903? (DAR)

SEYMOUR – Pinney, Mrs. Maria Watson
Richard Seymour, Hartford, 1640; a paper read before the Connecticut chapter, Daughters of founders and patriots of America, at Norwalk, Conn., February 13th, 1903. By Mrs. Maria Watson Pinney... (New Haven, the Tuttle, Morehouse & Taylor Press, 1903?). (LoC)

SEYMOUR – Seymour, Malcolm
Puritan migration to Connecticut: the saga of the Seymour family, 1129-1746. By Malcolm Seymour; with illustrations by Donald Bowman. Canaan, N. H.: Phoenix Pub., c1982. (LoC)

SEYMOUR – Seymour, Morris W.
Richard Seymour of Hartford. By Morris W. Seymour. (Hartford, Conn., 1906. (FW)

SEYMOUR – Seymour, Morris Woodruff
A record of the Seymour family in the Revolution. Litchfield, Conn.: Seymour, 1912. (DAR)

SHARP – Sharpe, W. C.
Sharpe genealogy and miscellany. By W. C. Sharpe... Seymour, Conn.: Record Print, 1880. (LoC)

SHARP – Sharpe, William Carvosso
The Sharpes. No. 1-32. (By William Carvosso Sharpe. Seymour, Conn., Printed by the author). 1893-96. (LoC)

SHARPE – Sharpe (William C.)
Records of the Sharpe family in England and America, from 1580 to 1870. By (William C.) Sharpe. Seymour, Ct.: W. C. Sharpe, 1874. (NY)

SHARPLES – Knox, Katherine McCook
The Sharples, their portraits of George Washington and his contemporaries. New Haven: Yale University Press, 1930. (DAR)

SHATTUCK – Duncan, Maxene Shattuck
Homer and Pearl (Bingham) Shattuck: their ancestors and descendants. Maxene (Shattuck) Duncan. [Stamford, Conn.]: M. S. Duncan, 1984. (LoC)

SHELDON – Sheldon, John P.

Genealogy of the descendants of Joseph Sheldon of Suffield, Connecticut. By John P. Sheldon. Cheyenne, Wyo.: Neostyle Print, 1901. (FW)

SHELTON –
Brief memoir of the family of Shelton of Connecticut. Bridgeport, 1876. (LI)

SHELTON –
Reunion of the descendants of Daniel Shelton, at Birmingham, Conn., June 14th, 1877. Newburgh, N. Y.: E. N. Ruttenber & Son, Printers, 1877. (LoC)

SHELTON –
Brief memoir of the family of Shelton of Connecticut. Boston, 1857. (LoC)

SHELTON – Shelton, Jane De Forest
Reunion of the descendants of Daniel Shelton at Birmingham, Conn., June 14th, 1877. Newburgh, N. Y.: E. M./Ruttenber & Sons, 1877. (DAR)

SHEPARD – Shepard, Gerald Faulkner
The Shepard families of New England. Compiled by Gerald Faulkner Shepard. Edited by Donald Lines Jacobus. New Haven, New Haven Colony Historical Society, 1971-1973. (LoC)

SHERMAN –
Genealogy of one branch of the Sherman family from Samuel Sherman of Stratford, Conn., the first American ancestor, in 1640, down to Jotham Sherman of Newtown, Conn., of the fifth generation, and most of his descendants down to the eighth and ninth generation. Compiled by Walter S. Booth... and Mrs. Hosea B. Northrop... (Milwaukee, Wis.: Press of the Evening Wisconsin Co.) 1900. (LoC)

SHERRILL – de Forest, Louis Effingham
The Sherrill genealogy. New Haven, Conn.: Tuttle, Morehouse & Taylor Co., 1932. (DAR)

SHERWOOD – Carlson, M. Beatrix
Thomas Sherwood of Fairfield, Conn. and descendants. By M. Beatrix Carlson. N. p., H. F. Johnston, 1950. (FW)

SHIPMAN –
History of the Shipmans, descended from Edward Shipman... born in Nottinghamshire, England... moved to Saybrook, Conn., about 1635...

died at Saybrook, Sept. 15, 1697. (Compiled by Rita Shipman Carl, Angela Shipman Crispin, and William Henry Shipman. Ann Arbor? Mich.: Shipman Historical Association, 1955). (LoC)

SHIPMAN – Cody, Edward Perrine
Genealogy of the Shipman family. By Edward Perrine Cody. (Wethersfield? Conn., 1949?). (LoC)

- Additions to the Genealogy of the family of Edward Shifton (Shipman) and his first wife Elizabeth Comstock of Wethersfield, Connecticut. (Wethersfield? 1951). (LoC)

SILL –
Sill Family of Connecticut (1897), 32 pgs.[1]

SILL – Burt, Sarah S. W.
Old Silltown, something of its history and people; being principally a brief account of the early generations of the Sill family, their settlements in Connecticut, etc. By Sarah S. W. Burt. (Evanston, Ill.), 1912. (LI)

SKEEL – Thoesen, Edythe Wilson
The Skeel (Skeele, Skiel) family of Connecticut. 1960? (DAR)

SKIDMORE – Hawley, Emily C.
A genealogical and biographical record of the pioneer Thomas Skidmore (Scudamore). Brookfield Center, Conn.: Emily C. Hawley, c1911. (DAR)

SKIDMORE – Hawley, Emily C.
A genealogical and biographical record of the pioneer Thomas Skidmore (Scudmore) of the Massachusetts and Connecticut Colonies in New Englon (sic) and of Huntington, Long Island, and of his descendants through the branches herein set forth; including other related branches of the Skidmore family, with historical sketches of places where the several branches settled and of events in which representative members participated. Compiled... by Emily C. Hawley. (Brookfield Center, Conn.): E. C. Hawley, 1911. (LoC)

SKIDMORE – Hawley, Emily C.
A genealogical and biographical record of the pioneer Thomas Skidmore (Scudamore) of the Massachusetts and Connecticut colonies in New England, and Huntington, Long Island. By Emily C. Hawley. (2d Ed. with supplement). (Brattleboro, Vt.). 1911 (1912). (LI)

SKIDMORE – Skidmore, Warren
Thomas Skidmore (Scudamore), 1605-1684, of Westerleigh,
Gloucestershire, and Fairfield, Connecticut. Akron, Oh., 1980. (NGS)

SKIDMORE – Skidmore, Warren
Thomas Skidmore (Scudamore), 1605-1684, of Westerleigh,
Gloucestershire, and Fairfield, Connecticut: his ancestors and his
descendants to the ninth generation. By Warren Skidmore. 2nd Ed.
(Akron, Ohio): W. Skidmore, 1985. (LoC)

SKILTON –
Skilton Family Association. Family reunion. Middlebury, Conn. (MH)

SKILTON – Skilton, George Warner
The teeth of the rake. Farmington, Conn.: Skilton, 1964. (DAR)

SKILTON – Skilton, George Warner
The teeth of the rake. By George Warner Skilton. Artist: N. William
Petersen. (Farmington? Conn., 1964?). (LoC)

SKILTON – Skilton, John Davis
Doctor Henry Skilton and his descendants. New Haven, Conn.: S. Z.
Field, 1921. (DAR)

SKILTON – Skilton, John Davis
Doctor Henry Skilton, and his descendants. Ed. by John Davis Skilton...
New Haven, Conn.: Press of S. Z. Field, 1921. (LoC)

- Supplement I... by The Doctor Henry Skilton Association; editors,
George Warner Skilton, B. S., secretary of the... Association, and Henry
Irving Skilton, B. S., registrar. (New Haven, Conn.), 1927. (LoC)

SKILTON – Skilton, John Davis
...The Doctor Henry Skilton house, Southington, Hartford County,
Connecticut... (By John Davis Skilton). (Hartford? 1930?). (LoC)

SKINNER – Fernold, Natalie R.
The Skinner kinsmen, the descendants of John Skinner of Hartford, Conn.
By Natalie R. Fernold. Washington: Pioneer Press, n.d. (LA)

SKINNER – Wahl, Doris S.
The Skinner kinsmen; the descendants of Joseph and Martha (Kinne)
Skinner of Connecticut, New York and Pennsylvania. By Doris S. Wahl.
Niagara Falls, N. Y. (1958). (FW)

SKINNER – Wahl, Doris Seymour
The Skinner Kinsmen; descendants of Joseph and Martha (Kinne) Skinner of Connecticut, New York and Pennsylvania. Niagara Falls, N. Y. ?1956. (NGS)

SKINNER – Wahl, Doris Seymour
The Skinner Kinsmen; descendants of Joseph and Martha (Kinne) Skinner of Connecticut, New York and Pennsylvania. Also by Cynthia W. Rummel. Kenilworth, Il., 1958. (NGS)

SLADE – Peck, Thomas Bellows
William Slade of Windsor, Conn. Keene, N. H.: Sentinel Printing Co., 1910. (DAR)

SLOSSON – Patterson, David W.
A genealogical memoir of Nathaniel Slosson, of Kent, Connecticut, and his descendants, 1696-1872. Reprinted from The New York genealogical and biographical record, July and Oct., 1872. With Nathan Slosson's descendants continued to Aug., 1896. (By David W. Patterson). Bridgeport, Conn.: The Marigold Prtg. Co., 1896. (LI)

SMITH –
A record of the family of Roswell Smith, son of Steel Smith of Farmington, Conn., Windsor, Vermont, and other localities, with residence of descendants, so far as is known to date. (Washington, D. C.), 1919. (LoC)

SMITH –
Smith Family of Stonington, Connecticut (1870), 53 pgs.[1]
Smith Family of Connecticut (1871), 7 pgs.[1]
Smith Family of New London, Connecticut (1889), 318 pgs.[1]
Smith Family of E. Haddam, Connecticut (1890), 269 pgs.[1]

SMITH –
A new edition of the record of the family of Roswell Smith and Roswell Smith, second of the family of Steel Smith of Farmington, Conn., Windsor, Vermont, and other localities, with residence of descendants so far as is known to date. (Rutland, Vt.: The Tuttle Co.), 1921. (LoC)

SMITH –
Ancestry of Henry Boynton Smith, Frederick Southgate Smith, Horatio Southgate Smith. Comp. by Henry Smith Munroe, with aid from Alice Durant Smith. Litchfield, Conn.: Printed for private distribution, Enquirer Press, 1922. (LoC)

SMITH –

The Record of my ancestry. (Genealogical memoranda in manuscript of the family of Robert Smith and others arranged in album designed by the Rev. Frederick W. Bailey). New Haven, Conn.: F. W. Bailey, 1894. (NY)

SMITH – Anderson, Mary Audentia Smith

Ancestry and posterity of Joseph Smith and Emma Hale, with little sketches of their immigrant ancestors, all of whom came to America between the years 1620 and 1685, and settled in the states of Massachusetts and Connecticut. Compiled and written by Mary Audentia Smith Anderson. Independence, Mo. (Herald Publishing House), 1929. (LoC)

SMITH – Brewer, Duane E.

A genealogical record of the descendants of Alexander Smith and Elizabeth Hastings. By Duane E. Brewer. Bridgeport, Conn., 1880. (LI)

SMITH – Hook, James William

Lieut. Samuel Smith and related families. New Haven, Ct., 1953. (NGS)

SMITH – Hook, James William

Lieut. Samuel Smith. New Haven, Conn.: Hook, 1953. (DAR)

SMITH – Kendall, John Smith

The Smith family of Withcote, and Wethersfield, Conn. By John Smith Kendall). (Berkeley, Calif., 1945). (LoC)

SMITH – Martin, Sophia Smith

A complete genealogy of descendants of Matthew Smith of East Haddam, Conn. Rutland, The Tuttle Company, 1890. (DAR)

SMITH – Martin, Mrs. Sophia (Smith)

A complete genealogy of the descendants of Matthew Smith of East Haddam, Conn., with mention of his ancestors, 1637-1890. By Mrs. Sophia (Smith) Martin... Rutland, The Tuttle Company, Printers, 1890. (LoC)

SMITH – Schmidt, Richard Gary

Sixteen Maryland families: a history and genealogy of sixteen of the Maryland families in the direct ancestry of the compiler and author, 1733-1980, in Maryland, from the early 1600's, with related families in New Jersey, Connecticut, and Europe. By Richard Gary Schmidt. Baltimore: Gateway Press: Glen Burnie, Md., 1981. (LoC)

SMITH – Seversmith, Herbert F.
The ancestry and kindred of Herbert Francis Smith. Being a genealogical account of the families of Smith, Weeks, Wicks, Furman, Ackerly, Hulse, Youngs, Baldwin, and many others, of Long Island, New York, Westchester, and also of Connecticut, Mass., and Pa. ... By Herbert F. Seversmith. Brooklyn,, N. Y., 1922. (NY)

SMITH – Smith, Alven M.
John Smith of Lancaster, Mass., and his descendants in Lyme, Conn. (Marlow, N. H., Vermont and the West). By Alven M. Smith. S. Pasadena, Cal.: A. M. Smith, 1931. (LA)

SMITH – Smith, George C.
A genealogical record of the family of Nathan Smith, of Connecticut. By George C.Smith. Cambridge, Ill., 1871. (MH)

SMITH – Smith, H. Allen
A genealogical history of the descendants of the Rev. Nehemiah Smith of New London County, Conn. Albany, N. Y.: Joel Munsell's Sons, 1889. (DAR)

SMITH – Smith, H. Allen
A genealogical history of the descendants of the Rev. Nehemiah Smith of New London County, Conn., with mention of his brother John and nephew Edward. 1638-1888. By H. Allen Smith... Albany, N. Y.: J. Munsell's Sons, 1889. (LoC)

SMITH – Snow, Helen (F.)
The Smith-Chaffee family of Ashford, Connecticut, and Marcellus, New York. By Helen (F.) Snow. Madison, Conn. (1954?). (NY)

SMITH – Tuckerman, Bayard
A sketch of the Cotton Smith of Sharon, Connecticut. Boston: s.n., 1915. (DAR)

SMITH – Tuckerman, Bayard
A sketch of the Cotton Smith family of Sharon, Connecticut; with genealogical notes. By Bayard Tuckerman. Boston, Priv. print. (Plimpton Press, Norwood, Mass.), 1915. (LoC)

SPELMAN – Barbour, Mrs. Fannie Cooley (Williams)
Spelman genealogy; descendants of Richard Spelman of Middletown, Connecticut, 1700. New York, N. Y., 1910. (NGS)

181

SPENCER –
Spencer Family of Cromwell, Connecticut (1896), 44 pgs.[1]

SPENCER – Spencer, Arthur C., III
Genealogy of Spencer family of Conn. and Oregon; Champlin of R. I. and
Conn.; Davis and Mansfield families of Conn.; Chamberlain of Conn. By
Arthur C. Spencer, III. Portland, Or., 1970. (LoC)

SPENCER – Spencer, William Henry
Spencer family record of the Springfield, Vt. and Evansville, Wis.
Spencers. Descendants of Garrard Spencer of Haddam, Conn. Emigrant
of 1630. By William Henry Spencer... New York: T. A. Wright, 1907.
(LoC)

SPENCER – Starr, Frank Farnsworth
The Thomas Spencer family in Hartford, Connecticut, in the line of
Samuel Spencer, of Cromwell, Connecticut, 1744-1818. Compiled by
Frank Farnsworth Starr for James J. Goodwin. Hartford, Conn.
(Cambridge, J. Wilson and Son), 1896. (LoC)

SPICER –
History of the descendants of Peter Spicer, a landholder in New London,
Connecticut, as early as 1666, and others of the name. With appendix
containing short accounts of allied families. Compiled by Mrs. Susan
Spicer Meech and Miss Susan Billings Meech... (Boston: F. H. Gilson
Company), c1911. (LoC)

SPICER – Meech, Susan Billings
A supplement to the descendants of Peter Spicer. Groton, Conn.: s. n.,
1923. (DAR)

SPICER – Meech, Susan Spicer
History of the descendants of Peter Spicer. S.1.: S. B. Meech, c1911.
(DAR)

SPINING – Thoesen, Edythe M. (W.)
The Spining-Spinning family of New Haven, Guilford, Conn. and
Elizabethtown, N. J. ... By Edythe M. (W.) Thoesen. Boulder, Col.
(1954). (DP)

SPINING – Thoesen, Edythe Wilson
The Spining-Spinning family of New Haven and Guilford, Connecticut,
and Elizabethtown, New Jersey. 1955? (DAR)

SPINING – Thoesen, Edythe Wilson
The Spining-Spinning family of Connecticut and New Jersey. 1962?
(DAR)

SPRAGUE – Sprague, Thomas Spencer
A Sprague family genealogy: the ancestors of Thomas Spencer Sprague,
IV, and Franklin Wiatt Sprague in America. Compiled by Thomas
Spencer Sprague, III. Hartford, Conn.: T. S. Sprague, III, 1987. (LoC)

SPRAGUE – Sprague, Thomas Spencer, III
A Sprague family genealogy, ancestors of Thomas Sprague, IV, and
Franklin Wiatt Sprague in America, also Phelps, Hubbell, and Andrews
family. Hartford, Ct., 1987. (NGS)

SQUIRE – Gardiner, Tiger
The Gardiner-Squires connection: an account of the Gardiner family of
Gardiner's Island, Long Island, New York, and the Squires family of
Squiretown, Long Island, New York and West Haven, Connecticut, their
connections and allied families – Wiggins, Miner, Beer, Wines, and
Raynor, 1559-1989. By Tiger Gardiner. Baltimore: Gateway Press, 1989.
(LoC)

ST. JOHN –
St. John of Bridgeport Biog. (1864), 10 pgs.[1]

STAFFORD – Stafford, Frederic Luther
A Stafford genealogy with index and a Stafford story. Hartford, Conn.:
Stafford, 1980. (DAR)

STAFFORD – Stafford, Frederic Luther
A Stafford genealogy; and A Stafford story. By Frederic Luther Stafford.
(Hartford, Conn.): F. L. Stafford (1980?). (LoC)

STANLEY – Warren, Israel P., D. D.
The Stanley families of America as descended from John, Timothy, and
Thomas Stanley of Hartford, Ct., 1636. Compiled by Israel P. Warren,
D. D. Portland, Me.: Printed by B. Thurston & Co., 1887. (LoC)

- First supplement... Compiled by Comdr. Emory Day Stanley, U. S. N.
  (N. p., 1924). (LoC)

- Revision to 1946 of the First supplement to the Thomas Stanley section of
  the Stanley families of America... Compiled by E. D. Stanley.
  Minneapolis, Minn., Stanley Iron Works, Inc. (1946). (LoC)

STANTON – Baldwin, John D.
Thomas Stanton of Stonington, Conn. Worcester: Tyler & Seagrave, 1882.
(DAR)

STANTON – Baldwin, John D.
Thomas Stanton of Stonington, Conn. An incomplete record of his
descendants. Prepared by John D. Baldwin of Worcester, Mass.
Worcester: Printed by Tyler & Seagrave, 1882. (LoC)

STANTON – Stanton, William A.
A record, genealogical, biographical, statistical, of Thomas Stanton of
Connecticut. Albany, N. Y.: Joel Munsell's Sons, 1891. (DAR)

STANTON – Stanton, William A., Ph.D., D. D.
A record, genealogical, biographical, statistical, of Thomas Stanton, of
Connecticut, and his descendants. 1635-1891. By William A. Stanton,
Ph.D., D. D. Albany, N. Y.: J. Munsell's Sons, 1891. (LoC)

STAPLES – Ralston, Mrs. Raymond
The ancestry of Job Staples of Canterbury, Connecticut, and Butler
County, Pennsylvania. Compiled by Mrs. Raymond H. Ralston. Slippery
Rock, Pa.: Mrs. R. H. Ralston, 1983-1988. (LoC)

STARK –
Stark Family Association – Year book. Year 1 –57. (New London, Conn.,
etc. 1895 – 1953. (LI)

STARK –
Stark family of N. H., Va., Ky., and Conn. N.p., n. d. (FW)

STARK – Stark, Charles R.
The Aaron Stark family: seven generations of the descendants of Aaron
Stark of Groton, Connecticut. By Charles R. Stark... (Boston, Wright and
Potter), 1927. (LoC)

STARKWEATHER – Starkweather, Carlton Lee
A brief genealogical history of Robert Starkweather of Roxbury and
Ipswich, Massachusetts, who was the original American ancestor of all
those bearing the name of Starkweather, and of his son John Starkweather
of Ipswich, Mass., and Preston, Conn., and of his descendants in various
lines, 1640-1898. By Carlton Lee Starkweather... (Auburn, N. Y.: Press
of Knapp, Peck & Thomson), 1904. (LoC)

STATES – States, James Noyes
Genealogy of the States family. New Haven, Conn.: States, 1913. (DAR)

STATES – States, James Noyes
Genealogy of the States family. Compiled by James Noyes States... New Haven, Conn., 1913. (LoC)

STEBBINS –
Reprint of: A genealogy of the familly of Mr. Samuel Stebbins... Hartford, Conn., 1771. (PH)

STEBBINS – Stebbins, Luke
A genealogy of the family of Mr. Samuel Stebbins and Mrs. Hannah Stebbins, his wife, from the year 1707 to the year 1771. With their names, time of their birth, marriages and deaths of those that are deceased. (By Luke Stebbins). Hartford: Printed by Ebenezer Watson, for the use of the descendants now living. 1771. (LoC)

STEBBINS – Wheeler, A. S.
An inquiry as to the heirs at law of Maria Stebbins, who died intestate, in New York, April 8th, 1875... Which is necessarily a genealogical table of the descendants of her two grandfathers Theophilus Stebbins and Robert Whitlock, both of Ridgefield, Fairfield County, Connecticut. Being a list of their descendants down to and including a living representative of each branch. Compiled by A. S. Wheeler... New York: P. Eckler, printers, 1880. (LoC)

STEELE – Barnett, Steele
The Steele family in America, a genealogical history of John and George Steele, settlers of Connecticut in 1635, and their descendants, with an appendix containing genealogical information respecting other families of the name in America... Copyright... by Steele Barnett... Tulsa, Okl., c1935. (LoC)

STEELE – Durrie, Daniel Steele
Steele family. A genealogical history of John and George Steele (settlers of Hartford, Conn.) 1635-6, and their descendants. With an appendix, containing genealogical information respecting other families of the name who settled in different parts of the United States. By Daniel Steele Durrie... Albany, N. Y.: Munsell & Rowland, 1859. (LoC)

STEEVENS – Barlow, Claude W.

John Steevens of Guilford, Connecticut, five generations of 17th and 18th century descendants with surnames Steevens, Stevens, Stephens, Kelsey... By Claude W. Barlow. Rrochester, N. J.: J. M. Stephens, 1976. (NY)

STERRETT – Sterrett, T. Woods
The Sterrett genealogy. New Haven, Conn.: Tuttle, Morehouse & Taylor Co., 1930. (DAR)

STERRETT – Sterrett, T. Woods
The Sterrett genealogy; families of Pennsylvania, Virginia, Canada & others. Compiled by T. Woods Sterrett... New Haven, Conn.: The Tuttle, Morehouse & Taylor Company, 1930. (LoC)

STETSON –
Stetson kindred of America incorporated. (New Haven) Priv. print. (Yale University Press), 1932. (LoC)

STETSON – Wilson, Kate De Normandie
Dolly Witter Stetson, a sketch of her life (with genealogical charts). By Kate De Normandie Wilson. (Brooklyn, Conn.), 1907. (LI)

STEVENS –
Record of the Stevens family presented to Charles Tracy Stevens and Emeline N. Upson, by Oliver Stevens. 1844. Meriden, Conn.: Reprinted, H. W. Lines, 1893. (LoC)

STEVENS –
A genealogy of the lineal dscendants of John Steevens, who settled in Guilford, Conn., in 1645. Compiled by Charlotte Steevens Holmes, 1906. Edited by Clay W. Holes, (sic) A. M., Elmira, N. Y. (Elmira, Advertiser Press, 1906). (LoC)

STEVENS – Barlow, Claude W.
John Steevens of Guilford, Connecticut, five generations of 17th and 18th century descendants with surnames Steevens, Stevens, Stephens, Kelsey... By Claude W. Barlow. Rochester, N. Y.: J. M. Stephens, 1976. (FW)

STEVENS – Barlow, Claude W.
John Steevens of Guilford, Connecticut: five generations of the 17th and 18th century descendants with surnames Steevens, Stevens, Stephens, Kelsey... By Claude Willis Barlow. Rochester, N. Y.: J. M. Stephens, c1976. (LoC)

STEVENS – Hill, Frank A.

To the descendants of Robert and Mary Stevens of Canterbury, Conn.,
1881. (By Frank A. Hill) (New York, 1881). (LI)

STEVENS – Stephens, Clarence Perry
The Stevens genealogy and family history: Richard of Taunton, Mass.,
Henry of Stonington, Conn., and their descendants in N. C., Ind., and
N. Y., including some named Stephens. By Clarence Perry Stephens.
Escalon, Calilf., c1950. (LoC)

STEVENS – Stevens, Nathaniel B.
Ancestral genealogical record and history of the Stevens family of Norfolk,
Conn. Winsted, Conn.: Stevens, 1896. (DAR)

STEVENS – Stevens, Nathaniel B.
Ancestral genealogical record and history of the Stevens family of Norfolk,
Conn. By Nathaniel B. Stevens. Winsted. Conn., 1896. (LoC)

STEVENS – Stevens, Oliver
Record of Stevens family, presented to Charles Tracy Stevens and Emeline
M. Upson. By Oliver Stevens. Meriden, Conn.: H. W. Lines, 1893. (FW)

STEVENS – Stevens, Plowdon
Stephens-Stevens genealogy, lineage from Henry Stephens or Stevens of
Stonington, Connecticut, 1668. By Plowdon Stevens. New York: Frank
Allaben Genealogical Company, 1909. (LoC)

STEVENS – Stevens, Casimir P.
Stevens family of Fairfield County, Conn.; descendants of Thomas and
Ann (--) Stevens of Stamford-Darien, 1649-1658. By Casimir P. Stevens.
(Shawnee, Okla.), 1921. (FW)

STEVENS – Whitcomb, Susannah Stevens
Descendants of John Stevens of Stamford, Conn. Corning, N. Y.:
Whitcomb, 1973. (DAR)

STILES – Stiles, Henry R.
Connecticut family of Stiles. By Henry R. Stiles. (New York: Norton,
1859). (FW)

STILES – Stiles, Henry Reed
The Stiles family in America. Genealogies of the Connecticut family.
Descendants of John Stiles, of Windsor, Conn., and of Mr. Francis Stiles,
of Windsor and Stratford, Conn., 1635-1894; also the Connecticut-New
Jersey families, 1720-1894; and the southern (or Bermuda-Georgia)

family, 1635-1894. With contributions to the genealogies of some New
York and Pennsylvania families... By Henry Reed Stiles... Jersey City:
Doan & Pilson, Printers, 1895. (LoC)

STILLMAN – Stillman, Francis D. (Francis Duane)
The Stillman family: descendants of Mr. George Stillman of Wethersfield,
Connecticut and Dr. George Stillman of Westerly, Rhode Island.
Compiled by Francis D. Stillman, Jr. [Greensburg, Pa.]: F. D. Stillman,
1989. (LoC)

STIMSON – Boyd, George A.
Three Stimsons and a Bartlett. By George A. Boyd. Stonington, Conn.:
Priv. print, Pequot Press, 1967. (NY)

STODDARD –
Stoddard Family of N. London (1872), 36 pgs.[1]
Stoddard of Woodbury, Connecticut (1893), 86 pgs.[1]

STODDARD – Deacon, Edward
Some of the ancestors of Rodman Stoddard, of Woodbury, Conn., and
Detroit, Mich. A compilation by Edward Deacon... Bridgeport, Conn.:
Press of Stiles & Tucker, 1893. (LoC)

STODDARD – Patterson, D. Williams
John Stoddard of Wethersfield, Conn., and his descendants. 1642-1872. A
genealogy. By D. Williams Patterson... Author's ed. (Newark Valley?
N. Y.) 1873. (LoC)

STODDARD – Stoddard, Rev. E. W.
Ralph Stoddard, of New London and Groton, Ct., and his descendants: a
genealogy. Compiled by Rev. E. W. Stoddard... New York: Press of
Poole & Maclauchlan, 1872. (LoC)

STONE –
Stone of Guilford, Vol. 2 (1898), 349 pgs.[1]

STONE –
Stone Family of Guilford (1888), 192 pgs.[1]
Stone Family of Watertown (1892), 78 pgs,[1]
Stone Family of Watertown (1899), 8 pgs.[1]

STONE –
Proceedings of the tenth annual reunion of The Stone Family Assoc. at
Guilford, Conn., 1896. N. p. (1896). (LI)

STONE –
Ancestors and descendants of Anson Parmilee Stone; descended from John Stone of Guilford, Conn. By Christine Rose and Seymour T. Rose. San Jose, Calif., 1963. (FW)

STONE – Handrick, G. Richard
Descendants of Canfield Stone of New Preston, Conn. Lexington, Mass.: Handrick, 1970. (DAR)

STONE – Handrick, George R.
Descendants of Canfield Stone of New Preston, Conn. By George R. Handrick. (Lexington, Mass.), 1970. (FW)

STONE – Stone, Edward P.
The family of William Stone, one of the first settlers of Guilford, Connecticut, 1639. Baltimore, Md.: Gateway Press, 1980. (DAR)

STONE – Stone, Edward P.
The family of William Stone, one of the first settlers of Guilford, Connecticut, 1639. By Edward Perry Stone, Sr. Baltimore, Md.: Gateway Press; Cortland, N. Y. 1980. (LoC)

STONE – Stone, Truman Lewis
Book II of the family of John Stone, one of the first settlers of Guilford, Conn. Buffalo, N. Y.: Charles Wells Moulton, 1898. (DAR)

STONE – Stone, Truman Lewis
Book II. of the family of John Stone, one of the first settlers of Guilford, Conn.; also, names of all the descendants of Russell, Bille, Timothy and Eber Stone. By Truman Lewis Stone. 1639... 1897. Buffalo, N. Y.: C. W. Moulton, 1898. (LoC)

STONE – Stone, William L.
The family of John Stone, one of the first settlers of Guilford, Conn. Albany: Joel Munsell's Sons, 1888. (DAR)

STONE – Stone, William L.
The family of John Stone, one of the first settlers of Guilford, Conn. By William L. Stone... Albany: J. Munselll's Sons, 1888. (LoC)

STOWE – Stowe, Nathan
Ancestry and some of the descendants of Capt. Stephen Stowe of Milford, Conn. New York, N. Y., 1924. (NGS)

STOWE – Stowe, Nathan
Ancestry and some of the descendants of Capt. Stephen Stowe of Milford,
Conn. S.1.:s..n., 1924. (DAR)

STOWE – Stowe, Nathan
Ancestry and some of the descendants of Capt. Stephen Stowe of Milford,
Conn. Collected by Nathan Stowe. (Milford: the Lyon Printer) 1924.
(LoC)

STOWE. See also:

	Adams	Ranney
	Chaffee, 1911	Skinner, 1935
	Chaffee, 1952	Sullens, 1942

STROUD – Lowell, Harriet D.
The Stroud family history; descendants of Captain Richard Stroud of New
London, Connecticut. By Harriet D. Lowell. Rutland, Vt.: The Tuttle
Company, 1934. (LoC)

STUART – Hamel, Claude Charles
Genealogy of John Stewart, brother of Walter Stewart, of Londonderry, N.
H., Boxford, Hopkinton, and Blandford, Mass., and Suffield, Conn. By
Claude Charles Hamel. Amherst, Ohio, 1951. (LoC)

STUDWELL –
Studwell family of Fairfield County, Connecticut. (Stamford? Conn.),
1899. (LoC)

STUDWELL –
Studwell family of Fairfield County, Connecticut. S.1.:s.n., 1899. (DAR)

STUDWELL – Andrews, Julia Isabelle Studwell
Studwell family of Fairfield County, Connecticut, 1640. Andrews family
of Bartholomew County, Indiana, 1834. By Julia Isabelle Studwell
Andrews. (Fort Wayne, 1967). (LoC)

STURGES – Whitmore, Harriet E. Goulden
A memorial of the kindred and ancestry of Harriet L. Sturges Gouldon.
Hartford: Whitmore, 1899. (DAR)

STURGES – Whitmore, Harriet E. Goulden
A memorail of the kindred and ancestry of Harriet L. Sturges Goulden, of
Fairfield, Conn. By Harriet E. Goulden Whitmore. (Hartford) 1899,
Plimpton Print. (FW)

SUTCLIFFE – Sutliffe, Bennett Hurd
A genealogy of the Sutcliffe-Sutliffe family in America from before 1661 to 1903. Hartford, Conn. ... R. S. Peck & Co., 1903? (DAR)

SUTHERLAND – Sutherland, Clyde F. (Clyde Foster)
A Sutherland genealogy: starting with William Sutherland of Greenwich, Fairfield Co., Conn., and Bangall, Dutchess Co., N. Y., through Manchester, Vt., Palatine, Ill., and west, spanning 11 generations to 1981. (Sandy, Or.) (C. F. Sutherland, 1981). (LoC)

SUTLIFF – Sutliffe, Bennett Hurd
A genealogy of the Sutcliffe-Sutliffe family in America from before 1661 to 1903. the descendants of Nathaniel Sutcliffe, with a brief account of their English ancestry back to 1500... also the ancestry of families related by intermarriage. By Bennett Hurd Sutliffe... Hartford, Conn.: R. S. Peck & Co., printers and engravers (1903?). (LoC)

SWEETLAND –
The descendants of Aaron and Patience Sweetland of Hebron, Conn. (Denver, col., 1890). (LoC)

T

TABER – Wright, Anna (A.)
Descendants of Joseph and Philip, sons of Philip Taber from Rhode Island, Connecticut and Long Island; with notes on their sister, Lydia Tabor (sic) Tillinghast. By Anna (A.) Wright. Ithaca, N. Y., 1952-57. (NY)

TAFT – Ross, Ishbel
An American family: the Tafts, 1678 to 1964. Ishbel Ross. Westport, Conn.: Greenwood Press, 1977, c1964. (LoC)

TAINTOR –
Taintor Family of Fairfield, Connecticut (1847), 82 pgs.[1]

TAINTOR – Taintor, Starr
Genealogy of the Taintor family of Connecticut, descendants of Charles Taintor of Wethersfield and Fairfield, Conn. By Starr Taintor. (Chicago, 1949). (FW)

TALCOTT – Talcott, Sebastian V.
Manuscript letter to Samuel G. Drake, giving genealogical information from the gravestones and monuments in Wethersfield and Glastonbury,

Conn., and Springfield, Mass. relating chiefly to the Wright, Goodrich and Talcott families. By Sebastian V. Talcott. N.p.:n.d. (FW)

TANNER – Tanner, Elias F.
The genealogy of the descendants of Thomas Tanner, Sr., of Cornwall, Connecticut, with brief notes of several allied families; also short sketches of several towns of their early residence. A Columbian memorial, by Rev. Elias F. Tanner... Lansing, Mich.: D. D. Thorp, Printer, 1893. (LoC)

TAYLOR – Meins, Alice J.
Poems and writings of Henry Wyllys Taylor of Hartford. Compiled and arranged by Alice J. Meins... Hartford, Conn.: Press of the Case, Lockwood & Brainard Company, 1895. (LoC)

TAYLOR – Pollock, Edwin Taylor
Descendants of John Taylor of Windsor, Connecticut. 1928. (DAR)

TEEPLE – Lewis, Alonzo N.
Celebration of the one hundredth birthday of Mrs. Orphany Teeple, at Woodbury, Conn., 1872. By Alonzo N. Lewis. New Haven, 1872. (LI)

TERRY – Steen, Marguerite
A pride of Terrys: family saga. By Marguerite Steen. Westport, Conn.: Greenwood Press, 1978, c1962. (LoC)

TERRY – Terry, Stephen
Notes of Terry families in the United States of America. Hartford, Conn.: Terry, 1887. (DAR)

TERRY – Terry, Stephen
Notes of Terry families, in the United States of America, mainly descended from Samuel, of Springfield, Mass., including also some descended from Stephen, of Windsor, Conn., Thomas, of Freetown, Mass., and others. By Stephen Terry... Hartford, Conn.: The compiler, 1887. (LoC)

THAYER – Thayer, Geo. Burton
Ancestors of Adelbert P.Thayer, Florine Thayer McCray and Geo. Burton Thayer, children of John W. Thayer and Adaline Burton. Compiled by Geo. Burton Thayer. Also, reminiscences of a Christmas eve at Windermere and some early events in the life of the writer... Hartford, Conn.: Press of the Plimpton Mfg. Co., 1894. (LoC)

THOMPSON –
Memorials of the families of Mr. James Thompson and of Dea. Augustus Thompson, of Goshen, Connecticut. Hartford: Press of Case, Tiffany and Company, 1854. (LoC)

THOMPSON – Amy, Henry J.
Descendants of John and Dorothy Thompson of East Haven, Conn.; seven generations of Thompsons descended from John Thompson... who died East Haven, 1655. By Henry J. Amy. Eastchester, N. Y., 1958. (NY)

THOMPSON – Amy, Henry J.
Anthony, William and John Thompson of New Haven, Conn.; being a record of seven generations of descendants of Anthony Thompson, some of whom migrated to Dutchess Co., N. Y. By Henry J. Amy. Eastchester, N. Y., 1960. (NY)

THOMPSON – Elliott, Mary A.
Thompson genealogy, the descendants of William and Margaret Thomson, first settled in that part of Windsor, Connecticut, now East Windsor and Ellington. 1720-1915, including many of the names of Chandler, Trumbull, Marsh, Pelton, Allen, Harper, Osborn, Hooker, Ellsworth, Stiles, Phelps, Bartlett, etc. Compiled by Mary A. Elliott. (New Haven, Conn.), The Thompson Family Association (1915?). (LoC)

THOMPSON – Lainson, D. A. S.
John, William, and Anthony Thompson and relatives of New Haven, Conn., 1637 and some of their descendants. By D. A. S. Lainson. Huntsville, Ark.: Century Enterprises, 1971. (FW)

TIBBALS – Barber, Gertrude A.
Tibbals family of New York State (and Connecticut). By Gertrude A. Barber. N. p., 1966. (NY)

TIFFANY – Wright, Ella F.
Genealogical sketches of the Tiffany family. Waterbury, Conn.: Mattatuck Press, 1904. (DAR)

TIFFANY – Wright, Ella F.
Genealogical sketch of the Tiffany family, as collected and arranged by Ella F. Wright. Waterbury, Conn. Mattatuck Press, The Waterbury Blank Book Mfg. Co., 1904. (LoC)

TILLEY – Tilley, Milton Popple

Progeny and ancestry of Milton Popple Tilley of New Canaan,
Connecticut. S.1.: s.n., 1955. (DAR)

TILLEY – Tilley, Milton Popple
Progeny and ancestry of Milton Popple Tilley of New Canaan,
Connecticut. By Milton Popple Tilley. (New Canaan? 1955). (LoC)

TILSON – Tilson, John Q.
The Tilson family. New Haven, Conn.: Tilson, 1954. (DAR)

TILSON – Tilson, John Q.
Tilson family; being a brief history of the family of William Erwin Tilson
and Katherine Sams Tilson... By John Q. Tilson. New Haven, Conn.,
1954. (FW)

TOMLINSON – Orcutt, Rev. Samuel
Henry Tomlinson, and his descendants in America, with a few additional
branches of Tomlinson, later from England. By Rev. Samuel Orcutt...
New Haven, Conn.: Press of Price, Lee and Adkins Co., 1891. (LoC)

TOMPKINS – Walker, Grace Tompkins
Travels in search of an ancestor. Fairfield, Conn.: s. n., 1975. (DAR)

TOWNER – Towner, James W.
A genealogy of the Towner family, the descendants of Richard Towner,
who came from Sussex County, Eng., to Guilford, Conn. before 1685...
By James W. Towner... Los Angeles, Cal.: Times-Mirror Printing and
Binding House (1910?). (LoC)

TOWNSEND – Townshend, Doris B.
Townshend heritage; a genealogical, biographical history of the
Townshend family and of their old homestead on the east shore of New
Haven harbor. By Doris B. Townnshend. New Haven, New Haven
Colony Historical Society, 1971. (LoC)

TOWNSHEND – Townshend, Charles Hervey
The Townshend family. Mew Haven, Conn.: Tuttle, Morehouse & Taylor
Printer, 1882. (DAR)

TRACY – Abbey, Matilda O.
Genealogy of the family of Lt. Thomas Tracy, of Norwich, Conn.
Milwaukee: D. S. Harkness & Co., 1888. (DAR)

TRACY – Dickson, Tracy Campbell
Some of the descendants of Lieutenant Thomas Tracy of Norwich, Connecticut. S.1.: Dickson: B. Abbott Dickson, c1936. (DAR)

TRACY – Dickson, Tracy Campbell
Some of the descendants of Lieutenant Thomas Tracy of Norwich, Connecticut. Compiled by Tracy Campbell Dickson... (Philadelphia: Printed by the John C. Winston Company, c1936). (LoC)

TRACY – Ripley, Charles Stedman
The ancestors of Lieutenant Thomas Tracy of Norwich, Connecticut. Boston: Alfred Mudge & Son, 1895. (DAR)

TRACY – Ripley, Lieutenant Charles Stedman
The ancestors of Lieutenant Thomas Tracy of Norwich, Connecticut. By Lieutenant Charles Stedman Ripley... Boston: A. Mudge & Son, Printers, 1895. (LoC)

TRACY – Tracy, Everet E.
Tracy genealogy. Ancestors and descendants of Lieutenant Thomas Tracy of Norwich, Conn. 1660. Compiled by Everet E. Tracy... Albany, N. Y.: J. Munsell's Sons, 1898. (LoC)

TRACY – Tracy, Dwight
Leiutenant Thomas Tracy and "The widow Mason" of Wethersfield, Connecticut, and Edward Mason's Wethersfield record, by Dwight Tracy... Boston, 1907. (LoC)

TRACY – Tracy, Dwight
Recently discovered English ancestry of Governor William Tracy of Virginia, 1620, and of his only son, Lieutenant Thomas Tracy of Salem, Massachusetts, and Norwich, Connecticut. By Dwight Tracy... New Haven, Conn.: The Journal of America History, 1908. (LoC)

TREMAN –
The history of the Treman, Tremaine, Truman family in America; with the related families of Mack, Dey, Board, and Ayers; being a history of Joseph Truman of New London, Conn. (1666); John Mack of Lyme, Conn. (1680); Richard Dey of New York City (1641); Cornelius Board of Boardville, N. J. (1730); John Ayer of Newbury, Mass. (1635); and their descendants. By Ebenezer Mack Treman and Murray E. Poole... (Ithaca, N. Y.): Press of the Ithaca Democrat, 1901. (LoC)

TREVETT – Sinclair, Jacqueline M.

Captain John Trevett. Greenwich, Conn.: John C. Sinclair: J. M. Sinclair, 1969. (DAR)

TRIPP –
Tripp-Wilcox and allied families: genealogical, biographical. Hartford, Conn.: States Historical Co., for author, 1943. (FW)

TROWBRIDGE –
Trowbridge Family, N. Haven (1872), 461 pgs.[1]

TROWBRIDGE – Chapman, F. W.
The Trowbridge family. New Haven: Punderson, Crisand & Co., 1872. (DAR)

TROWBRIDGE – Chapman, Rev. F. W.
The Trowbridge family; or, The descendants of Thomas Trowbridge, one of the first settlers of New Haven, Conn. Compiled at the request of Thomas Rutheford Trowbridge, of New Haven, Conn., by Rev. F. W. Chapman... New Haven: Punderson, Chrisand & Co., Printers, 1872. (LoC)

TROWBRIDGE – Trowbridge, Francis Bacon
The Trowbridge genealogy. New Haven: Tuttle, Morehouse & Taylor, 1908. (DAR)

TROWBRIDGE – Trowbridge, Francis Bacon
The Trowbridge genealogy. History of the Trowbridge family in America. By Francis Bacon Trowbridge... New Haven, Conn.: Printed for the compiler (Press of the Tuttle, Morehouse & Taylor Company), 1908. (LoC)

TRUBEE – Garlick, Harriet Trubee
...History of the Trubee family. By Harriet Trubee Garlick. Bridgeport, Conn.: the Marigold Printing Company, 1894. (LoC)

TUBBS – Tubbs, Charles M.
Tubbs ancestral notes: a genealogy traced from William Tubbs of Duxbury, Mass., through Isaac Tubbs of Lyme, Conn., with the descendants of Alvan Tubbs of Hanover, N. H. By Charles M. Tubbs. Bath, Me., 1957? (FW)

TULL – Tull, James Porter
John Porter Tull and his descendants, 1796-1942. Hartford, Ct., 1942. (NGS)

196

TULL – Tull, James Porter
A biographical sketch of the life of John Porter Tull and his descendants, 1769-1942. Hartford, Conn.: Morton B. Hadlock, 1942. (DAR)

TUPPER – Gundry, Eldon P.
John Tupper, his ancestors and descendants. This is the John Tupper who was born in Middlesex County, Conn., 1776... By Eldon P. Gundry. Flint, Mich., 1960. (NY)

TURNER –
Turner Family of N. Haven (1894), 4 pgs.[1]

TURNEY –
The ancestry of Benjamin Turney of Concord, Mass., and Fairfield, Conn. S.1.: s.n., 1936. (DAR)

TUTTLE –
Tuttle Family of N. Haven (1873), 22 pgs.[1]
Tuttle Family of N. Haven (1883), 814 pgs.[1]

TUTTLE – Tuttle, Joseph F.
1635. William Tuttle of New Haven: an address delivered at the Tuttle gathering, New Haven, Conn., September 3d, 1873. By Joseph F. Tuttle... Newark, N. J.: Printed at the office of the Daily Advertiser, 1873. (LoC)

TUTTLE – Tuttle, George Frederick
The descendants of William and Elizabeth Tuttle, who came from old to New England in 1635, and settled in New Haven in 1639, with numerous biographical notes and sketches; also, some account of the descendants of John Tuttle of Dover, N. H.; Richard Tuttle, of Boston; John Tuttle of Ipswich; and Henry Tuthill, of Hingham, Mass. ...By George Frederick Tuttle... Rutland, Vt.: Tuttle & Company, 1883. (LoC)

TYLER –
Daniel Tyler: a memorial volume containing his autobiography and war record, some account of his later years, with various reminiscences and the tribute of friends. New Haven, Priv. print., 1883. (LoC)

TYLER – Lawton, Frederick Tyler
Tyler families of early Branford, Connecticut; lineage of Joel Ford Tyler (1802-1878) of North Haven, Conn., and Oswego, New York. By Frederick Tyler Lawton. Jamaica, N. Y., 1951. (LoC)

TYLER. See also:

Castle, 1922	Hunter, 1934
Crooke, 1942	James, 1912
Henshaw, 1894	Stansbury, 1933
Hildreth	Ungrich

U

UNDERHILL –
Bulletin of the Underhill Society of America Education and Publishing Fund. Greenwich, Conn.: The Society, 1967. (DAR)

UPSON –
Upson Association of America (Directory) 1935. (Southington, Conn.), 1935. (FW)

UPSON –
The Upson family in America. Compiled by the Upson Family Association of America. New Haven, Conn.: The Tuttle, Morehouse & Taylor Company, 1940. (LoC)

UPSON – Upson Family Association of America
The Upson Family in America. New Haven, Conn.: Tuttle, Morehouse & Taylor Co., 1940. (DAR)

V

VAN ANDEN – Prindle, Paul Wesley
Van Anden family. By Paul Wesley Prindle. (Darien, Conn., 1951). (LoC)

VANDERBILT – Burden, Shirley
The Vanderbilts in my life: a personal memoir. By Shirley Burden. New Haven, Conn.: Ticknor & Fields, 1981. (LoC)

VAN DUZEE – Van Duzee, Frederic P.
A genealogy of the Van Duzee family. Also Van Deurzen and Van Deuzen families. Hartford, Ct., 1964. (NGS)

VAN DUZEE – Van Duzee, Frederic P.
A genealogy of the Van Duzee family. By Frederic P. Van Duzee. (West Hartford, Conn.): Chedwato Service, 1964. (NY)

VANHOOSEAR – Van Hoosear, David Hermon
A complete genealogy of the Van Hoosear family. Wilton, Conn.: Van Hoosear, 1902. (DAR)

VAN HOOSEAR – Van Hoosear, David Hermon
A complete genealogy of the Van Hoosear family embracing all descendants of Rinear Van Hoosear, an officer in the revolutionary army, and a resident of Norwalk, Weston, Conn., Ballston, N., Y.; and Wilton, Conn. By David Hermon Van Hoosear... Norwalk, Conn.: Printed for the author, 1902. (LoC)

VAN VALKENBURGH – Van Valkenburgh, Franklin B.
"Grandpapa's letter," to his children; being the story of a boy's life in a country village from 1835 to 1847... tog. with notes of interest to the family. By Franklin B. Van Valkenburgh. (Branford, Conn.), 1958. (NY)

VAN VALKKENBURGH – Van Valkenburgh, Franklin Butler
Grandpapa's letter to his children/from Franklin Butler Van Valkenburgh; additional material compiled and edited by Charles H. Vilas. 2nd Ed. (Bradford, Conn.): Vilas, 1978. (LoC)

VAN WYCK – Hijmans, Hendrick
Wijk bij Duurstede. By Hendrick Hijmans. English translation (prepared by Mrs. G. R. Peereboom-Chambers... Wilton, Conn., priv. print., 1961). (NY)

VARS – Vars, Nelson Byron
The genealogical history of the Vars family in America. New London, Conn.: Harold A. Vars, 1976. (DAR)

VIBBER – Vibber, Ruth Williams Staples
A rough outline of the Vibber family of Montville, Connecticut, from 1711 to the present day, designed for the second phase. (Ruth Williams Staples Vibber, John R. Vibber; editor, Pat Vibert). [S.1:s.n.], 1976. (LOC)

VIENS – Dare, Norma Thornley
The Viens family. By Norma Thornley Dare. (West Haven? Conn., 1968). (LoC)

VIETS – Viets, Francis H.
Viets family. Dr. John Viets of Simsbury, Connecticut (1710) and his descendants. By Francis H. Viets... Providence: E. A. Johnson & Co., printers, 1879. (LoC)

VIETS – Viets, Francis Hubbard
A genealogy of the Viets family. Hartford, Conn.? Hartford Press, Case, Lockwood & Brainard, 1902. (DAR)

VIETZ – Viets, Francis Hubbard
The genealogy of the Vietz family with biographical sketches; Dr. John Viets of Simsbury, Connecticut, 1710, and his descendants. Written and compiled by Francis Hubbard Viets. (Hartford): The Case, Lockwood & Brainard Co., 1902. (LoC)

W

WADE – Newsom, E. Earl
Sergeant Wade's letters, 1863-1865. Salisbury, Ct., 1968. (NGS)

WADSWORTH – Day, Thomas
A historical discourse, delivered before the Connecticut Historical Soc. ... (with genealogy). By Thomas Day. Hartford, 1844. (LI)

WAKEMAN – Wakeman, Robert P.
Wakeman genealogy, 1630-1899. Meriden, Conn.: Journal Pub. Co., 1900. (DAR)

WAKEMAN – Wakeman, Robert P.
Wakeman genealogy. 1630-1899. Being a history of the descendants of Samuel Wakeman, of Hartford, Conn., and of John Wakeman, treasurer of New Haven colony, with a few collaterals included. By Robert P. Wakeman. Meriden, Conn.: Journal Publishing Co., 1900. (LoC)

WALDO – Hall, Joseph D.
The genealogy and biography of the Waldos of America. Danielsonville, Conn.: Press of Scoville & Hamilton, 1883. (DAR)

WALDRON –
Genealogy of Frederick H. Waldron, from the time of the settlement of New Amsterdam (New York) through the Waldrons, Whitneys and Riggses. New Haven, Conn.: Tuttle, 1909. (FW)

WALBRIDGE – Wallbridge, William Gidney
Descendants of Henry Wallbridge, who married Anna Amos, December 25th, 1688, at Preston, Conn., with some notes on the allied families of Brush, Fassett, Dewey, Fobes, Gager, Lehman, Meech, Stafford, Scott,

Compiled by William Gedney Wallbridge... (Philadelphia: Press of
Franklin Printing Company, 1898). (LoC)

WALKER – Elston, James Strode
George Walker. West Hartford, Conn.: Elston, 1952. (DAR)

WALKER – Paine, Gustavus Swift
Walker wives. By Gustavus Swift Paine. Southbury, Conn., 1946. (LoC)

WALKLEY – Walkley, Stephen
Genealogical index of some descendants of Richard Walkley of Haddam.
Compiled by Stephen Walkley. Plantsville, Conn. (1911?). (LoC)

WANZER – Brincherhoff, Mrs. H. Winship
Record of research. Wanzer family of Connecticut. 19--? (DAR)

WARNER – Warner, Andrew F.
One of the Warner family in America. Compiled by Andrew F. Warner.
Hartford, Conn.: Printed for J. J. Warner by Case, Lockwood & Brainard
Co., 1892. (LoC)

WARNER – Warner, James Alfred
History of John Warner of 'Increase', 1635. Hartford, Connecticut. 1950.
(DAR)

WARNER – Sandiford, Edward R.
Some more descendants of John Warner, the immigrant, of Farmington,
Conn., through Daniel Warner... By Edward R. Sandiford. (Bloomfield,
N. J., 1956). (MH)

WARNER – Strong, Doris Wolcott
Ancestry and descendants of Justus Warner, 1756-1856, one of the first
group of settlers in 1811 to Liverpool (now Valley City) Medina County,
Ohio, in the "Connecticut western reserve." Edited and compiled by Doris
Wolcott Strong... Washington, D.C. (1941). (LoC)

WARNER – Warner, Lucien C.
The descendants of Andrew Warner. New Haven, Conn.: Tuttle,
Morehouse & Taylor, 1919. (DAR)

WARNER – Warner, Lucien C.
The descendants of Andrew Warner, compiled by Lucien C. Warner... and
Mrs. Josephine Genung Nichols. New Haven, Conn.: The Tuttle,
Morehouse & Taylor Co., 1919. (LoC)

WARREN – Warren, Pickett
Warren genealogy (descendants of Jabez Warren of Lebanon, Ct. and Brimfield, Mass). By Pickett Warren. N. p.: n. d. (FW)

WASHBURN – Sharpe, W. C.
The Washburn family. Descendants of John of Plymouth, Mass., and William of Stratford, Conn., and Hempstead, L. I. Compiled by W. C. Sharpe... Seymour, Conn.: Record Print, 1892. (LoC)

WASHINGTON –
Sulgrave Manor... Read at a meeting of Colonial dames in New Haven, Connecticut... December 5, 1923, by Mrs. Wm. H. Smith. Hartford, Conn., 1924. (LoC)

WATERHOUSE – Waterhouse, George Herbert
Descendants of Richard Waterhouse of Portsmouth, N. H., with notes on the descendants of Jacob Waterhouse of New London, Conn., Joshua Waterhouse of New Jersey and others. Also a sketch of the Waterhouse family in England. Compiled by George Herbert Waterhouse... (Wakefield, Mass., 1934). (LoC)

WATERMAN – Jacobus, Donald Lines
The Waterman family. New Haven, Conn.: Waterman, 1939, 1942, 1954. (DAR)

WATERMAN – Jacobus, Donald Lines
The Waterman family. By Donald Lines Jacobus. New Haven: E. F. Waterman, 1939-54. (LoC)

WATERMAN – Waterman, Charles E.
The Maine Watermans, with an account of their ancestors in Massachusetts, Rhode Island and Connecticut. By Charles E. Waterman... Mechanic Falls, Me.: Ledger Publishing Company, 1906. (LoC)

WATERS – Jenkins, Philomene
David Waters and Consider Law of Lebanon and Hebron, Conn., and Oneida Co., N. Y., their ancestors and some descendants. (By Philomene Jenkins). Lincoln, Neb., 1929. (LI)

WATSON –
Watson Family of Hartford (1865), 47 pgs.[1]

WATSON –
Additions and corrections to: John Watson of Hartford, by Thomas
Watson, 1865. West Winstead, Conn., 1866. (LI)

WATSON – Watson, Joseph M.
A history and some biographies of the following families: Watson,
Pendell, Curry, Bliss, Hazard, Bogardus. Madison, Conn.: Watson, 1969.
(DAR)

WATSON – Watson, Thomas
John Watson, of Hartford, Conn., and his descendants. A genealogy, by
Thomas Watson. New York: Printed for the U. Q. Club, 1865. (LoC)

WAUGH –
Waugh family of Litchfield, Conn., Ross County, Ohio, Henry County,
Missouri. Lapeer, Mich.: J. Dee Ellis, 1969. (FW)

WAUGH – Waugh, Patricia Lee Russ
A Waugh family history: John of Litchfield, Connecticut, Milo and
Elizabeth (Kious) Waugh of Ohio and Indiana: allied lines of Bowers,
Bucher, Hamilton, Hopkins, Kious, Minor & Ward. Compiled by Patricia
Lee (Russ) Waugh. Kansas City, Kan.: P. L. Russ Waugh, c1986. (LoC)

WEBB – Greene, R. H.
William Webb September 19, 1746-September 23, 1832 – his war service
from Long Island and Connecticut – ancestry and descendants. New York:
Greene, 1914. (DAR)

WEBB – Greene, Capt. R. H.
William Webb, September 19, 1746 – September 23, 1832; his war service
from Long Island and Connecticut, ancestry and descendants. (by) Capt.
R. H. Greene... New York (Press of J. C. Hassel) 1914. (LoC)

WEBSTER –
Webster Family of Connecticut (1836), 8 pgs.[1]
Webster Family of Connecticut (1879), 9 pgs.[1]

WEBSTER – Webster, J. C.
Memorial poems and brief ancestral record of the Webster family and
descendants. Hartford, Conn.: Hartford Printing Co., 1904. (DAR)

WEBSTER – Webster, J. C.

Memorial poems and brief ancestral record of the Webster family and
descendants. By J. C. Webster. Hartford, Conn. (Press of the Hartford
Printing co.), 1904. (LoC)

WEBSTER – Webster, William Holcomb
History and genealogy of the Gov. John Webster family of Connecticut.
Rochester, N. Y.: E. R. Andrews Printing Co., 1915. (DAR)

WEED – McSweeney, Henry
Weed family of Stamford and Greenwich, Conn. By Henry McSweeney.
N. p., 1934. (FW)

WEIDNER – Ayres, Thomas D.
Weidner genealogy: some of the descendants of Wilhelm Johann Georg
Weidner of Ammertsweiler, Germany. Thomas D. Ayres. Simsbury, Ct.:
T. D. Ayres, 1990. (LoC)

WELD – Fowler, Mrs. Charlotte Weld
History of the Weld family, from 1632 to 1878. Written by Mrs. Charlotte
Weld Fowler, at the advanced age of 86. Middletown, Conn.: Pelton &
King, Printers, 1879. (LoC)

WELLES – Welles, Theodore W.
Ancestral tablets from Colonial days to the present era. A record of the
descendants of Gov. Thomas Welles of Connecticut, Capt. Gerrit Janes
Hardenbergh of New York, Fiscaal Hendrick Van Dyck of New
Amsterdam, Jan Tysse Goes of Beaverwyck... By Theodore W. Welles.
Paterson, N. J.: The Press Print. and Pub. Co., 1893. (MH)

WELLS –
Wells Family of Hartford (1848), 27 pgs.[1]

WELLS –
Welles Family Association Bulletin. 1939, 1940, 1942, 1952.
Wethersfield, Conn., 1939-52. (MH)

WELLS –
History of the Welles family in England; with their derivation in this
country from Governor Thomas Welles, of Connecticut. By Albert
Welles... (Assisted by H. H. Clements, Esq.). With an account of the
Welles family in Massachusetts, by Henry Winthrop Sargent... Boston:
Press of J. Wilson and Son, 1874. (LoC)

WELLS –
List of ancestors and descendants of John Howell Welles, of Gilead Parish, town of Hebron, County of Tollard, and state of Connecticut, grandson of Thomas Wells, the emigrant of Dudley, Worcestershire, England, who landed in Saybrook, Conn. in 1712. (Washington, D. C., 1898). (LoC)

WELLS – Reynolds, Gwen Fuller
A Welles genealogy: ancestors and descendants of Francis Raymond Welles and his wife Anna Frances Thomas: one line of descent from Governor Thomas Welles of Connecticut: allied families include many in New England and in Pennsylvania, Hollenback, Page, and Thomas. Compiled by Gwen Fuller Reynolds. Berkeley, Calif.: Merryall Manse Books, 1983. (LoC)

WELLS – Welles, Edwin Stanley
The life and public service of Thomas Welles, fourth governor of Connecticut. By Edwin Stanley Welles. A paper read at the fourth annual meeting of the Welles Family Association, South Coventry, Connecticut, Saturday, June 8, 1940. Wethersfield, Conn.: The Welles Family Association, 1940. (LoC)

WELLS – Wells, Heber
A limited genealogy of the Wells family of the Colchester, Conn. branch. By Heber Wells. (Malden, Mass., 1923). (NY)

WELLS – Welles, Lemuel A.
The English ancestry of Gov. Thomas Welles of Connecticut. By Lemuel A. Welles... Boston, 1926.

WELLS – Wells, John W.
Wells genealogies. An enumeration of the descendants of Nathaniel Wells and Mary Dudley. By John W. Wells. Waterbury, Conn., 1890. (PH)

WELLS – Wells, Katherine E.
Our Wells ancestors. (By Katherine E. Wells). (New Milford, Conn., 1911). (LI)

WELTON – Welton, John
John Welton and his wife Mary Upson came from England about 1667 and settled in Waterbury, Ct. in 1679. (By John Welton)... (N.p., 185-). (LoC)

WHEAT – Wheat, Silas Carmi

<u>Wheat genealogy.</u> Guilford, Conn.: Shore Line Pub. Co., 1960. (DAR)

WHIPPLE – McGuigan, Clara Hammond
<u>The antecedents and descendants of Noah Whipple of the Rogerene
community at Quakertown, Connecticut.</u> By Clara Hammond McGuigan.
with additional sections by Robert W. Merriam. Ithaca, N. Y.: J. M.
Kingsbury (c1971). (LoC)

WHISTLER – Shaw, Margaret Race
<u>Abstracts of Whistler family probate records; originals found in
Connecticut State Library.</u> By Margaret Race Shaw. Hartford, 1946.
(LoC)

WHITE –
White Family of Hartford (1860), 322 pgs.[1]

WHITE –
White Family, Andover, Ct. (1905), 155 pgs.[1]

WHITE – Kellogg, Allyn S.
<u>Memorials of Elder John White.</u> Hartford, Conn.: Case, Lockwood & Co.,
1860. (DAR)

WHITE – Kellogg, Allyn S.
<u>Memorials of Elder John White, one of the first settlers of Hartford,
Conn., and of his descendants.</u> By Allyn S. Kellogg. Hartford: Printed for
the family by Case, Lockwood and Co., 1860. (LoC)

WHITE – White, Carlyle Snow
<u>The book of White ancestry.</u> By Carlyle Snow White. (Guilford? Conn.,
195-?). (LoC)

WHITE – White, John Bartlett
<u>A genealogical record of the family of White.</u> By John Bartlett White, of
East Killingly, Conn. Danielsonville, Greenslitt & Hamilton, Printers,
1878. (LoC)

WHITE – White, (Joseph H.)
<u>Ancestors and descendants of Joseph White, born March 29, 1752... A
memorial of Elder John White, one of the first settlers of Hartford, Conn.
...</u> By (Joseph H.) White. Canajoharie, 1883. (LI)

WHITE – White, Carlyle S.

(Histories of the White family). By Carlyle S. White. Guilford, Conn. (1954). (NY)

WHITE – White, Mary Edna
Joseph White of Derby, Connecticut, his descendants and allied families. Montrose, Ala.: White, 1972? (DAR)

WHITEHEAD – Shepard, James
John Whitehead of New Haven and Branford, Conn. By James Shepard. (Reprinted from New England historical and genealogical register for April, 1901). Republished by the author, New Britain, Conn., 1902. Boston, Press of D. Clapp & Son (1902). (LoC)

WHITING -
Whiting Family of Hartford (1888), 8 pgs.[1]

WHITING – Whiting, Andrew F.
Genealogical notes of the Whiting family... By Andrew F. Whiting. (Hartford, Conn., 1888). (LI)

WHITMORE – Bacon, William Plumb
Ancestors of Rev. William Howe Whittemore, Bolton, Ct., 1800 – Rye, N. Y., 1885, and of his wife Maria Clark, New York, 1803 – Brooklyn, 1886. Compiled by William Plumb Bacon. (New Britain, Conn.: Adkins Printing Co., 1907). (LoC)

WHITNEY – Phoenix, S. Whitney
The Whitney family of Connecticut, and its affiliations; being an attempt to trace the descendants, as well in the female as the male lines, of Henry Whitney, from 1649 to 1878; to which is prefixed some account of the Whitneys of England. By S. Whitney Phoenix... New York: Priv. print (Bradstreet Press) 1878. (LoC)

WHITNEY – Phoenix, Stephen W.
Record of one branch of the Whitney family of Connecticut. By Stephen W. Phoenix. (La Grange, Ill., 1964). (FW)

WHITON – Whiton, Augustus Sherrill
The Whiton family in America. New London, Conn.: Whiton Family Association, 1932. (DAR)

WHITTELSEY – Whittelsey, Charles Barney
Genealogy of the Whittelsey-Whittlesey family. Hartford, Conn.: Whittelsey, 1898. (DAR)

WHITTEMORE – Bacon, William Plumb
Ancestors of Rev. William Howe Whittemore. New Britain, Conn.:
Adkins Printing Co., 1907. (DAR)

WHITTEN – Whiton, Augustus Sherrill
The Whiton family in America, the genealogy of the descendants (!) of
Thomas Whiton (1635). Compiled by Augustus Sherrill Whiton... (New
London, Conn.): The Whiton Family Association, Inc., 1932. (LoC)

WHITTLESEY –
Address of Elisha Whittlesey delivered at a meeting of the Whittlesey
family, which convened at Saybrook, Connecticut, September 30, 1855.
Washington, 1855. (LoC)

WHITTLESEY –
Memorial of the Whittlesey family in the United States. (Hartford, Conn.):
The Whittlesey Association, 1855. (LoC)

WHITTLESEY –
Military record of the descendants of John Whittlesey and Ruth Dudley,
who were married at Saybrook, Conn., June 20, 1664. Cleveland, O.:
Fairbanks, Benedict & Co., Printers, 1874. (LoC)

WHITTLESEY – Whitttelsey, Charles Barney
Genealogy of the Whittlesey-Whittlesey family. Compiled and published
by Charles Barney Whittelsey.,.. Hartford, Conn.: C. B. Whittelsey, Press
of the Case, Lockwood & Brainard Company, 1898. (LoC)

WHITTLESEY – Whittelsey, Charles Barney
Genealogy of the Whittlesey-Whittelsey family. By Charles Barney
Whittelsey... 2d Ed. New York, London, Whittlesey House, McGraw-Hill
Book company, Inc., 1941. (LoC)

WHITNEY –
Whitney Family of Watertown (1857), 26 pgs.[1]
Whitney Family of Connecticut (1878), 2762 pgs.[1]
Whitney Family of Watertown (1890), 101 pgs.[1]
Whitney Family of Watertown (1895), 692 pgs.[1]
Whitney Family of Watertown (1898), 156 pgs.[1]

WICKWARE – Wickwire, Arthur Manley
Genealogy of the Wickware family: containing an account of the origin
and early history of the name and family in England, and the record of
John Wickware, who emigrated to New London, Connecticut, in 1675, and

of his descendants in America. By Arthur Manley Wickwire... (New York and Meriden: Press of the Curtiss-Way Company, c1909). (LoC)

WIGGINS – Gardiner, Tiger
The Gardiner-Squires connection: an account of the Gardiner family of Gardiner's Island, Long Island, New York, and the Squires family of Squirestown, Long Island, New York and West Haven, Connecticut, their connections and allied families – Wiggins, Miner, Beer, Wines, and Raynor, 1559-1989. By Tiger Gardiner. Baltimore: Gateway Press, 1989. (LoC)

WILCOX – Savage, Albert Wilcox
Descendants of Elisha Bacon Wilcox of Middletown, Connecticut. Albert Wilcox Savage. Baltimore, Md.: Gateway Press; Las Vegas, Nv.: A. W. Savage, 1990. (LoC)

WILCOX – Wilcox, Owen N.
Wilcox family history. Being some account of the first five generations in direct line from William Wilcockson of Stratford, Connecticut, to Josiah Wilcox of Brecksville, Ohio. Comp. by Owen N. Wilcox. Cleveland, O., 1911. (LoC)

WILCOX – Wilcox, Thomas
A preliminary report on the descendants of William Wilcoxson, "Father of Connecticut"... Compiled and issued by Thomas Wilcox... Los Angeles, Calif. (1937). (LoC)

WILCOX – Wilcox, Thomas
Descendants of William Wilcoxson of Derbyshire, England, and Stratford, Connecticut. By Thomas Wilcox. Pasadena, Calif., 1963. (LoC)

WILCOX. See also:

Barber, 1911	Hughes, 1917	Stebbins, 1940
Brockway	Mead, 1945	Wallace, 1928
Card	Merrill, 1888	Whitmore, 1875
Coates, 1901a	Nash, 1902	Willcox
Curtis, 1912	Ranney	

WILCOX – Wulfeck, Dorothy Ford
Wilcoxson and allied families: Willcockson, Wilcoxen, Wilcox. Compiled and published by Dorothy Ford Wulfeck. Waterbury, Conn., Printed (by) Commercial Service, 1958. (LoC)

WILCOXSON – Wulfeck, Dorothy (Ford)

Wilcoxson and allied families: Willcockson, Wilcoxen, Wilcox.
Waterbury, Ct., 1958. (NGS)

WILFORD – Gregory, Elizabeth Hitchcock
The Wilfords of Branford. By Elizabeth Hitchcock Gregory. Branford,
Conn.: Gregory, 1975. (LoC)

WILKINSON – Wilkinson, Rev. Israel, A. M.
Memoirs of the Wilkinson family in America. Comprising genealogical
and biographical sketches of Lawrence Wilkinson of Providence, R. I.;
Edward Wilkinson of New Milford, Conn.; John Wilkinson of
Attleborough, Mass.; Daniel Wilkinson of Columbia Co., N. Y... and their
descendants from 1645-1868. By Rev, Israel Wilkinson, A. M. ...
Jacksonville, Ill., Davis & Peniman, Printers, 1869. (LoC)

WILLARD – Willard, Stephen E.
Descendants of Josiah (2) Willard of Wethersfield, Connecticut. Boston:
Willard Family Association, 1972. (DAR)

WILLARD – Willard, Stephen F.
Family of Stephen Franklin Willard, Wethersfield, Conn., 7 generations
removed from Major Simon Willard, settler of Concord, Mass. By
Stephen F. Willard. Wollaston, Mass., 1960. (FW)

WILLEY – Willey, Henry
Preliminary outline of the descendants of Isaac Willey, of New London,
Conn. By Henry Willey... New Bedford, Mass.: E. Anthony & Sons,
1886. (LoC)

WILLEY – Willey, Henry
Isaac Willey of New London, Conn.., and his descendants. By Henry
Willey... New Bedford, Mass., Printed for the author (by E. Anthony &
Sons), 1888. (LoC)

WILLIAMS – Favretti, Rudy J.
Once upon Quoketaug, the biography of a Connecticut farm family; 1712-
1760. By Rudy J. Favretti. (Storrs, Conn., Paraousia Press, 1974). (FW)

WILLIAMS – McLean, Mary Dyer (Williams)
The ancestors and descendants of Ezekiel Williams of Wethersfield, 1608-
1907. Comp. by Mary Dyer (Williams) McLean. (Hartford: The Case.
Lockwood & Brainard Company Print), priv. print., 1907. (LoC)

WILLIAMS – Williams, Charles Fish

Genealogical notes of the Williams and Gallup families. Hartford, Conn.:
Case, Lockwood & Brainard Co., 1897. (DAR)

WILLIAMS – Williams, Samuel H.
An unpredictable grandfather: Solomon Williams of Lebanon and
Manchester, Conn. By Samuel H. Williams. Glastonbury, Conn., 1946.
(MH)

WILLIAMS – Williams, Samuel H.
Who's who in the family of Solomon Williams. By Samuel H. Williams.
Glastonbury, Conn., 1947. (MH)

WILLIAMS – Williams, Samuel H.
The House that James built. By Samuel H. Williams. Glastonbury, Conn.,
1948. (MH)

WILLIAMS – Williams, Samuel H.
A James Baker Williams family album. By Samuel H. Williams.
Glastonbury, Conn., 1949. (MH)

WILLIAMS – Wright, Alexander Hamilton
The descendants of Veach Williams. New Haven, Conn.: Tuttle,
Morehouse & Taylor, Printers, 1887. (DAR)

WILLIAMS – Wright, Alexander Hamilton
The descendants of Veach Williams of Lebanon, Conn., who was of the
fifth generation from Robert Williams, who came from England in 1637,
and settled at Roxbury, Mass. Also, the ancestry of Lucy Walsworth, wife
of Veach Williams. By Alexander Hamilton Wright... New Haven:
Tuttle, Morehouse & Taylor, Printers, 1887. (LoC)

WILLIAMS – Starr, Frank Farnsworth
The Williams and Cobb families in the line of Caleb and Mary (Cobb)
Williams of Barnstable, Mass., and Hartford, Conn. 1896. Comp. by
Frank Farnsworth Starr for James J. Goodwin. Hartford, Conn.
(Cambridge, University Press, J. Wilson & Son) 1896. (LoC)

WILLIS –
The first wife of Governor Willys of Connecticut, and her family. By a
descendant. (Charles Atwood White. Boston, 1899). (LoC)

WILLOUGHBY – Willoughby, Miranda G.
The Willoughbys of Connecticut. By Miranda G. Willoughby. Riverside,
R. I., 1976. (LA)

WILMOT –
Wilmot Family of New Haven (1904), 9 pgs.[1]

WILMOT – Jacobus, Donald Lines
The Wilmot family of New Haven, Conn. By Donald Lines Jacobus.
Boston, New England Historic Genealogical Society, 1904. (LoC)

WILSON – Roberts, W. Willard
Historical review of the Wilson family in America. By W. Willard
Roberts. Bridgeport, Conn. (Columbia Printing Co.) 1935. (LoC)

WILSON – Stevens, Ken
Five families from Hartford County, Connecticut. Ken Stevens. Walpole,
N. H.: K. Stevens., c1989. (LoC)

WINCHESTER – Hotchkiss, Mrs. Fanny Winchester
Winchester notes, by Mrs. Fanny Winchester Hotchkiss. New Haven,
Conn. Printed by the Tuttle, Morehouse & Taylor Co., 1912. (LoC)

WOLCOTT –
The two sister's poems and memoirs. Composed by Eliza and Sarah G.
Wolcott, of Connecticut. New Haven, Baldwin and Treadway, printers,
1930. (LoC)

WOLCOTT – Rudd, Alice Bohmer
Wolcott genealogy; the family of Henry Wolcott, one of the first settlers of
Windsor, Connecticut. By Alice Bohmer Rudd. Washington, Guild Pub.
Co., 1950. (LoC)

WOLCOTT. See also:

Bishop, 1877	Smith, 1924
Blake, 1948	Toll, 1961
Gibbs, 1933	Tuckerman, 1914
McCurdy, 1892	Wallcott
Salisbury, 1892	

WOLCOTT – Wellner, Louis V.
Genealogical table. Showing the lineage of Margaret Wyatt, wife of
Matthew Allyn, Devonshire, Eng.., later of Windsor, Conn. Also the
descent of Henry Wolcott, Devonshire, Eng., later of Windsor, Conn.,
down to the compiler, Louis V. Wellner... New York, N. Y., 1934. (LoC)

WOLCOTT – Wolcott, Chandler
Wolcott genealogy; the family of Henry Wolcott, one of the first settlers of
Windsor, Connecticut. By Chandler Wolcott. Printed for the Society of

descendants of Henry Wolcott. Rochester, N. Y., The Genesee Press, 1912. (LoC)

WOLCOTT – Wolcott,Samuel
Memorial of Henry Wolcott, one of the first settlers of Windsor, Connecticut, and some of his descendants. By Samuel Wolcott... New York, A. D. F. Randolph & Co., 1881. (LoC)

WOOD – Wheat, Edwin W.
The first two generations of the descendants of Joseph Wood (1755-1836) of New Canaan, Conn., and Walton, New York. By Edwin W. Wheat. Mount-Vision, N. Y., 1924. (NY)

WOOD – Wood, Frederick
Chart of descendants of Dr. Samuel Wood. One of the pioneer settlers of Danbury, Conn. By Frederick Wood. Comp. between 1875 and 1930? (PH)

WOODIN – Woodin, Wallace I.
Unfinished genealogy of the Amos Woodin family. By Wallace I. Woodin. Hartford, Conn., 1928. (SP)

WOODIN – Woodin, Wallace I.
Descendants of Amos Woodin. By Wallace I. Woodin. (Andover, Conn.), 1934. (DP)

WOODRUFF –
Woodruff genealogy; Matthew Woodruff of Farmington, Conn., 1640-1, and ten generations of his descendants, together with genealogies of families connected through marriage, Abbe genealogy, Sturtevant genealogy, Stevens genealogy, Burke genealogy, briefs from Kelly, Franklin and Folger genealogies. Compiled by George N. Mackenzie... George S. Stewart... assisted by Frederick O. Woodruff... Boston, Mass.: The Everett Print, 1925. (LoC)

WOODRUFF –
Woodruffs; from Matthew, 1640, to Morgan and Franklin, 1961, a genealogy. From records of the church at Southington, Conn., with reference only to those records containing the name Woodruff, by Frankkin Kenneth Woodruff and Morgan Lewis Woodruff, Jr. (N. p., 1961 or 2). (LoC)

WOODRUFF – Abbott, Susan Woodruff

Descendants of Mathew Woodruff of Farmington, Conn. Milford, Ct., 1963. (NGS)

WOODRUFF – Abbott, Susan Woodruff
Woodruff genealogy. New Haven, Conn.: Harty Press, 1963. (DAR)

WOODRUFF – Abbott, Susan Emma (Woodruff)
Woodruff genealogy; descendants of Mathew Woodruff of Farmington, Connecticut. By Susan Emma (Woodruff) Abbott. Milford, Conn., 1963. (LoC)

WOODRUFF – Woodruff, Norris C.
Twelve generations from the colony of Connecticut in New England and the province of Upper Canada, 1636-1959; a Woodruff genealogy. By Norris C. Woodruff. (Hamilton? Canada, 1958 or 9). (FW)

WOODRUFF – Woodruff, Norris Counsell
Twelve generations from the Colony of Connecticut in New England and the Province of Upper Canada. S.1.:s..n., 1959? (DAR)

WOODWORTH – Miller, Margaret Porter
Some descendants of Robert Porter, Farmington, Connecticut, 1640: with female lines. Compiled by Margaret Porter Miller. Baltimore: Gateway Press; Easton, Md.: M. Miller, 1986. (LoC)

WOOLSEY –
Letters of a family during the war of the union. 1861-1865. (New Haven, Conn.: Tuttle, Morehouse & Taylor) 1899. (LoC)

WOOLSEY – Howland, Mrs. Eliza Newton (Woolsey)
Family records; being some account of the ancestry of my father and mother, Charles William Woolsey and Jane Eliza Newton. (By Mrs. Eliza Newton (Woolsey) Howland). (New Haven, Conn.: The Tuttle, Morehouse & Taylor Press, 1900). (LoC)

WOOLWORTH – Woolworth, Charlotte R.
The descendants of Richard and Hannah Huggins Woolworth, who landed at Newbury, Mass., 1678; removed to Suffield, Conn., in 1685. Comp. by Charlotte R. Woolworth, assisted by her daughter, Josephine L. Kimpton. New Haven, Conn. (Press of C. H. Ryder) 1893. (LoC)

WORCESTER –
The descendants of Rev. William Worcester, with a brief notice of the Connecticut Wooster family. First edition published by J. Fox Worcester,

of Salem, Mass., in 1856. Rev. by Sarah Alice Worcester... Boston: E. F. Worcester, 1914. (LoC)

WORCESTER – Wooster, David
Genealogy of the Woosters in America, descended from Edward Wooster of Connecticut; also an appendix containing a sketch relating to the author, and a memoir of Rev. Hezekia Calvin Wooster, and public letters of General David Wooster. By David Wooster... San Francisco: M. Weiss, Printer, 1885. (LoC)

WORCESTER – Worcester, J. F.
The Worcester family; or, The descendants of Rev. William Worcester, with brief notice of the Connecticut Wooster family. Collected by J. F. Worcester. Lynn: W. W. Kellogg, Printer, 1856. (LoC)

WRIGHT –
Wright Family of Guilford, Ct. (1901), 16 pgs.[1]

WRIGHT –
History of the Wright family who are descendants of Samuel Wright (1722-1789) of Lenox, Mass., with lineage back to Thomas Wright (1610-1670) of Wethersfield, Conn. (emigrated 1640) and showing a direct line to John Wright, lord of Kelvedon Hall, Essex, England. Ed. by William Henry Wright and Gertrude Wright Ketcham. Denver: The Williams-Haffner Co. (c1913). (LoC)

WRIGHT – Wright, Curtis
Genealogical and biographical notices of descendants of Sir John Wright of Kelvedon Hall, Essex, England; in America, Thomas Wright, of Wethersfield, Conn., Dea. Samuel Wright, of Nothampton (sic), Mass., 1610-1670, 1614-1665. Compilation and annotations by Curtis Wright. Carthage, Mo., 1915. (LoC)

WRIGHT – Wright, Rev. Henry W.
Genealogy of the Wright family from 1639 to 1901. Eight generations. Comp. and written by Rev. Henry W. Wright... Middletown, Conn.: Pelton & King, Printers, 1901. (LoC)

WRIGHT – Wright, Noel Woodworth
Wright families of Massachusetts, Connecticut, New York, and points west. By Noel Woodworth Wright. (Ventura, Ca.): Wright (c1979). (LoC)

WYLLYS –
   The Wyllys papers; correspondence and docuements chiefly by
   descendants of Gov. George Wyllys of Connecticut, 1590-1796. Hartford
   Connecticut Historical Society, 1924. (LoC)

WYLLYS – Seymour, George Dudley
   Captain Nathan Hale, 1755-1776; Yale College 1773; Major John
   Palsgrave Wyllys, 1754-1790; Yale College 1773; friends and Yale
   classmates, who died in the country's service, one hanged as a spy by the
   British, the other killed in an Indian ambuscade on the far frontier. A
   digressive history now told with many antiquarian excursions,
   genealogical, architectual, social, and controversial; with an account of
   some members of a great patrician family, their monorial establishment in
   Hartford, their custody for generations of the Charter of King Charles the
   Second, and the story of the hiding thereof. By George Dudley Seymour.
   New Haven, Priv. print. for the author (The Tuttle, Morehouse & Taylor
   Company) 1933. (LoC)

Y

YALE – Carnevale, Alphonse J.
   The royal and noble heritage of Elihu Yale of Plas Grono, Denbigh, Wales.
   By Alphonse J. Carnevale. New Haven, Conn.: Yale Heritage
   Publications, 1962. (NY)

YALE – Yale, Elihu
   The Yale family. New Haven: Storer & Stone, 1850. (DAR)

YALE – Yale, Elihu
   The Yale family, or The descendants of David Yale, with genealogical
   notes of each family. By Elihu Yale... New Haven, Storer & Stone,
   Printers, 1850. (LoC)

YORK – York, Ervine D.
   York of Yorke of New Haven, Conn., an escerpt (sic) from "The York
   book" in mss (sic). By Ervine D. York. (Glendale, Cal., 1921). (NY)

---

[1] This book is listed in **'INDEX TO AMERICAN GENEALOGIES'** (A
reprint of the fifth Edition, 1900 with Supplement, 1900 to 1908). Printed by
Joel Munsell's Sons, Albany, N. Y. Location of libraries is not shown. Each
book listed has some facts about the family mentioned but such information is
frequently limited to a few pages.

MAJOR CONNECTICUT LIBRARIES

Connecticut Historical Society Library
One Elizabeth Street
Hartford, CT 06105

Connecticut State Library
231 Capitol Avenue
Hartford, CT 06106

Godfrey Memorial Library
134 Newfield Street
Middletown, CT 06457

New Haven Colony Historical Society Library
114 Whitney Avenue
New Haven, CT 06510

Pequot Library
720 Pequot Avenue
Southport, CT 06490

CODES TO LIBRARY ABBREVIATIONS & GLOSSARY

CH -   Cincinnati Historical Society

DP -   Denver Public Library

FW -   Allen County Library, Fort Wayne, Indiana

GF -   Genealogical Forum of Portland, Oregon

LA -   Los Angeles Public Library

LI -   Long Island Historical Society, Brooklyn, N. Y.

MH -   Minnesota Historical Society, St. Paul

NY -   New York Public Library

OH -   Ohio Historical Society, Columbus

OS -   Oregon State Library, Salem

PH -   The Historical Society of Pennsylvania, Philadelphia

PP -   Library Association of Portland, Oregon

SP -   Seattle Public Library

SL -   St. Louis Public Library

SU -   Sutro Branch of the California State Library,
          San Francisco

GLOSSARY

sic   thus; used to indicate that the previous word has been copied
        directly, despite an apparent misspelling.

s. l.   sine loco; without named place of publication.

s. n.   sine nomine; without named publisher.

n. d.   no date.

STATE OF CONNECTICUT GENEALOGICAL SOCIETIES

Connecticut Society of Genealogists
P. O. Box 435
Glastonbury, CT 06033

Connecticut Ancestry Society
P. O. Box 249
Stamford, CT 06940

Genealogy Roundtable/Hebron
Douglas Library
22 Main Street
Hebron, CT 06248

Middlesex Genealogical Society
P. O. Box 1111
Darien, CT 06820

Southington Genealogical Society
239 Main Street
Southington, CT 06485

BIBLIOGRAPHY

DAUGHTERS OF THE AMERICAN REVOLUTION (DAR)
State and Local Histories and Records. Compiled under the Supervision of Eric G. Grundset and Ana Antolin. National Society of the Daughters of the American Revolution. DAR Library, Washington, D. C. Volume Two. 1986.

HOFFMAN, Marian
Genealogical & Local History Books in Print. 5th Edition. Compiled & edited by Marian Hoffman. Genealogical Publishing Co., Inc. Baltimore, Md. (4 Volumes).

KAMINKOW, Marion J.
Genealogies in The Library of Congress. Baltimore: Magna Carta Book Company. 1972.

KAMINKOW, Marion J.
Genealogies in The Library of Congress, Supplement 1972-1976. Baltimore: Magna Carta Book Company. 1977.

KAMINKOW, Marion J.
Genealogies in The Library of Congress, Second Supplement 1976-1986. Baltimore: Magna Carta Book Company. 1987.

KAMINKOW, Marion J.
A Complement To Genealogies in The Library of Congress. Baltimore: Magna Carta Book Company. 1981.

LIBRARY OF CONGRESS
Genealogies Cataloged By The Library of Congress Since 1986. Cataloging Distribution Service, Library of Congress, Washington, D. C. 1992

MICHAELS, Carolyn Leopold and Scott, Kathryn S.
Library Catalog DAR Family Histories and Genealogies. Washington: National Society Daughters of the American Revolution. 1982.

NATIONAL GENEALOGICAL SOCIETY.
National Genealogical Society Library Book List. Marion Rollins Beasley, Librarian. 5th Edition. Arlington, VA. 1988.

AMES – 7
Benjamin-7; Dorcas-7

AMOS – 200
Anna-200

ANABLE – 7

ANDERSON – 44

ANDREW – 7

ANDREWS – 7, 8, 93, 183, 190
Asa-7, 8; Chester-7; John-7, 8;
Mary-7; Nelson-7; Schuyler-7;
Rev. Wells-7; William-7, 8,
93; Wm.-8

ANDRUS –8
John-8; Grace (Rood)-8

ANTISELL – 8
Christopher-8; Lawrence-8;
Mary-8

ARCHIBALD – 65

ARMES – 116
Ethel-116

ARNOLD – 8, 9
ARNOLD – 8, 9

ASHLEY – 9

ATKINS – 9
John, III-9

ATKINSON – 9
Stephen-9

ATWATER – 9, 10
David-9, 10; Francis-9

ATWELL – 10

AUGUR – 10
Robert-10

AUSTIN – 10
John-10

AVERY – 10, 11

AXTELL – 11

AYE – 104
Rebecca Hyde-104

AYER – 11, 195
John-195

AYERS – 12, 195
John-195

BABCOCK – 12

BACKHOUSE (BACKUS) – 12
Elijah-12; James-12

BACKUS – 12
Elijah-12; James-12; William-
12

BACON – 12
Hannah-12; John-12

BAILEY – 13
Thomas-13

BAIRD – 13
Martha-13

BALDWIN – 13, 14, 61, 63, 141,
181

Deac. Aaron-13; Eunice-141; Francis-13, 14; Jesse-13; John-13; Joseph-13

BALL – 14
Alling-14

BALLARD – 14

BANCROFT – 5
Thomas-5

BANKS – 3, 14

BANNING – 14
(Banning-Bradley)

BARBER (BARBOUR) –14, 209
Sylvester-14

BARBOUR – 14

BARET – 16
Margaret-16

BARKER – 15
Edward-15; James-15; John-15; Robert-15; Samuel-15; Virginia-15

BARLOW – 15, 33
William Howard-15

BARNES – 15, 55, 100
Julius Elizer-15; Thomas-15; William-100

BARNHART – 15
Jeremiah-15

BARRETT – 15, 16, 51, 95
Margaret (Baret)-16

BARTHOLOMEW – 16

Hon. Andrew J.-16; Lieut. William-16

BARTLETT – 16, 38, 88, 131, 188, 193
John-16; Mary-38

BARTRAM – 16

BASS – 16

BASSETT – 17
Annie (Preston)-17; Edward M.-17; Howard Murray-17; Preston Rogers-17

BATEMAN – 17
William-17

BATES – 17, 18
Benjamin-18; Calvin-18; Elias-18; Henry-18; Capt. Lemuel-17; Rufus-18

BATTERSON – 18

BAYLEY – 18
Joshua-18

BEACH – 18, 19
John-18; Rev. John-18, 19; Richard-18; Thomas-18, 19

BEAMAN – 19
Thomas-19

BEARD – 13, 19
Martha-13, 19

BEARDSLEY – 19, 61
William-19

BEARSE – 19
(Bearse or Bearss)

Dea. John-19; Molly
(Beardsley)-19

BECHTEL – 20
Judge Karl-20

BECK – 20
Thomas, Esq.-20

BECKLEY – 20
Richard-20

BECKWITH – 20, 114
Albert C.-114; Matthew-20

BEEBE – 20

BEECHER – 21

BEEMAN – 21
Thomas-21

BEER – 133, 183, 209

BEERS – 21, 157
Anthony-21; Barnabas-21;
Ephraim-21; Dea. Nathan-21;
Sarah-157

BEHAIM – 21

BELCHER – 61

BELDING – 22
Richard-22

BELOTE – 22

BENEDICT – 129

BENJAMIN – 22

BENNET – 22
James-22

BENNETT – 22
Calvin Goddard-22; John-22

BENTLEY – 22, 165
William-22

BENTON – 22, 25
Arthur Hotchkiss-22

BERRY – 22, 23
Hosea-22, 23

BERTRAND – 23

BETTS – 23
Annie Rebecca-23

BILLARD – 23
Mary Elizabeth-23

BINGHAM – 23, 24
Thomas-23

BIRCHARD – 24
(Birchard-Burchard)
Thomas-24

BIRD – 24

BISHOP – 24, 25, 212
James-25; John-24, 25; Rev.
John-25

BISSELL – 25, 139
John-25

BIXBY – 52
Capt. Jonathan, Sr.-52

BLACKMAN – 25
(Blackman-Blackmore)
Rev. Adam-25

BLACKMER – 25

David-25; Reuben-25; Samuel-25

BLACKMORE – 25
Rev. Adam (Blackman)-25;
David (Blackmer)-25; James-25; Reubenn (Blackmer)-25;
Samuel (Blackmer)-25;
William—25

BLACKSTONE – 25, 26
James-25; William-26

BLAKE – 26, 167, 212
Amos S.-26; Theophilus-167

BLAKESLEY – 26
Samuel-26

BLANKMAN – 26
Pieter-26

BLIN – 26, 27
Peter-26, 27

BLINN – 26, 27

BLISH – 27

BLISS – 27, 203
Ephraim-27; Thomas-27

BLODGETT –27
Hon. William A.-27

BLOSS – 79
John B.-79; Sarah Rebecca (Gilbert)-79

BOARD – 195
Cornelius-195

BOARDMAN – 27, 28, 76, 84, 122

Samuel (Boreman)-28;
Thomas (Boreman)-28;
William Francis Joseph-27, 84

BOGARDUS – 139, 203

BOGUE – 28
James Hubbard-28; John-28

BOLTON – 28
James-28

BONAPARTE – 28

BOND – 28, 123
Rev. Alvan-28

BONTECOU – 29
Pierre-29

BOOTH – 29
(Booth-Boothe)
Richard-29

BOOTHE – 53

BOREMAN – 27, 28
(Boreman-Boardman)
Samuel-28; Thomas-28

BOSTWICK – 30
Arthur-30

BOTSFORD – 16, 30

BOUGHTON – 30
(Bouton-Boughton-Boution)
John Boution-30

BOURNE – 30

BOUTION – 30
John-30

BOUTON – 30

BOWEN – 30, 31
Griffith-31; Esq. Silas-31

BOWER – 31
Rev. John-31

BOWERS – 103, 203
Mrs. Rebecca-103

BOWNE – 31

BRADFORD – 31
Governor William-31; Major
William-31

BRADLEY – 14, 31, 32
Aaron-32; Isaac-32; Leland-
32; Sarah-32

BRAINERD – 32

BREED – 33

BREWER – 33
Erastus-33

BREWSTER – 33
James-33; Mary-33; William-
33

BRIGHT – 33
Henry-33

BRINLEY – 33
Grissell-33

BRISTOL – 33

BRITTAINE – 33
(Brittaine-Britton)
William-33

BRITTIN – 33, 34
Lewis Hotchkiss-33

BRITTON – 33, 34
(Britton-Brittin-Brittaine)
Lewis Hotchkiss (Brittin)-33;
William (Brittaine)-33

BROCKETT – 34
John-34

BROCKWAY – 34, 209
Wolston-34

BROMLEY – 34
Luke-34

BRONCK – 139

BRONSON – 137

BROOKS – 29, 53
Nathaniel-29, 53

BRONSON – 34, 35
**(Bronson-Brownson-
Brunson)**

BROWN – 35, 43
David Arms-35; John-35; Max
L.-35; Sarah-43

BROWNE – 35

BROWNELL – 35

BROWNSON – 35
John-35; Richard-35

BRUCE – 42

BRUNSON – 35, 41

BRUSH – 200

BRYAN – 35
Alexander-35

BUCHANAN – 122

BUCHER – 203

BUCK – 35, 36, 129
Emanuel-36; Samuel-36;
Thomas-36

BUCKINGHAM – 36, 88
Thomas-36

BUDINGTON – 36
(Budington-Buddington)

BULKELEY – 5, 36
Peter-36

BULL – 36, 37
Suusannah-37; Captain
Thomas-37

BUNCE – 37

BURBANK – 37
John-37

BURCHARD – 24

BURGIS – 112

BURHAMS – 75

BURLINGAME – 63

BURNAP – 132
Agnes or Ann (Miller)-132

BURNHAM – 37, 138
Thomas-37

BURRITT – 38
Rev. Blackleach-38; William-
38

BURROWS – 95

BURTON – 192
Adaline-192

BURWELL – 38

BUSHNELL – 38
Francis-38

BUTLER – 38, 39
Eleazer-39; John-38; Lydia
(Durkee)-39; Patrich-38; Sarah
(Cross)-39; Lt. William-39

BUTT – 161

BYAM – 39
George-39

CABLER – 39

CALAWAY – 39

CALDWELL – 39, 40
**(Coalwell, Coaldwell,
Caldwell or Coldwell)**
William-39, 40

CALHOUN –40

CALKINS – 169

CALLAWAY – 40

CAMERON – 30, 40
Mrs. Donald-30

CAMP – 40, 61
Edward-40

CAMPBELL – 65

CANFIELD – 35

CANTINE – 40
Moses-40

CAPEN – 61

CARD – 209

CARPENTER – 19, 40, 41, 165

CARRIER – 41
Martha (Allen)-41; Thomas-41

CARTER – 41
(Chartier)
Samuel-41

CASE – 41
John-41

CASTLE – 198

CASTO – 41

CARVER – 48

CATES – 78

CHAFFEE – 42, 170, 181, 190
Jerome Stuart-42; G. D. K.-42

CHAMBERLAIN – 182

CHAMPION – 42
Henry-42

CHAMPLIN – 182

CHANDLER – 193

CHAPIN – 42

Calvin-42; Dea. Samuel-42

CHAPMAN – 42, 43
Rev. Benjamin-43; Edward-43;
Ichabod-43; John-43; Robert-
43; Robert, Sr., 43; William-43

CHARTIER – 41

CHATFIELD – 43, 44

CHENEY – 44
William-44

CHESEBROUGH – 10, 11, 44,
62
William-44

CHESTER – 44, 50
Leonard-44

CHEVALIER – 44

CHITTENDEN – 35, 44, 45
William-45

CHRISTOPHERS – 45
Christopher-45; Jeffrey-45

CHURCH – 45
Henry (Shutts)-45; Richard-45;
Simeon-45

CHURCHILL – 61

CLAPP – 45
Col. John B.-45

CLARK (e) – 4, 45, 46, 47, 48,
207
Daniel-46, 47, 48; Ebenezer-
46; Edmund, Jr.-46; George-
46; Dea. George-46; John-4,
46, 47; Maria-207; Dea.

Maj. James-52; Maj. Jas.-52;
Samuel, Jr.-52

COACH – 171

COOK-COOKE – 52, 139

COONLEY – 139

CORBIN – 52
Clement-52

CORLISS – 52, 53

CORNELL – 53

CORNWALL – 29, 53
(Cornwell, Cornell)
William-53

CORNWELL – 53

COSSITT – 53
Rene-53

COTTON – 53
Lucius Storrs-53

COWLES – 49, 54
Lucy-54

COYNE (COAN) – 54
George-54; Peter-54

CRAMPTON – 54

CRANKSHAW – 54
Ann-54; Charles-54

CRAWFORD – 131

CRITES – 41

CROOKE – 198

CROSBY – 54
John-54

CULVER (COLVER) – 51, 54
Edward-54

CUMMINS – 54

CURRY – 203

CURTIS – 55, 56, 209
(Curtiss-Curtice)
Clifford Clarke-55; Elizabeth-
56; Grace Lillingston-55; Dr.
Holbrook-55; Judge Holbrook-
55; Thomas-55, 56; Walter
Stanley-55; William Edmond-
55; Judge William Edmond-55

DALTON – 56

DANIELS – 56
John-56

DARROW – 56, 57
Mary-57; Richard-57

DART – 57

DASKAM – 57
William-57

DAVENPORT – 57
Rev. John-57

DAVIES – 58, 111
John-58; Rev. Thomas-58

DAVIS – 55, 57, 58, 182
Gaius-57; Geo. T.-57; John-58;
Col. John-57; Rev. Thomas-
58; Wilson Kies, Jr.-57

DAVISON – 65

DAWSON – 58
Robert-58

DAY – 58, 59, 123
Alfred—58, 59; Rev.
Jeremiah—58, 59; John-58,
59; Cpt. John-59; Lydia
Calkins-58; Robert-58, 59;
Thomas-59

DAYTON – 59, 60
Henry, Jr.-59, 60; Ralph-59

DEACON – 60

DEAN – 60
Ezra-60; James-60; Thomas-
60; Walter-60; William-60

DECHMAN – 60

DEFOREST – 60, 61
Anthony-61

DEKARAJAN – 61

DELAVAN – 61
Cornelius-61

DEMING – 61, 107
John-61

DEMMOND – 19

DENISON – 61, 62, 63, 106
Ann Borodell-62; Lady Ann-
63; Esther-106; George-62;
Cpt. George-62, 63; James
Post-62; Robert-62

DENNIS – 66

DE VAUX – 143

DEVEREAUX – 63
Jonathan-63

DEWEY – 63, 200
Thomas-63

DE WOLF – 63, 64, 123
(D'Wolf-de Wolf)
Charles-63; Balthasar-63;
Bradford Colt-64; Joseph-63;
Simon-63

DEY – 195
Richard-195

DIAMOND – 64

DICKERMAN – 64

DICKERSON – 133

DICKINSON – 61, 64
Anna Gull-64; Nathaniel-64;
Thomas-64

DICKSON – 65

DIGBY – 122

DILLON – 55

DIMAN – 64
(Dimond-Dimon-Dymont)

DIMONS – 65

DINSMORE – 158

DIODATE (DIODATI) – 65, 122
William-65

DIXON – 42, 52, 65
Amelia Bishop-65; Charles-65;
Courtland Palmer-65

DODD – 65
Daniel-65

DOLBERE (DOLBIAR) –80
Mary-80

DOMMERICH – 65

DORRANCE – 66

DOTY – 66, 118, 151
Edward-66, 118, 151; Harrison
Parmelee-66, 118, 151; Leete
Parmelee-66, 118, 151

DOUBLEDAY – 133

DOUDE – 66
Henry-66

DOWD – 66
Henry-66

DRAKE – 66, 112, 123, 139, 191
John-66, 112; Samuel G.-191

DRIGGS – 66
Alfred Waldo-66

DUDLEY – 205, 208
Mary-205; Ruth-208

DUFAY – 20

DUNBAR – 123

DUNCAN – 66, 67
Charles-67; Hazle (Bartram)-
67

DUNHAM – 51, 67
Jacob-67

DUNN – 67

Harvey Dunn-67

DUNNAM – 67

DUNNING – 67
Rev. Benjamin-67; Ebenezer-
67

DURAND – 67
Dr. John-67

DURANT – 67
Elizabeth-67; George-67

DUVAL – 55

DURKEE(s) – 39
Lydia (Burler)-39

EAMES – 68

EASTON – 68
Joseph-68

EATON – 68, 161

EDGECOMB – 68

EDMOND – 55
Judge William-55

EDSON – 68
Josiah-68

EDWARDS – 68, 69
Hon. Bulkeley-69; Richard-69;
Stella Lee-69; William-69;
William Lemly-69

EELLS – 40

EGGLESTON – 69

ELDREDGE – 69

Jonathan-79; Sarah Rebecca-79; Thomas-79

GILDERSLEEVE – 79
Philip-79

GILLESPIE – 79, 80
John-80; Mary Jane (Cunningham)-80

GILLETT – 80
(Gillet-Gillette)
Jeremiah-80; Jonathan-80; Joseph-80; Nathan-80; Salmon Cone-80

GILMAN – 80

GODDARD – 80

GOES – 204
Jan Tysse-204

GOLDTHWAITE – 81

GOODFELLOW – 81
Thomas-81

GOODING – 19

GOODLOCK – 133

GOODRICH – 76, 81, 192
John-81; Richard-81, William-81

GOODSELL – 81

GOODWIN – 42, 81, 82, 141, 146
Clarinda (Newberry)-141; Eunice (Olcott)-146; James-82; Lucy (Morgan)-82; Ozias-81; William-81

GORDON – 82
(Gorden-Gaordon-Gordan-Gorden-Gordien-Gordins-Gordton-Gorndon-Gorton)

GORHAM – 82
Ephraim-82

GOULDEN – 82, 190
Harriet L. Sturges-82, 190

GOWDY – 82

GRAHAM – 83
Henry-83; Mary (Graham or Grimes)-83

GRANBERRY – 83
Helen (Woodward)-83

GRANGER – 83
Launcelot-83

GRANNIS – 83
Edward-83

GRAVES – 83
George-83; Thomas-83

GRAY – 84
Rev. Walter Henry-84

GRAYBILL – 70

GREEN – 48, 84
Ezra-84

GREENLEAF – 84
Jane-84

GREGORY – 106, 170
Henry-170

GRENVILLE – 66

GRIFFIN – 107
Lydia-107

GRIFFING – 84
Jasper-84

GRIMES (GRAHAM) – 83

GRISWOLD – 85, 105, 122
Col. Charles-85; Matthew-85;
Thomas—85

GROSVENOR – 5, 85
Nathan-85

GUERNSEY – 85, 86
(Garnsey-Guersie)
Henry-86; Joseph-86

GUILD – 86
Jeremiah-86

GUTHRIE – 86

HAIGHT – 86

HALE – 86, 87, 180, 216
Emma-180; Josiah-87; Cpt.
Nathan-87, 216; Samuel-87

HALL – 5, 65, 87, 88, 89
Daniel Hubbard-88; John-88,
89; Lt. Nathaniel-88;
Nathaniel, Jr.-88; Noah-88,
Sophia Fidelia-88

HALLOCK – 89
Rev. Jeremiah-89; Rev.
Moses-89

HALSEY – 133

HALSTED – 89
Caleb-89

HAMBLY – 20

HAMILTON – 203

HAMLIN – 89
Cpt. Giles-89

HAND – 89
Daniel-89

HANDY – 89
Richard-89

HANFORD – 89
Rev. Thomas-89

HANKS – 89

HARDENBERGH – 204
Cpt. Gerrit Janes-204

HARLAKENDEN – 92
Mabel-92

HARPER – 193

HARRIES – 170
Jane Ceclia-170

HARRIS – 61, 90, 107
Ely-90; James-90; Joseph-90;
Cpt. Seers-90

HARRISON – 41, 90
Richard-90

HART – 55, 91
Dea. Stephen-91; William A.-
91

HARTWELL – 91

HASTINGS – 180
Elizabeth-180

HATCH – 91
Major Timothy-91

HAUGHEY – 52

HAUSER – 17
Helen Bassett-17

HAWES – 61

HAWK (S) – 91
John-91

HAWLEY – 91, 92
Joseph-92

HAY – 133

HAYDEN – 92

HAYES – 92
George-92; Richard-92; Titus-92

HAYNES – 92, 93
Gov. John-92; John Russell-93

HEARDS – 115

HAZARD – 203

HEATH – 132
Elizabeth (Miller)-132

HECOX (HICKOK) – 93
William-93

HEMPSTEAD – 93

HENDERSON – 65

HENSHAW – 198

HERRICK – 93

Rev. Claudius-93; James-93

HETHS – 88

HICKCOX – 93

HICKOK (S) – 93
William-93

HIGBIE – 133

HIGBY (HIGBE) – 94

HILDRETH – 198

HILL – 94
John-94; Melanchthon-94;
William-94

HILLIS – 94
Adam-94

HILLS – 94
William-94

HILLYER – 94, 95

HINDS – 161

HINE – 95
Thomas-95

HINMAN – 95
Edward-95; Edward, Jr.-95;
Sergt. Edward-95; Hannah-95;
Havilah Burritt-95

HINTON – 128
Hessina-128

HITCHCOCK – 95, 96
Luke-95, 96; Matthias-95, 96

HOADLEY – 96

William-96

HOBART – 154
Edmund-154

HODGKINS (HOTCHKIN) – 96
John-96

HOLBROOK – 96

HOLCOMB – 96

HOLLENBACK – 205

HOLLY – 96

HOLMES – 20, 27, 96, 97
George-97; Israel-27; John-97

HOLT – 48, 97
Charlotte A.-48

HOLTON – 97
Joel-97; William-97; Dr.
William-97

HOO – 122

HOOK – 70, 98
James-98; Humphrey-98

HOOKE – 98
Humphrey-98

HOOKER – 98, 193
Com. Edward-98; John-98;
Rev. Thomas-98

HOPKINS – 98, 99, 203
James-99; Jean-99; Samuel
Miles-99

HORSFALL – 99

HOSMER – 99

HOTCHKIN (HODGKIN) – 96
John-96

HOTCHKISS – 34, 99
Samuel-34

HOUGHTALING – 139

HOUSE – 87

HOUSTON – 99
William-99

HOWARD – 99
Susanna-99; Thomas-99

HOWE (HOW) – 99
James-99

HOWELL – 34
William-34

HOWLETT – 35, 137

HOYT – 73, 99, 100
Charles Davenport-100;
David-100; Elizabeth-73;
John-100; Linus-100; Simon-
100

HUBBARD – 100
George-100; Hon. William-
100

HUBBELL – 73, 183
Rev. Stephen-73

HUGGINS – 101
James-101

HUGHES – 62, 209

HULL – 34, 101
  George-34; Richard-101

HULSE – 181

HUNGERFORD – 101
  Thomas-101; William-101

HUNT – 102
  Thomas-102

HUNTER – 198

HUNTINGTON – 16, 102, 103
  Margaret-102; Simon, 16, 102

HUNTLEY – 103
  John-103

HURD – 103

HURLBURT – 103, 104
  Thomas-103

HUSTON – 104
  William-104

HUTCHINS – 104

HUTCHINSON – 138
  Hannah-138

HYDE (HIDE) – 104
  Andrew-104; Humphrey-104;
  Rebecca-104; William-104

INDICOTT – 104
  Dr. John-104

INMAN – 104
  Daniel-104

INSLEY – 105
INSLEY – 105

Andrew-105; Ceclia Ann
Whitmore-105; William
Quinn-105

IRONMONGER – 133

ISBELL – 105
  Robert-105

ISHAM – 105
  Jirah-105

JACKSON – 105, 106
  Com. Charles Hunter-105;
  Edward-105; Esther-105;
  Joseph-105; Michael-106

JACOBS – 106
  John Clark-106

JAGGER (GAGER) – 106
  John-106; Dr. William-106

JAMES – 62, 106, 198
  Alice-106; Bob-106; Henry-
  106; Cpt. John-106; Wilkie-
  106

JARVIS – 1006

JENNINGS – 106
  Gershom-106; Jonathan-106;
  Nathan Tileston-106

JEPSON – 106

JEROME – 107
  Eugene Murray-107

JEWELL – 107

JOHNSON – 107, 122

Albert-107; Charles Frederick-107; Elisha (Johnston)-107; Rev. Jacob-107

JOHNSTON (JOHNSON) – 107
Elisha—107

JONES – 108
Benjamin-108; Cpt. Israel-108

JOY – 108

JUDSON – 108, 137
Dea. Benjamin-108

KAMPE – 20

KEELER – 108, 167
Ralph-108, 167

KELLEY – 108, 109
Joseph-109

KELLY – 213

KELSEY – 109, 185, 186
William-109

KEMP – 109

KEMPER – 127
John Mason-127

KENDALL – 109, 110
William-110

KENNEDY – 110

KENNEY – 110
Gen. George C.-110

KENT – 110
Benjamin-110

KERCHAL – 110

KRIS – 57
Wilson, Jr.-57

KILBOURN – 110, 111

KILLAM – 161

KILLORAN-GURRY – 29, 53

KIMBERLY – 111
Thomas-111

KING – 111
James-111; Roger-111;
William-111

KINGSBURY – 111

KIOUS – 203

KIRBY – 36, 112
John-112; Joseph-112; Mary-36; Richard-112

KNAPP – 112
Roger-112

KNIFFEN – 11

KNOWLTON – 112, 161
Richard-112; Sewell-112;
Thomas-112; Col. Thomas-112

KNOX – 112
Mjr. Gen. Henry-112

LACKEY – 113

LACY – 113

LADD – 169
Samuel-169

LOCKE – 122

LOCKWOOD – 119, 120
Edmund, Sr.-119, 120;
Edmund, Jr.-119, 120

LONGWELL – 48

LOOMER – 120
Stephen-120

LOOMIS – 120, 121, 139
Joseph-120, 121

LORD – 121, 122
Thomas-121

LOVELAND – 121
Thomas-121

LOWE – 121, 122
Lt-Col. Alfred Edward
Lawson-121, 122

LOWREY – 122
Mary-122; Thomas-122

LUDINGTON – 122
Ethel Saltus-122; William-122

LUITWEILER – 17
Marion Bassett-17

LYNDE – 122

LYON – 122
Henry-122; Richard-122

MCCRAY – 192
Florine Thayer-192

MCCURDY – 122, 123, 212

MCDONALD – 123

MCEWAN (MCEWEN) – 123
George-123

MCGILLIVRAY – 123
Clan McGillivray-123

MCGUIRE – 123
Elisha Whipple-123

MCINTOSH – 123
Andrew-123; Robert-123

MCKAY – 65

MCKEE – 133

MCLEAN – 123

MCNAIR – 123, 124

MCNEIL – 70

MACDONALD – 124

MACFARLANE – 123, 124
Clan MacFarlane-124

MACK – 124, 195
John-124, 195

MACKENZIE – 65

MACLAREN – 112

MACLEAN – 124
Allan-124; Doctor Neil-124

MAIN-MAINE – 124, 125
Ezekiel-124, 125

MALTBY – 125
George Ellsworth-125;
Georgia Lord (Morehouse)-
125

242

MANLEY – 129

MANN (MAN) – 125
  John-125

MANSFIELD – 125, 182
  Gillian-125; Richard-125

MANSON – 135

MANY – 125
  Jean-125

MAPES – 125

MARBLE – 30

MARCY – 125, 126
  John-126

MARKS – 126

MARSH – 126, 193
  John-126; Samuel-126;
  William-126

MARTIN – 126
  Ira Jay-126

MARTINDALE – 167
  John-167

MARVIN – 122, 126
  Edward-126; Matthew-126;
  Reinold-126

MASKELL – 127
  Thomas, Sr.-127; Thomas, Jr.-
  127

MASON – 127, 128, 195
  Edward-195; Elisha-127; Cpt.
  Hugh-127; Mjr. John-127, 128;
  "The Widow Mason"-195

MATHER – 128
  Rev.Richard-128

MATTINGLY – 128
  Joseph-128

MAUGHAM – 128
  Somerset-128

MAULSBY – 133

MAXIM – 117, 128

MAXWELL – 128

MAY – 148
  Mary Ann-148

MEACHAM – 128, 129
  Charles-128

MEAD – 129, 130, 209
  Jeremiah, Jr.-129, 130;
  Jonathan-129

MEARS – 130
  John-130; Lucy Rockwell-130

MECORNEY – 130

MEECH – 200

MERES – 60, 130

MERRILL – 130, 209

MERRIMAN – 130, 131
  Nathaniel-130, 131

MERRITT – 131, 168
  James-168; Katherine-168

MERWIN – 131
  Miles-131

Josiah-139

MUNSELL – 139

MUNSON – 135, 139, 140
Cpt. Thomas-135, 139

MURDO – 140
John-140

MURDOCK – 140
George-140; John-140; Peter-
140; Robert-140; William-140

MURPHY – 140

MURRAY – 140
Jonathan-140

MYGATE – 140
Joseph-140

NASH – 141, 209
Thomas-141

NEIL – 42

NETTLETON – 141
Daniel-141

NEUKIRK – 141

NEWBERRY – 141

NEWBURY – 141
Clarinda (Goodwin)-141

NEWCOMB – 141, 142
Andrew-141, 142

NEWDIGATE – 122

NEWELL – 114, 142
Elisha R.-114; Thomas-142

NEWSOM – 142
John Edward-142

NEWTON – 142, 143, 214
Abner-143; David-143; Jane
Eliza-214; Richard-142; Rev.
Roger-142, 143; Thomas-142,
143

NICHOLS – 143
Ezra-143; Sigurd the
Northman-143

NICHOLS-NICHOLLS – 143
Caleb-143; Sgt. Francis-143

NOBLE – 33
Nancy-33

NODINE – 143
(Maudin)

NOELL – 145

NORTH – 144
Dea. Frederick-144; Harriet-
144; James-144; John-144;
Mary-144

NORTON – 61, 144, 145
Charles-144, 145; James, Sr.-
145; John-145

NOWELL-NOELL – 145
Peter-145; Thomas-145

O'DALY – 145

OGDEN – 89, 122, 145, 146
John-145, 146; Rebecca-89

OKIE – 146
Reginald-146

OLCOTT – 146
Thomas-146

OLDS – 146
Alfred Allen-146

ORMSBY – 146, 147

ORTON – 147
Thomas-147

OSBORN – 193

OSTERHOUTS – 88

OTIS – 147
Dea. Joseph-147

OVERMAN – 147
Jacob-147

OWEN – 147
John-147

PAGE – 148, 205
George-148

PAINE-PAYNE – 139, 148
James-148; John-148

PALGRAVE – 148

PALMER – 10, 11, 148, 149
Gershom-149; Walter-148, 149

PARADISE – 149

PARCHER (PARKER) – 151
Elias-151

PARDEE – 149, 150

PARISH – 150

John-150

PARK – 11, 150
(Parke, Park, Parks, etc.)
Edward-150; Robert-150;
Thomas Kinnie-150

PARKE – 150, 151
Edward-151; Robert-151

PARKER – 151
Elias (Parcher)-151; Dea.
Lovel-151; Samuel-151

PARMELEE – 66, 89, 118, 122,
151
Anna-89; John-66, 118, 151

PARMLEY – 151
(See: Parmelee, Doty, Leete,
Wilson)

PARSONS – 152, 172
Cornet-152; Cornet Joseph-
152; Eli-152; Jonathan-152;
Mehitable-172; Thomas-152

PARTCH – 123, 152
Quinten-152

PARTRICK (PATRICK) – 152
Richard-152

PATCH (PARTCH) – 152
Quinten-152

PATCHIN-PATCHEN – 152

PATRICK or PARTRICK – 152
Richard-152

PATTERSON – 65, 152, 153
Andrew-153; George
Washington-153

PAWLING – 75

PAYNE – 153
James-153

PEABODY – 153

PEALE – 153
Charles Wilson-153

PEARSON – 153
Stephen-153

PEASE – 153, 154
Hon. Calvin-154; John-153,
154; Laura Grant Risley-154

PECK – 151, 154
John Hudson-154; Mehitable-
154; William-154

PEET – 155
John-155

PELTON – 193

PENDELL – 203

PERCY – 155, 157

PERKINS – 155
Edward-155

PERRIN – 155, 156
John-155; Thomas-155, 156

PERRY – 156

PETERS – 125
Margaret-125

PETTIBONE – 156
John-156

PETTIS – 112
Deborah Tracy-112

PHELPS – 156, 183, 193
Jemima (Post)-156; Joseph-
156; Josiah-156; William-156

PHILLIPS – 28, 156
Noah-156; Polly Adelaide-28

PHINNEY – 105
Mary Allen-105

PHIPPEN – 61

PICKETT – 156
John-156; Margaret-156

PIERCE – 4, 156, 157
Pres. Franklin-157; Jane M.-4,
156, 157; Mary M. (Aiken)-4,
157

PIERPONT – 93, 157
(de Pierrepont)
Hannah-93; Hezekiah-157; Sir
Hugh de Pierrepont-157; Rev.
James-157; John-157

PIERREPONT – 157
Sir Hugh de-157

PIERSON – 153, 157
Stephen-153

PINNEY – 68
Sarah-68

PITKIN – 122, 157, 158
Martha-158; William-157, 158

PLANT – 158

PLATT – 126, 158

Arthur-163

REYNES – 60

REYNOLDS – 163, 164
Charissa (Huntington)-164;
Christopher-164; John-164;
Sarah (Backus)-164

RICHARDSON – 57, 164
Amos-164; Mary (Darrow)-57

RIDER (RYDER) – 165

RIDGWAY – 165

RIGGS – 200

RISDON – 165
Josiah-165

RISING – 165
Jonathan-165; Justus-165

RISLEY – 165
Richard-165

ROACH – 65

ROBBINS – 165
Cpt. Elisha-165; John-165;
William-165; Rev. William
Randolph-165

ROBENS – 165

ROBERTS – 166
Cpt. Lemuel-166; Nancy Hoyt
(Bean)-166

ROBINS – 166
John-166

ROBINSON – 166, 167

Edward-166; John-166; Rev.
William-166, 167

ROCKWELL – 61, 167
John-167

RODMAN – 167

ROE – 167
David-167

ROGERS – 167, 168
Adam-168; David-167; James-
167, 168; Katherine-168

ROLFE – 139

ROLLO – 168
Alexander-168

ROOSEVELT – 168

ROOT – 168

ROSE – 168
Robert-168

ROSENBERGER – 133

ROUSSEAU – 168, 169

ROWLEY – 169
Eleazer-169; Thomas-169

ROYCE – 169
Mary-169; Robert-169

RUGGLES – 169
Thomas-169

RUSSELL – 169
John-169; Stephen-169

RYDER – 165

SHEPARD – 176

SHERMAN – 176
Jotham-176; Samuel-176

SHERRILL – 176

SHERWOOD – 176
Thomas-176

SHIFTON – 177
Edward (Shipman)-177

SHIPLEY – 158

SHIPMAN – 176, 177
Edward-176, 177

SILL – 177

SKEEL (SKEELE-SKEIL) –
177

SKIDMORE – 177, 178
Thomas (Scudamore)-177, 178

SKILTON – 178
Dr. Henry-178

SKINNER – 178, 179, 190
John-178;Joseph-178,179;
Martha (Kinne)-178, 179

SLADE – 179
William-179

SLOAT – 69

SLOSSON – 179
Nathaniel-179

SMITH – 20, 30, 61, 62, 114,
129, 169, 170, 179, 180, 181,
212

Alexander-180; Alitheah-169;
Cotton-181; Edward-181;
Frederick Southgate-179;
Henry Boynton-179; Herbert
Francis-181; John-181;
Joseph-180; Mrs. Joseph F.-
114; Matthew-180; Nathan-
181; Nehemiah-20; Rev.
Nehemiah-181; Richard-20;
Robert-180; Roswell, 2d.-179;
Lt. Samuel-180; Simon-20;
Steel- 20, 179

SNOW – 14

SOLLE – 172
Dorothee-172

SOUTHERLAND – 20

SOUTHWORTH – 158

SPELMAN – 181
Richard-181

SPENCER – 182
Garrrard-182; Samuel-182;
Thomas-182

SPICER – 182
Peter-182

SPINING-SPINNING – 182, 183

SPRAGUE – 183
Franklin Wiatt-183;Thomas
Spencer IV-183

SQUIRE-SQUIRES – 133, 183,
209

ST. JOHN – 183

STAFFORD – 105, 183, 200

251

STANLEY – 61, 183
John-183; Thomas-183;
Timothy-183

STANSBURY – 198

STANTON – 184
Thomas-184

STAPLES – 184
Job-184

STARK – 184
Aaron-184

STARKWEATHER – 30, 184
John-184; Robert-184

STATES – 185

STEBBINS – 185, 209
Hannah-185; Maria-185;
Samuel-185; Theophilus-185

STEELE – 185
George-185; John-185

STEEVENS – 185, 186
(Steevens, Stevens, Stephens,
Kelsey)
John-186

STEPHENS – 185, 186, 187
Henry (Stevens)-187

STERNE – 158

STERRETT – 186

STETSON – 186
Dolly Witter-186

STEVENS – 163, 186, 187, 213

(Steevens-Stevens-Stephens-
Kelsey)
Ann(--)-187; Charles Tracy-
186, 187; Elizabeth-163;
Henry-187; John-186, 187;
Mary-187; Richard-187;
Robert-187; Thomas-187

STEWART (STUART) – 190
John-190; Walter-190

STILES – 139, 187, 193
Francis-187; John-187

STILLMAN – 188
George-188; Dr. George-188

STIMSON – 188

STODDARD – 188
John-188; Ralph-188;
Rodman-188

STOKER – 70

STONE – 39, 188, 189
Anson Parmilee-189; Canfield-
189; Eber-189; John-189; Rev.
Samuel-39; William-189

STORY – 69

STOTT – 52

STOUGHTON – 16
Lieut. Thomas-16

STOW – 3

STOWE – 189, 190
Cpt. Stephen-190, 190

STRATTON – 113

WHITING – 207
WHITLOCK – 185
Robert-185

WHITMORE – 105, 207, 209
John-105; Rev. William
Howe-207

WHITNEY – 200, 207
Henry-207

WHITON – 207

WHITTELSEY – 207
(Whittelsey-Whittelsey)

WHITTEMORE – 207, 208
Rev. William Howe-207, 208

WHITTEN – 208
Thomas-208

WHITTINGTON – 70

WHITTLESEY-WHITTELSEY
– 207, 208
Elisha-208; John-208

WHITNEY – 208

WICKRICH –WIDRIG – 69

WICKS – 181

WICKWARE – 208, 209
John-208

WIGGINS – 133, 183, 209

WIGHTMAN - 20

WILCOCKSON – 209, 210
William-209

WILCOX – 133, 196, 209, 210
(Wilcoxson-Willcockson-
Wilcoxen-Wilcox)
Elisha Bacon-209; Josiah-209;
William-209

WILFORD – 210

WILKINSON – 210
Daniel-210; Edward-210;
John-210; Laurence-210

WILLARD – 210
Josiah-210; Mjr. Simon-210;
Stephen Franklin-210

WILLCOX – 209

WILLEY – 210
Isaac-210

WILLIAMS – 20, 65, 66, 78,
129, 210, 211
Alice May-66; Caleb M.-78;
Ezekiel-210; Hannah
Elizabeth-65; James-211;
James Baker-211; Robert-211;
Sarah Gallup-78; Solomon-
211; Veach-211

WILLIAMSON – 211
Caleb-211; Mary (Cobb)-211

WILLIS – 211

WILLOUGHBY – 122, 211

WILLYS – 211
Govenor-211

WILMOT – 212

WILSON – 34, 66, 118, 151, 212

Carol Parmelee Doty-66, 118, 151

WINCHESTER – 212

WINES – 133, 183, 209

WINKLEY – 26

WINSTON – 16

WITTER – 161

WOLCOTT – 122, 158, 212, 213
Henry-212, 213; Simon-158

WOLFE – 41

WOOD – 213
Joseph-213; Dr. Samuel-213

WOODIN – 213
Amos-213

WOODMANCY – 133
(Thomas)-133

WOODRUFF – 213, 214
Matthew-213, 214

WOODWORTH – 214

WOOLSEY – 214
Charles William-214

WOOLWORTH – 214
Hannah Huggins-214;
Richard-214

WOOSTER – 214, 215
Edward-215; Hezekia Calvin-215; General David-215

WORCESTER – 214, 215
(Wooster)

Rev. William-214, 215

WRIGHT – 53, 105, 192, 215
John-215; Sir John-215;
Samuel-215; Dea. Samuel-215;
Thomas-215

WRIGLEY – 11

WYATT – 6, 212
Margaret-6, 212

WYLLYS – 216
Gov. George-216; Mjr. John
Palsgrave-216

YALE – 170, 216
David-216; Elihu-216;
Thomas-170

YORK – 216

YOUNG – 181

Heritage Books by Lu Verne V. Hall:

Delaware Bible Records, Volume 6

New England Family Histories and Genealogies: State of Massachusetts

Heritage Books by Lu Verne V. Hall and Donald O. Virdin:

Delaware Bible Records, Volume 5

New England Family Histories and Genealogies: Miscellaneous New England States

New England Family Histories and Genealogies: States of Maine and Rhode Island

New England Family Histories and Genealogies: States of New Hampshire and Vermont

New England Family Histories: State of Connecticut

Texas Family Histories and Genealogies

www.ingramcontent.com/pod-product-compliance
Lightning Source LLC
Chambersburg PA
CBHW070806270326
41927CB00010B/2323